A NATURAL HISTORY OF JERSEY

To my husband
whose love for his native Island
made this book possible

Yellow horseshoe vetch above Le Pinnacle, St. Ouen.

A Natural History of Jersey

by

FRANCES LE SUEUR

with illustrations by

Richard Le Sueur

PHILLIMORE

1976

Published by
PHILLIMORE & CO., LTD.,
London and Chichester

Head Office: Shopwyke Hall, Chichester,
Sussex, England

ISBN 0 85033 238 9

Text in 11/12pt. Baskerville

Printed in England by

Butler & Tanner Ltd.,
Frome and London

CONTENTS

List of illustrations and maps vii

Preface ix

Chapters

1   Jersey and the Jerseyman 1

2   Plants, Flowering and Flowerless 18

3   Mammals 59

4   Birds 106

5   Insects and Some Related Species 154

6   Amphibians and Reptiles 178

7   Fish of Ponds and Streams 188

8   Molluscs of Inland Areas 197

9   The Future 204

Bibliography 207

Index 211

ILLUSTRATIONS

Horseshoe vetch above Le Pinnacle, St Ouen *frontispiece*

Burnet rose in fruit 25

Burnet rose in flower 25

Leaves of three *Oxalis* species 42

Lattice stinkhorn 56

Lesser white-toothed shrew 74

Bank vole 102

Diagram showing status of birds in Jersey at different seasons 107

Brent geese feeding at West Park, St Aubin's Bay .. 112

Head of a snipe 119

Dartford warbler on gorse 135

Privet hawkmoth caterpillar 165

Three moths: garden tiger; cream-spot tiger; Jersey tiger 167

Colorado beetle 171

Common toad 179

Agile frog 180

St Ouen's Pond, 1975 189

White-lipped ramshorn snail 199

Pfeiffer's amber snail 199

Chrysalis snail 199

Hairy snail 201

Pointed snail 201

Two-toothed door snail 201

MAPS

1 Maps showing how different falls in sea level
would affect the Channel Islands 4

2 Simplified geological map showing areas of blown
sand overlying the main rocks 7

3 Maps showing distribution of mammal species in
the Channel Islands 63-5

4 Maps showing distribution of records of both
shrew species 77

5 Map showing distribution of stoat records 84

6 Map showing distribution of red squirrel records .. 96

7 Map showing possible routes of brent geese
between their breeding grounds in the high
Arctic and Jersey 111

8 Map showing migration of swallows 132

9 Map showing migration of linnets 148

10 Map showing migration of starlings 150

11 Map showing distribution of glow-worm records .. 170

12 Map showing distribution of green lizard records .. 183

13 Map showing distribution of wall lizard records .. 185

PREFACE

This is the first book devoted entirely to a general account of Jersey's natural history and indeed only three books dealing with specific aspects of it have ever appeared. All are out of print. Two were Floras, C. C. Babington's *Primitiae Florae Sarnicae* in 1839, and L. V. Lester-Garland's *Flora of Jersey* in 1903. These now provide historical records and work on a new Flora is almost complete. The third book was R. Dobson's excellent *Birds of the Channel Islands* which was published in 1952. A great deal of information exists on the mammals, reptiles, etc., of Jersey, but, so far, much of it has only been available in scientific journals. Each group is therefore discussed separately here, for ease of reference, but their interdependence is stressed. The treatment within the chapters is different and habitats are described in the chapter on vegetation.

The Botanical Society of the British Isles has recently published a recommended list of English names for flowers. These have been used, and occasionally, in addition, others well known in Jersey or elsewhere. Latin names have not normally been given for plants unless they do not occur on this list. There should be no ambiguity with birds or mammals. In other groups the position is not so clear and Latin names have been given when thought necessary. There has been no attempt at consistency.

The book could not have been written without the help of a great number of people. The records of the Société Jersiaise from 1873 have obviously been used extensively, but also discussions within the botanical and ornithological sections of the Société have proved invaluable. I am much indebted to the transcribers of early documents, such as the *Lettres Closes,* and to the Société for publishing them. As more of these documents become available, more references to the natural history of Jersey in the past will almost certainly be found.

Since I began writing articles on natural history for the *Jersey Evening Post* many readers have told me items of interest. While it is impossible to mention by name all who have helped I should like to thank in particular David Clennett, Margaret and Roger Long, and Joan Stevens for their help over the years, Madge Tubby for typing the manuscript, and Robert Paton for preparing the basic map of Jersey used to show the distribution of selected species. My husband and our two children, Richard (16) and Alexander (12) have helped in innumerable ways. The remaining maps and the illustrations were drawn by Richard, all from Jersey specimens, except that of the (French) Colorado beetle which it is illegal to have in one's possession in the Island whether it be alive or dead.

Les Hâtivieaux,   FRANCES LE SUEUR
Val de la Mare,
St Ouen, Jersey
August 1975

1

JERSEY AND THE JERSEYMAN

> . . . this interesting group of islands . . . connected
> geographically with France, and politically with England:
> their natural history has been neglected by scientific men
> of both countries . . .
>
> C. C. Babington,
> *Primitiae Florae Sarnicae* 1839

THE LAND WE CALL JERSEY is now an island, but at
various times in the distant past it was joined to the
Continent and, unless man interferes with nature on a
colossal scale, the time will come when it will be joined
again. The earth, during the course of the last million
years, has had alternate cold and warm periods, the
glaciations and the interglacials. During each glaciation a
good deal of the earth's total water supply is locked up in
the form of ice at the poles or in alpine regions. This lowers
the level of the sea which, at times, becomes sufficiently
low for Jersey to be connected to the Continent. As the earth
warms up again and the ice melts, the sea rises. The dry
land between Jersey and the Continent becomes progres-
sively wetter and marshier until finally the sea closes in
and Jersey is once more an island. This is a considerable
simplification of events, for superimposed on it are possible
movements of the land, but, nevertheless, the sea is high
relative to the land in warm interglacials and its heights
in the past are shown by where ancient beaches were formed.
Between St Aubin and Belcroute and in many other places
there are raised beaches eight metres above present sea level.
In the vertical face of the deep cutting forming Snow Hill
car park, there is one at 18 metres, and at South Hill there is
a yet higher beach, about 40 metres above present sea
level.

There have been four major glaciations, and we are probably living in a warm period between the fourth and a fifth.

But men were living in, or at least visiting, Jersey[1] as far back as about 100,000 to 115,000 years ago at the end of the third glaciation. No bones of the men of this occupation have as yet been found, but a pile of huge pieces of animals, excavated at the Société Jersiaise's archaeological site, La Cotte de St Brelade, by Dr C. B. M. McBurney and students of the Cambridge Department of Archaeology indicate that man was then using the cave as a storing place, perhaps a larder. In a preliminary report McBurney and Callow state that in the pile were three woolly rhinoceros' skulls and pieces of at least five mammoths, and that there was much to suggest that the chunks were deliberately assembled and that the work was done in one operation. All three woolly rhinos died of severe blows to the head. The stratification of the cave deposits is such that it is possible to date the pile of bones to the end of the third glaciation. The question arises as to why no one returned for this very large quantity of meat, the acquiring of which must have taken a vast amount of effort. These are animals of a cold climate and they may have been hunted in the tundra-like plain that would then exist between Jersey and France. But the climate was beginning to warm up and it has been suggested that this plain had become too water-logged for the hunters to come back for their catch, i.e., Jersey was becoming isolated once more. After this warm interval in which the sea rose relative to the land, the next glaciation began. As the severity of the fourth glaciation increased, so the level of the sea fell and eventually hunters were again able to walk to Jersey. More than 50,000 years had passed. The old occupation layer in the cave had been covered by deposit, the sea had washed against it and had also formed the eight metre beach. But the cave was still there, and the new hunters used it at a higher level. Some teeth of the first known Jerseyman, one of these hunters of about 50,000 to 60,000 years ago, were found in this upper occupation layer. He was Neanderthal man and belonged to the same species *Homo sapiens* as today's man, modern man, but his kind in western Europe eventually died out without issue. He could perhaps be described as belonging to a collateral branch of our ancestors.

1 As this book goes to press, alternative theories about the age of this occupation are being discussed.

Mrs. J. Hawkes states in *The Archaeology of Jersey*, that from the available evidence, Neanderthal man lived here for some considerable time, but he had no immediate successor and Jersey must have remained uninhabited through the whole time of the final retreat of the ice. So far, man had been purely a hunter and a gatherer of wild fruits and berries, and his presence can have made little difference to the fauna and flora. These varied with the climate and, to determine the vegetation, an analysis of pollen in the deposits at various archaeological sites is in progress. Remains of the animals on which Neanderthal man lived or which came into his cave for shelter included woolly rhinoceros, mammoth, reindeer, Irish elk, cave hyaena, fox, hare, red deer and a palaeolithic ox. Various birds, all of cold climates, have also been identified. Abundant remains of rodents were found above the habitation layers, and among these were three species of field voles *Microtus*, none of which occurs in the Island today. M. A. C. Hinton, who identified the rodents, commented on the absence of the bank vole and the wood mouse, both of which are here now.

Exactly at what stage man returned is unknown. There were fluctuations of climate during its overall amelioration and the land itself may have moved, so that, as had happened so often in the past, Jersey was sometimes connected to the Continent and sometimes it was not. Comparatively small differences in sea level had important consequences within the Channel Islands, for at times Jersey could be Continental, but Guernsey, lying in deeper seas, would still be insular. Plants and animals, including man, moving westwards across Europe could therefore sometimes reach Jersey, but not Guernsey, and this, in part, accounts for the difference in the present-day flora and fauna of the islands. J. Sinel was first to draw attention to this, and he illustrated his argument with various maps showing the islands in relation to the present depth of the sea. The position of the 10, 20 and 30 fathom lines are given in the illustrations on page four. Men had also been slowly advancing westwards across the Mediterranean, through the Iberian peninsula and up the coast of Europe. These men had boats so could reach both

1.— Maps showing how different falls in sea levels would affect the Channel Islands.

Present Coastline

Coastline if sea fell 10 fathoms
below present level

Coastline if sea fell 20 fathoms
below present level

Coastline if sea fell 30 fathoms
below present level

Jersey and Guernsey. Broadly speaking, the new Jerseymen were neolithic farmers and, whether they belonged to those arriving by land from the east or by sea from the south, they had a much more advanced culture than any previous inhabitants and immediately set about changing Jersey to suit their needs, and Jersey has been changing, with increasing momentum, ever since.

Many sites are known where neolithic man settled in Jersey. The best known is probably at Le Pinnacle, St Ouen, where the lowest habitation layer has been dated by radiocarbon to 3070 BC $\pm$ 100 years, i.e., approximately 5,000 years ago, and we know a little of what the Island looked like then. The forest of oak, alder and hazel, now submerged round the coast, had been flourishing for some time in a warm, humid climate, and Jersey was probably joined to the Continent during its formation and heyday.

Neolithic man would begin clearing whatever woodlands there were, either deliberately for crops or unwittingly, by letting his stock browse in them so preventing regeneration. That the Island was highly productive, at least in the megalithic stage of this new occupation, is shown by the dolmens. According to Mrs Hawkes there was established in the Island 'a society enjoying a settled existence with crops and herds which provided the requisite stability and available labour to indulge the religious extravagances of the people by the construction of vast imposing tombs for their dead'. Many of the present weeds of cultivation were spread across Europe by neolithic man and such weeds probably also flourished among the crops of these original Jersey farmers. Little work has been done on this in Jersey, but at neolithic sites in England seeds of weeds like common poppy have been found.

The coastal forest was destroyed by a rise in the sea relative to the land and Jersey may have been isolated again though not perhaps finally. The remains of the forest in St Ouen's Bay are high up the beach and the most likely time for it to be exposed is after a rough tide when the waves have had a strong eroding action and have pulled material down the beach rather than piled it up. The best places to

see stumps of trees are at the top of the beach by Kempt
Tower or just south of L'Ouzière Slip.

Exactly when the final isolation came is unknown but,
when it did come, the break was of immense importance
from a natural history point of view. Any plant species
slowly advancing across Europe was then unable to reach
Jersey naturally unless it had some special mechanism like
wind-borne or water-borne seed dispersal which could get
it across the wide gap. No mammal could walk here. Sedentary birds and insects, those which fly only short distances,
would find the gap too great to cross. Only creatures which
could fly long distances or could make use of man, either
by travelling with him in his ships or attached to his clothing
or person, could arrive. Man might also deliberately bring
a species which interested him. The effect was two-fold.
Few new species arrived until the comparatively recent
increase in man's movements to and from the Island. Equally
important, the gene pool of each species was limited to what
was then in the Island. In the same way that since last
century the Jersey cow has developed in isolation, though
helped in its case by selective breeding, so a few wild species
here are somewhat different from their equivalent species
elsewhere. Unfortunately, the original arrival date of most
species is unknown, but the wood mouse is slightly different
from its English counterpart, the bank vole is sufficiently
different for it to be called a subspecies, and the Jersey
grasshopper exists nowhere else.

The geology of the Island is at present the subject of a
major survey being carried out by the Department of
Geology of St Mary's College, London University on behalf
of the States of Jersey in conjunction with the Insititute of
Geological Sciences. As I write, their report has not yet been
published, but this account of Jersey's natural history is
concerned with the plants and animals which live here and
only with geology as far as it affects them. The main rocks
are of immense importance because the physical shape and
the contours of the Island depend on their differing
abilities to withstand weathering by water and wind, and
because the Island's soil is formed to a certain extent by the

products of that weathering. The principal rock of the Island is granite and because of its hardness, Jersey has roughly maintained its shape whether it has been, to use Dr A. E. Mourant's description, a hill on an extensive plain or a shallow area at the bottom of a deep sea. Now it is an island roughly 17km. east-west and 11km. north-south with its south-west corner lying at approximately 49 deg. 11 min. N, 2 deg. 15 min. W.

Apart from granite, the most extensive rocks are shale in the west and west-centre, rhyolite and andesite in the east-centre, and conglomerate in the north east.

A simplified map based principally on that of Père C. Noury in his *Géologie de Jersey* is given.

2.– Simplified geological map showing areas of blown sand overlying the main rocks.

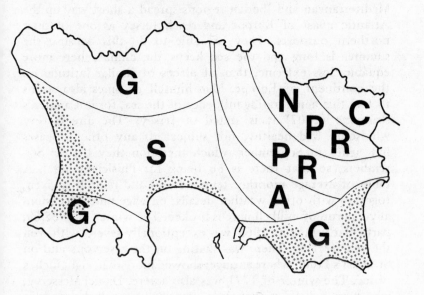

G=granite; S=shale; C=conglomerate; NPR=non-porphyritic rhyolite; PR=porphyritic rhyolite; A=andesite.

According to Dr Mourant, a layer of 'head', a mixture of rock rubble and brownish-yellow clay, forms a thick layer over a good deal of the rock surface of the Island and this is usually overlain by a deposit of brick-earth or loess, a pre-historic wind-blown dust. The present soil is formed above these two layers. Dr Mourant considers that the district of Maufant takes its name from two old French words *mau* and *fanc*, meaning bad mud because of the presence of this brick-earth as the subsoil. If a slight slope is present, the top soil is fertile, but any large flat saucer-shaped region becomes water-logged. The coastal areas of the west, south, and particularly the south west have received considerable amounts of blown sand and the soil in these areas often has a high lime content because of broken-down mollusc shells. Elsewhere, because much of the rock is acid, the soil tends to be acidic.

Many plants and wild creatures belonging usually to the Mediterranean and Iberian regions spread a short way up the Atlantic coast of Europe and reach Jersey as one of their northern outposts. They are able to do this because the summer is long and the sea keeps the climate here more equable, less extreme, than at places of similar latitude on the continent of Europe. Man himself at times also seems to feel this ameliorating influence of the sea, for in Camden's *Britannia* (1607) it is stated of Jersey, 'The aire is very wholsome and healthy, not subject to any other diseases but agues in September, which therupon they tearme Settembers, so that there is no being for Phisicians here'. A table of average monthly temperatures and rainfall is given, together with other weather details, on page nine. Occasionally the run of mild climate is broken. The winter of 1962/63, particularly January 1963, was exceptionally severe, with even the sea freezing. There was skating on the reservoirs and on St Ouen's Pond, where an auger showed more than eight inches of ice. The winter of 1771 was also severe. Daniel Messervy, who kept a diary at that time, described how all the roads in Jersey were full of snow from one side to the other and at Town Mills the snow, which was frozen on top, was more than 17ft. deep *'ce qui n'avait este vu de memoire d'home...'*.

CLIMATE

Averages at Jersey Airport Meteorological Station, 276ft above sea level

(Tables compiled from figures issued by the Meteorological Department, States of Jersey)

	Jan.	Feb.	Mar.	Apr.	May	June	July	Aug.	Sept.	Oct.	Nov.	Dec.	Year
Temperature deg. C. (1951–72)													
Daily maximum	7.7	7.7	9.7	11.9	14.9	17.5	19.2	19.2	18.1	15.3	11.1	9.0	13.4
Daily minimum	3.6	3.2	4.5	6.2	8.7	11.3	13.2	13.7	12.8	10.5	7.1	5.0	10.9
Mean	5.7	5.5	7.1	9.1	11.8	14.4	16.2	16.5	15.4	12.8	9.1	7.0	8.3
Extreme maximum	12.9	16.2	20.1	21.8	27.3	29.0	34.6	31.2	30.7	22.9	17.3	15.7	34.6
Extreme minimum	−11.0	−7.1	−4.7	−0.4	3.0	6.2	8.4	9.6	6.8	3.4	−2.1	−8.2	−11.0
Sunshine in hours (1954–72)													
Total	59	92	152	189	240	240	248	218	169	130	71	53	1,861
Daily mean	1.90	3.24	4.90	6.29	7.74	8.00	8.01	7.02	5.63	4.20	2.36	1.72	5.08
Rainfall in mm. (1951–72)	94.7	70.0	56.9	51.9	53.5	40.1	43.1	63.6	71.7	75.3	113.5	105.3	840
No. of rain days (0.2 or more) (1951–72)	20.4	16.2	14.7	13.5	12.9	10.5	11.0	12.9	14.1	14.5	18.9	20.3	180
No. of days of snow or sleet (1951–72)	3.4	3.9	2.5	0.5	0.0	0.0	0.0	0.0	0.0	0.0	0.5	2.2	13.0
Snow lying at 09.00	0.8	1.5	0.5	0.0	0.0	0.0	0.0	0.0	0.0	0.0	0.0	0.6	3.4
Air frost	4.1	4.6	2.3	0.0	0.0	0.0	0.0	0.0	0.0	0.0	0.0	2.8	13.8

Wind (1951–72)

Hourly mean speed : : : 12.9 knots (15 m.p.h.).

Highest hourly wind : : : 68 knots (78 m.p.h.) from 280deg. for hour ended 14.00 on 9 October 1964.

Highest gust : : : 94 knots (108 m.p.h.) from 270deg. at 13.25 on 9 October 1964.

In all these untypically severe winters there is great loss of wild life, but the populations usually build up again to normal within a few years except for new immigrants, particularly plants of warmer areas, which may have been doing well during a run of mild winters and are then killed off. This happened to Marvel of Peru, *Mirabilis jalapa,* sometimes called *Belle de Nuit,* which in the late 1950s and early 1960s could be found regularly on consolidated rubbish dumps and on many waste places and seemed to be seeding freely. No plants were found for several years after the hard frost, but a few have been seen recently. These are presumably from a new set of garden throw-outs.

The winds are perhaps as much responsible for the 'look' of Jersey as any other weather factor. Severe gales from the south west, west or north west, blow sometimes for a week at a time, as they have done for centuries, and create a totally different landscape on the west coast of the Island from that elsewhere. Native trees are unable to survive the desiccation of the salt-laden winds with the result that other species of plants and wild creatures which require full sun, and have some special adaptation to enable them to withstand the occasionally rigorous conditions, flourish superbly. As will be seen in the following chapters, much of the best of Jersey's natural history is contained within these areas.

There would appear to be little information about what was happening in Jersey during the period immediately preceding the Christian era and even less in the next millenium, the Dark Ages being as dark in Jersey as elsewhere in Europe. It is not until the Kings of England in early medieval times began trying to assess the value of their lands in the Channel Islands and to claim what they considered were their rights, with the inhabitants often resisting the claims, that once again there are items which tell us, accidentally, something of the vegetation and wild life, native or otherwise, which existed here. From then onwards, the *Extentes,* the Assize Rolls, the *Actes des Etats,* records of dues to the Seigneur, etc., tithes to the Church and a few contemporary descriptions allow us to build up a picture of how the present countryside evolved on the soil and rock of Jersey.

In very early days dues were levied and actually paid in kind and so much wheat, oats and barley are mentioned, together with chickens, geese and eggs, that the Island must have contained a flourishing agriculture except in the years when it was harried by raiders. This occurred fairly frequently and such comments as 'nought left to burn' in 1205, 'every blade of corn and all the houses burnt' in 1338, and 'the island hath been destroyed and burnt three times this year' in 1339, suggest that it was a rich island containing a fair amount of burnable crops like cereals. G. R. Balleine, from whose *History of Jersey* these dates come, considered from the Hearth Tax returns that there were over 2,000 houses in 1331. The houses would be thatched so they would burn easily.

Orders given in 1225 for a thousand trunks of trees to be cut in the wood of Bere near Porchester, and sent to Guernsey and Jersey, indicate that there was no appreciable woodland of any quality here. This shortage continued, for in 1558 the entry 'timber . . . cannot be had in the isle . . .' occurs in the State Papers of Elizabeth I. That all wood was scarce is evident from the way in which the tenants' rights to cut fuel of gorse and bracken on the commons was jealously guarded and how wooden planks washed up on the beach were highly prized. Dried seaweed had to be used to supplement wood for fires. On 9 March 1601/2 the States asked the Governor to get coal for the Castles because of *'la grande escarcité du boys et plantes de lysle, qui aultrement seroiet deffrauldrées et desolées'*. Even as late as 1631 Speed remarked that 'Wood is very scant'.

But the face of Jersey was changing rapidly, and according to Poingdestre it all happened in the hundred years between about 1582 and 1682. The Island 'lay almost open' at the beginning of this period, but by 1673 so much land had been enclosed for orchards that fierce regulations governing the planting of trees were introduced by the States. Farmers had found that there was more profit in apples than in the traditional corn so had made orchards with huge hedges

round them. The regulations forbade the planting of trees
on agricultural land because, as Poingdestre said in his
Caesarea 1682, 'the whole Island was in danger of becoming,
at last, a continued orchard, if care had not ben taken to put
a stopp to that vnlimited inclinatio of ye Inhabitants'. No
longer was wood scarce. Poingdestre went on to say: 'The
Ordinary fewell is wood, which groweth plentifully all ye
Island over, not onely in sett Rowes along the Highwayes,
affoarding shade in Summer and shelter in Winter, but alsoe
vpon the fences & hedges, & is lopped once in five or six
yearse for fewell. Besides which the hedges are planted with
white and blacke thorne & with willowes; & ye barren hills
affoard firzes and ferne, . . .'. Falle, writing in 1694, confirmed what Poingdestre had said: 'I mayn't have named
another great Obtrusion to Tillage, but such a one as can
hardly now be removed. 'Tis the prodigious augmentation
of Inclosures, Fences, Hedgerows and Highways, which, tho'
they add much to the Beauty, and perhaps strength of the
Island, yet hold no Proportion with the Bignesse thereof,
and waste a great deal of good land which may't be turned
to better Account. For I am of the opinion that these which
I have mentioned together with the Gardens, Orchards,
Situation, Avenues, and Issues of Houses, take up very near
one Third of the whole Island . . .
'The whole Island, especially the more inland Part, is so
thick Planted, that to any that takes a Prospect of it from
some higher ground, it looks like a continued Forest, altho'
that in walking through it, not a Wood, nor hardly a Coppice
is to be seen, but many hedgrows and Orchards. Nothing
can be imagined more delightful than the Face of the Island,
when the Trees, which are set among the High-ways, and
in the Avenues of Houses, are covered with verdure, and the
Orchards are full of Blossoms . . . But still it must be con-
fessed that so much shade is prejudicial to the growth of
Pasture and Corn'.

This change from open windswept farmland to small
sheltered fields and orchards would bring with it a corres-
ponding change in the natural vegetation and wild life. The
numbers of skylarks and other birds of open areas would

decrease while species such as chaffinches which nest in trees and bushes would increase. Flowers requiring full sun would partly be replaced by shade-loving species, and consequent on that change the insect fauna would change.

Descriptions of the Island from then onwards stress the wooded nature of the interior. Lyte in 1808 and Plees in 1817 said it was like a continuous forest, but with pollards instead of forest trees. During last century cider apple trees began to give way to potatoes. Though most orchards have now been felled, the many thousands of hedgerow trees and the wild wooded côtils remain. During the Occupation, 1940-45, coal, gas and electricity were scarce, so wood was used extensively. The Germans issued orders about tree-felling and re-planting soon after they arrived, but as conditions in the Island deteriorated, and the weather worsened during the last winter, the inhabitants became desperate. L. Sinel in his *Occupation Diary* noted on 14 March 1945 that people were chopping down the trees along St Aubin's Road and that: 'Discretion has been flung to the winds as far as tree-felling is concerned, and the countryside is disfigured by large numbers of mutilated tree-stumps. Even saplings are not spared'. Three days later the German Commandant of the Fortress of Jersey issued a notice saying that unauthorised tree-felling had increased to such an extent that it had led to spoliation of the Island and unequal distribution of the wood, so he ordered that 'all illicit cutting and gathering of wood is forbidden to all, whether owner or occupier of the land on which it stands, also in private grounds and farms, public parks and roads'. Most of these trees have since been replaced either by saplings or by regeneration from the root. Many of the wooded côtils contain mature-looking chestnut trees which on a close inspection will be found to have re-grown from stools of the war years.

The cliffs and cliff-top heaths have changed comparatively little. Records show that sheep and/or rabbits have grazed them for centuries and there were rights of furze-cutting and fern-cutting from earliest times. At the 1309 Assizes it was stated that in St Brelade the King had 'a certain common where there grows much fuel & . . . they call this

common Les Landes de la Moye & they call the rent sheep-
rent'. Sheep were still common in the 17th century, but
they were decreasing in number. In 1808 Lyte wrote that
land on the north coast fed a few sheep and produced large
quantities of furze which was sold at a high price to bakers.
By 1837, according to Durell, there were only a few sheep
left in the Island and they were on the north and west cliffs,
but in 1861 a few were still on La Motte, Green Island, and
they were still grazing at Noirmont much later. That the
north coast slopes were once an essential part of the farmed
land of Jersey is shown by the old walls and earth banks
which still exist among the gorse and bracken.

Land grazed by sheep is close-cropped so when rabbits,
which were introduced in the 12th or 13th centuries, spread
out of the warrens, they would not necessarily change the
look of the vegetation much. The most rapid change may
well have been during the years immediately after the first
attack of myxomatosis. Close-nibbled cliff turf, with
neither sheep nor rabbits to trim it, gave way to rank
growths of cock's-foot and other coarse plants, and in some
cases gorse and brambles invaded areas previously free from
them. Rabbits are now back in quantity, except when
a pocket of them is again wiped out by myxomatosis, and
most of the traditional rabbit areas are short-turfed once
more.

Some of these cliffs and cliff-heaths, where the vegetation
is not deliberately 'gardened' by man, provide a magnificent
landscape. Noirmont headland was bought by the States of
Jersey as a memorial to the islanders who gave their lives or
suffered during the Second World War. It has always been
a place of great beauty, Octavius Rooke describing it in 1857
in the glowing terms of Victorian writing '. . . nearer to
Noirmont point the land becomes barer, till at last an uncultivated common takes the place of tillage. Then Nature
comes again with all her beauty, shedding a glory of bright
hues upon the landscape; beautiful heathers and yellow
shining gorse climb over every steep, and mingling their
colours with the sombre rock, produce a scene that cannot
be surpassed . . .'.

The low-lying parts of the coast have changed most and the changes, many of them irreversible, have occurred mainly in the last 100 or 150 years. The coastal plains originally had sand dunes or *mielles* against the shore and behind them lay marshes. No records exist of what St Helier's marsh contained except perhaps the rare Jersey cudweed, but the other marshes were drained later and we know more of their flora. The St Peter–St Lawrence marsh, which was drained in the 1870s, and various wet areas in the south east, contained extremely interesting plants which have gone permanently. They included adder's-tongue spearwort, pillwort, bogbean, and marsh-mallow. It is possible that the water vole vanished at this time because of the loss of its habitat. Grouville Marsh and St Ouen's Pond and various smaller areas remain and, as will be seen in later chapters, these retain their natural history value.

The *mielles* of St Helier were levelled by General Don in the early 19th century to make a parade ground, now known as The Parade, but it was towards the end of that century and on into the 20th that the main changes in the coast were made. In 1903 Lester-Garland wrote in his *Flora*: 'elaborate and costly sea-walls are being built all round the low-lying parts of the coast, and the botanical features of the foreshore entirely obliterated'. The stabilising of the dunes meant it was possible to build on them. Who now can imagine sand hillocks and open downs between St Helier and St Aubin as there were only a hundred years ago? And not many remember that the shores of St Brelade's Bay were, 'everywhere covered with a small ground rose, of the finest colour, and emitting all the fragrance of the "rose d'amour" '. Fortunately much of the flora and consequently the fauna of sandy areas still remains on L'Ouaisné, Les Quennevais and inland from St Ouen's Bay. And strangely, the building of the sea-walls has increased, and even created in some areas, a type of habitat recently rare in Jersey—saltmarsh. There were saltmarshes in the past and the Fief of Samarès is named after one, drained about a century ago, which was near the Manor. In 1204 the family de Salinelles, meaning 'little saltpans' held the Fief. The new saltmarshes are thin strips just behind the sea-walls, and they occur here and there from St Catherine round the south coast to St Ouen and in them common sea-lavender, broad-leaved sea-lavender, herbaceous seablite, and sea-purslane occur. Three of these are not listed in Lester-Garland's 1903 *Flora*.

This century modern technology has enabled man to change his way of life more quickly than at any other time in the past. Modern transport makes it possible for him to live in the country, yet work in town, and, for his leisure hours, any part of the Island is but a short drive away. This spread into the countryside brings wider roads with all wild waysides cleared and with any streams which might overflow, culverted and covered over. It brings man's domestic animals, his dogs and his cats, which are predators not just of rats and mice, but equally of shrews, birds and green lizards, and most of all it brings his car. In 1974, more than 45,000 vehicles were taxed in Jersey which has an area of about 45 square miles. Car ferries are also running daily between Jersey and St Malo and Jersey and Weymouth, bringing visitors' cars. Any unfenced area, over which it is possible to drive a car, is driven over, and the erosion of parts of the Island which have been green for centuries is becoming serious.

Statistics on land use during the last centuries are given by Dury in various articles in the Société Jersiaise Bulletins and in his *Land Utilisation Survey* in 1950. But farming methods have also changed radically. Pesticides and herbicides are used on a large scale with the result that the weed flora of arable fields is changing. The more resistant species like scentless mayweed are sometimes able to cover whole fields later in the season in the absence of competition. Fortunately, most of the hedgebanks of Jersey have never been sprayed with selective weedkiller as they have in many parts of Britain. The Department of Public Works sprays the tarmacadam edge of the surface of the main roads and no more than six inches, if that, up the road wall or bank. The effect of pesticides is more difficult to see, more difficult to evaluate. Toads, for example, though still plentiful, have decreased in number. Is it because the slugs and insects which they eat are poisoned or because their breeding pools are polluted? It may be a combination of both, but yet again, neither may be the real reason.

The laws of inheritance have left their mark on Jersey's landscape. The obligatory sharing of an estate between sons and daughters was in operation for centuries. Peter Heylin, writing in 1656, commented that he hardly saw a field of corn bigger than an ordinary garden during his visit in 1628. Many of Jersey's fields are still small or divided into strips showing how a *partage* of years ago split the family land. Hedges and banks, which provide cover for wild life, still demarcate small areas, but there is a growing tendency to form larger units for ease of cultivation.

While this one species, man, has been changing Jersey to suit himself, how have the other living organisms fared? In the following chapters general up-to-date accounts have been given of flowers and birds, but more detailed histories, where known, have also been included for species in other sections.

2

PLANTS, FLOWERING AND FLOWERLESS

*. . . few . . .would have expected to find so bright a gleam
of the sunshine of the Mediterranean so far north.*
L. V. Lester-Garland
A Flora of the Island of Jersey 1903

THE NUMBER OF DIFFERENT PLANTS in a given area
depends to a large extent on the number of different habitats
within that area. Though a comparatively small island, Jersey
is fortunate in having a great diversity of habitat ranging
from salt marshes to wooded côtils, from high cliffs to wide
sandy plains, and from acid sphagnum marshes to base-rich
dunes. Added to these, Jersey has a mild climate and is
just off the edge of a huge land mass. A rich and varied flora
is therefore to be expected and, indeed, is to be found here.

The cliffs lie along the western half of the south coast
from Noirmont to La Corbière and from L'Etacq on the west
round the north to Rozel in the north east. Those of the
south and west, even as far as Grosnez, are sun-baked in
summer, sometimes for months on end, so are warm and
dry, but from Grosnez, along the north, the slopes are in
shade for a large part of every day and are cooler and more
moist. The species of plants growing on the cliffs reflect this
and range from the spotted rock-rose, which grows along the
south and west and is a warmth-loving plant of south Europe
and the Mediterranean region, to the bilberry, which grows
in one place along the north coast and is usually a plant of
moors and mountainous districts.

Jersey has one of the biggest tides in the world, about
40 feet on some springs, so only species specially adapted
to withstand occasional complete drenching with salt water
grow at the foot of the cliffs or on rocks round the coast.
If a gale accompanies one of these high tides, green water,
not just sea spray, may pour over the lower vegetation.
Plants growing higher up the cliffs must still be fairly tolerant
of salt, for sea spray will be driven by strong winds to

considerable distances. None of the cliffs presents a uniform surface but, instead, they have an infinite variety of slopes, outcrops, gullies, platforms and ledges and the vegetation in any area, however large or small, depends substantially on the exposure to which that area is subjected. Some species may positively need salt, but they are few and will be in the very lowest regions where small saltmarshes have formed when fresh water runs down the cliffs on to the beach. On the cliffs themselves it will be seen that many species flourishing at the top are unable to succeed lower down unless they have the protection of a rocky outcrop from the prevailing wind or they are at the bottom of a gully. Those species which can cope with both the desiccation of strong drying winds and the saline conditions produced by the salt-laden ones will grow profusely in the absence of competition. It will be noticed that near the cliff base some species produce leathery or sometimes almost succulent leaves much thicker than on plants further away from salt spray. Sea beet, which is eaten as wild spinach, illustrates this and so does rock samphire, of which a pickle used to be made, while the heart-shaped leaves of Danish scurvygrass become so thick that it is sometimes hard to recognise, compared with the same species a little further inland. This thickening of the leaves helps the plant to survive by reducing loss of water. Other plants like thrift, produce masses of fine leaves in a rosette at first, but later in a dense mat, the top layer sheltering the lower ones. Thrift also has an enormously long tap root, if necessary, both to anchor it and to obtain water. These species are common all round the rocky coast at the sea edge. Slightly higher up the cliffs, sea campion is usually mixed with the thrift and in May forms large masses of pure white among the drifts of pink. Near La Corbière and again at L'Etacq, prostrate broom spreads low over the ground, its mats of yellow flowers joining with the thrift and sea campion to produce a splendid natural rock garden in early summer. Rock sea-lavender will occasionally line a crack in the cliffs and sea spleenwort will frequently be found growing in the protection of overhanging rocks. Some plants are particularly fine, their fronds being up to two feet long.

On the higher reaches, the differences between the cliffs
of the south and west and those of the north become more
apparent. The south and west cliffs in the main carry low-
growing vegetation except for the cliff-top heaths or where
a valley cutting through the cliff produces a different habitat.
Many of the more interesting species which grow on these
cliffs finish their growing season in early summer and are
dormant in bulb or in seed form by the time the heat of full
summer parches the ground. In low open turf where soil
only thinly covers the granite a succession of minute plants,
with correspondingly small but delicately beautiful flowers,
occurs from February to May. The weather is then warm
but not too hot, and the soil is still moist. Many of these
species are normally at home much further south and Jersey
is on the northern fringe of their range.

In February the early sand-grass will be flowering. It is
one of the shortest of annual grasses, usually little more than
an inch or two high including the flower. The small green
tufts, often with a purple tinge, are abundant in some areas.
It occurs in the other Channel Islands, but elsewhere in
Britain it is native only in Anglesey. Two small chickweeds,
the sea mouse-ear and the little mouse-ear, produce tiny
flowers of pure dazzling white when they open full in
the sun, and Jersey has a dwarf form of corn spurrey
Spergula arvensis var. *nana* which bears white flowers very
freely early in the year. At the end of March and in April
these cliffs are worth a special visit to see the sand crocus
which on the mainland grows in only one place and then
sparingly. The flowers do not open in dull weather, so it is
essential to choose a day when the sun is shining. Find
an area where the short open turf is about an inch high,
preferably containing a good deal of moss, and sit down.
These plants are so small they can easily be overlooked
and it is essential to get one's 'eye in' for them. The dark
green moss may well, on a close inspection, be found to be
beautifully studded with pale bluish-purple stars of sand
crocus, about half an inch across. There will also be glints of
bright sapphire-blue, from flowers of the dwarf early wall
speedwell.

In some places there will be leaves of the Jersey buttercup which flowers in early May, by which time the sand crocus will be fruiting. This buttercup occurs nowhere else in the British Isles or the Channel Islands. It flowers irregularly, perhaps because it likes the soil to remain moist until late in spring and Jersey frequently has a hot spell in March or April. Some years a patch of it on a côtil on the foothills of St Ouen has more than a hundred flowers on it, and other years perhaps only two or three. In 1974, the spring was very dry and not a single plant in the Island was seen in flower. In a normal year the leaves are often withering by the time the plant flowers and, even if not, they are inconspicuous compared with the large flower which is borne well clear of the low turf on a bolt-upright stem six inches or more high.

Normally one associates rushes with wet meadows and fairly luxuriant vegetation, but these south and west cliffs have a minute rush, the dwarf rush, which like many of the other plants on the cliffs and dunes is a spring ephemeral, an annual which completes its life in the early months of the year. It is a tufted plant, often little more than an inch high, yet in that short space containing stem, leaves, flowers, and, later, fruit like any of the much larger rushes. Single plants grow here and there in open turf, but in the early 1960s there were so many plants near La Corbière that the surface of the ground over many square yards was reddish when they fruited. The spotted rock-rose, an annual, is at its best a little later in May and in June. The five petals of its lovely pale yellow flowers each have a small but conspicuous dark brown blotch near the throat of the flower. They fall shortly after midday, so a morning visit is necessary to see the flowers at their best. The spotted rock-rose is truly at home in the Mediterranean region and is a very rare and local plant in the British Isles. In the Channel Islands it.is locally common in some parts of Jersey and it occurs on a small area above the south cliffs of Alderney.

Common cat's-ear, ox-eye daisy, milkwort, and trailing St John's-wort add more colour and variety so that in spring and early summer these cliffs are a delight to any flower lover. In the heat of full summer they tend to be parched and bare, but in late summer they are worth visiting again. Heather and bell heather flower in profusion on the cliff-top heaths and spill over down the cliff slopes as does western gorse. The first flowers of autumn squill come up in July and some can be found right through to the end of September. They are relatives of the spring squill which does not grow in the Channel Islands, but whereas the spring squill puts its leaves up and then goes on to flower as is the more usual order, autumn squill behaves like the Jersey or belladonna lily, *Amaryllis belladonna* and begins its growing season by putting up its flowers first to be followed later by its leaves. It is dormant after the leaves have died. *La belle toute-nue* is the apt Jersey-French name for *Amaryllis belladonna* and could well be for the autumn squill.

The easiest time to explore the north coast cliffs is spring. The vegetation is so luxuriant during summer and autumn that it is virtually impossible to push a way through it unless one goes specially prepared. Where there is sufficient depth of soil a mixture of bracken and bramble usually clothes the slopes engulfing all but the wide paths maintained by the States of Jersey and the National Trust for Jersey. These paths are open all year round, but the steep narrow tracks used by ormerers in winter to get down to the smaller bays and inlets become completely overgrown in summer. By June the grandeur of the huge pink or grey granite masses projecting into the sea is offset by the lush vivid green of the vegetation which follows and emphasises the contours of the less steep slopes. As autumn comes, the bracken and bramble turn a golden or coppery brown and after the storms of winter have raged against the cliffs, clearing away or beating down the now dead vegetation of the previous summer, it is once again possible to explore the area. Many plants which are more usually associated with woodland, grow on the cliffs. They flower in spring and later bracken gives them the shade normally provided by trees. To me the most beautiful of them is the wild daffodil, a native wild flower which has been here for centuries and is not to be confused with any of the garden escapes of which there are literally thousands. It can be seen in woods in the inland valleys though to me it is the more striking on cliffs of the north coast when the sun picks out its yellow heads among dead bracken on a rough grassy slope above the sea. One of the most beautiful sights I have seen in Jersey was a herring gull sitting on a nest surrounded by fragile-looking wild daffodils at the foot of a huge grey lichen-covered boulder. Away below the sea was dazzling blue. Wood-sorrel, a common English plant, grows in few woods here but is in good quantity occasionally on the cliffs, for example, to the west of Le Petit Port at the foot of Egypt. This is the delicate, pale shell-pink native oxalis which does not make a nuisance of itself like most of the other oxalis species which have come in of late years. And it may seem strange but there are as many bluebells on the cliffs of Jersey as in the woods.

The high land of St Mary, St John and Trinity acts as a watershed in the Island, so that several small streams run the short distance northwards down to the sea. The sides of these streams down the cliffs are lined with dark green hemlock water-dropwort and hemp-agrimony. In one place the stream falls over the edge of a small quarry and forms a most impressive waterfall in winter. The spray creates an atmosphere so humid that the rocks, trees and bushes within the quarry are festooned with moss and the ferns are so luxuriant that the whole area is more reminiscent of a tropical forest than the north coast of Jersey. Few cliff faces are vertical and often a stream will reach a flat area where it will disperse, creating damp conditions. Moisture-loving plants grow in the wetter of these, including in one area the greater tussock-sedge, well-named from its huge three-foot-high tussocks. In other places yellow archangel and dog's mercury, both rare plants in Jersey, or opposite-leaved golden-saxifrage may be underfoot with willows and oaks above, the whole being intertwined with liana-like stems of honeysuckle and ivy. It is possible to survey a length of cliff and know from the tree cover which parts have water.

A daphne, the evergreen spurge-laurel, grows sparingly on the cliffs of St John, usually within the leaf-fall area of a stunted tree where the habitat is slightly different from that of the bracken and bramble-covered slopes. Small racemes of wax-like green flowers appear in the axils of the darker green leathery leaves in February and seem able to withstand the winter gales with ease. Ox-eye daisies and primroses grow in profusion on some of the grassier slopes and the lesser-known saw-wort, devil's bit scabious and spotted cat's-ear are local. In my experience there is only one flower which rivals an orchid in its appeal to the flower-loving public and that is a cowslip. Orchids have a fascination about them but cowslips a charisma. The Botanical Society of the British Isles is much concerned about the number of rare or unusual wild flowers now being picked and so being unable to set seed. Its most recent poster, issued at the time the Wild Flower Protection Bill received its second reading in the House of Lords, showed a group of cowslips with the caption *Please Leave Wild Flowers for Others to Enjoy.* We have cowslips in small quantity on one part of the north coast.

The cliff-top heaths and commons all round the Island are magnificent when gorse is in full bloom in spring. Sheets of yellow cover many vergées and the scent of the flowers fills the air. Later, on hot days in summer, the seed pods can be heard exploding as they open. About the end of July a different species, western gorse, a low-growing gorse of a deeper colour, comes into flower. It can be seen at its best on Les Landes where it mixes with heather and bell heather which are about the same height to give a rich carpet of orange and purple throughout most of August. At this time Grosnez is one of the sights of Jersey and well worth a special visit. Common gorse is unusual in that whereas most shrubs flower at one period of the year only, a few flowers of common gorse can be found at any time. Like western gorse, its flower buds are produced and are visible on the shoots in late summer. Western gorse follows the more normal pattern and goes straight on to flower and a few buds of common gorse do break into flower then and during the winter, but most are held back by some mechanism until the weather warms up the following spring.

The heaths where western gorse and heather grow are acidic as is most of the agricultural land in Jersey, for there

Burnet Rose *Rosa pimpinelli-folia* in fruit.

Burnet Rose *Rosa pimpinellifolia* in flower.

is little or no calcareous rock to break down into a basic soil. Occasionally a few lime-loving plants will grow together on the cliffs indicating a difference in pH value in some small pockets of soil, but the only naturally occurring extensive areas of calcareous soil are the dunes where crushed shells give a high lime content, in particular the dune system of Les Blanches Banques and Les Quennevais. Dunes in the process of formation are stabilised by marram whose rhizomes help to bind the loose moving sand. Marram flourishes when its growing points are continuously receiving a new covering of sand and it will be noticed that the older and more stable the dune the less the marram which grows on it. If the sand is firmer

sand sedge also helps. Its long runners can often be seen
crossing the bare floor of sand blow-outs. Once the surface
is fixed other plants gain a foothold, and botanists will
realise how base-rich the dune soil is when they see hutchinsia flourishing.

Other small springtime species, many rare elsewhere, will
also be found: dwarf pansy, spring vetch, early forget-me-not,
changing forget-me-not and small hare's ear which, though
often only about an inch high, belongs to the umbelliferae,
most of whose members are of considerable size. Creamy
white flowers of the burnet rose scent the air in June and are
followed later by their almost spherical black-purple fruits.
Occasionally the roses will have a pink tinge. Lady's-bedstraw,
sea-holly, the green-winged orchid and kidney vetch all
thrive as they have done for generations and at dusk
evening-primroses, a fairly new addition to Jersey's flora,
open their large scented flowers to attract night-flying moths.
Wild thyme, which spreads low over the ground, is smothered
with small flowers in late summer, and the short turf may
be pinkish-purple over a considerable area. Many gardeners
have attempted to establish lawns of low mat-forming peren-
nials like thyme, chamomile and pennyroyal which give off
an aromatic smell when crushed underfoot. At La Hague
Manor, for instance, a very successful chamomile lawn has
been created, yet in August, unnoticed by many people a
natural turf of unsurpassed beauty grows wild on the dunes
of St Ouen, St Peter and St Brelade.

Thrift flowers principally in May and has long fine leaves
less than an eighth of an inch wide. It occurs on rocky coasts
of north and west Europe, including Jersey which is towards
the southern end of its range. But Jersey is also just within
the range of another thrift, the Jersey thrift, a species more
often seen in the Mediterranean region and in south
Europe and which does not reach the other Channel Islands
or the British Isles. Its flowers are borne about nine or 10
inches high on much longer stouter stems than the usual
thrift and its leaves have a normal leaf shape, not being linear,
but perhaps its simplest difference is that it flowers almost
two or three months later. Holidaymakers in Britain in

summer do not normally see thrift at its best because it flowers in May and early June, but this Jersey thrift is in full flower on the dunes in August.

The dunes and other flat sandy areas are particularly rich in interesting grasses. The beautiful grey hair-grass, a grey-green tufted perennial shot with purple, is plentiful on Les Quennevais. Bulbous meadow-grass is almost as early as early sand-grass and both the normal and viviparous forms grow together as they do on the Continent. It dies down, sometimes as early as April, and stores its energy for the next growing season in a bulbous base which tends to get blown out of the light sandy soil. Large numbers of these straw-coloured bases of this normally rare grass are often blown about like chaff on L'Ouaisné and piled into mounds. Other, taller, native grasses, downy oat-grass and crested hair-grass, grow abundantly on parts of the dunes, the downy oat-grass in particular giving them a meadow-like appearance in June. Hare's-tail grass is used in enormous quantity to make exhibits for the Battle of Flowers. There are no certain records of it before the 1870s when J. Piquet brought some seed from Guernsey and sowed it in St Ouen. In 1877 he showed it to Dr Druce, a well-known English botanist, who reported that there was no more than could be covered by a pocket handkerchief, yet when he returned in 1906 he found that it filled the Bay. The great inroads made by exhibitors for the Battle of Flowers seem to make little impression on the amount the following year, and indeed they may accidentally be responsible for its spread. They carry it to all parts of the Island and while it does not survive in competition with the vegetation of inland areas, it has become established in other sandy bays. It is an annual grass, essentially Mediterranean in character, which occurs here and there up the west coast of France to the Channel. The frost of the winter 1962/63 killed off the greater part of the seedlings so the following summer it was scarce, but by 1964 the quantity was back to normal. Another grass of more southern regions, rough dog's-tail, often grows with hare's-tail and though it has one-sided, greener, rougher, less silky flower heads, it can easily be mistaken for hare's-tail.

Inland the Island is intensively farmed. Good arable land, well farmed for generations, obviously will hold little of the native flora though the wooded côtils of the inland valleys, the wet meadows of the valley floors and the hedge banks are full of interest. There is a marked pattern in the distribution of trees, the east and centre being well wooded, but the wind-blown west containing few. Of late years it has become fashionable to decry the lack of trees in Jersey. This I do not understand. The Island is not large enough for a forest, but from almost anywhere in the interior it is possible to gaze over a landscape containing innumerable trees in hedgerows, on wooded slopes and in private gardens. Admittedly there are few specimen trees and this is to be regretted. Also trees which fall in gales are seldom replaced and if they are, the fashion is now for conifers rather than the deciduous trees which were originally present.

Throughout historical times, a good deal of the coast has been treeless, providing a magnificent landscape with a totally different character from that of inland wooded areas. Attempts are now being made to change that character by the regimented planting of specially imported trees. Apart from blurring or smothering the shapes and outlines of the coast which have remained unchanged for centuries, the natural vegetation of the dunes and cliffs and the gorse commons, all of which are typical of Jersey, will be destroyed, and the insect, bird and animal fauna associated with them will vanish. Any further destruction of these habitats, some of the most valuable in Jersey from a natural history point of view, should be resisted by all people interested in the conservation of the Island's wild life. At the same time encouragement should be given to the replanting of trees in hedgerows and along road sides and to the maintenance and improvement of inland woods and copses.

The question as to which trees are native in the Island often arises and many present-day species have been claimed as native because they were present when the peat beds which underlie parts of the Island were laid down. While one may accept that some of these species have survived here unaided, for example, that some oaks may be direct descen-

dants of those in post-glacial times, equally others, like
cedar, did not survive and the present cedar trees are very
recent introductions. Most of the trees present in wild
situations today and maintaining themselves through seedlings, fall somewhere between these two extremes and their
detailed history is unknown.

Records of the recent past give oak, evergreen oak, sweet
chestnut and elm as the commonest trees of the Island. In
1975 they are still common, but sycamore must be added
to the list. The oaks are usually the pendunculate oak,
though a few planted sessile oaks are known and trees with
intermediate characters exist. Oaks occur in good quantity
as hedgerow trees, on côtils and as single trees on the cliffs
where they are often covered with marble galls after infes-
tation by a gall mite. From the 13th to the 17th centuries,
oak trunks, oak planks and oak beams were mentioned as
being imported from Bere near Porchester, or from Normandy. This may simply have been because the oaks here
were inferior in quality though they would still appear to
have been valued highly. Strong objections were raised when
the Governor, Sir George Carteret, in January 1647/8 gave
orders for some young oak trees to be removed from
Mr Herault's garden and replanted on both sides of Mont
Orgueil Castle. Eventually the trees were shared. A century
and a half later, in 1789, when the 200-ton vessel *Elisha
Tupper* was built at Bel Royal from oak grown in St Lawrence, the *Gazette de L'Ile de Jersey* claimed, just before
the launching, that there was more than a hundred times as
much oak left in the parish. While this is the parish which
contains the Fief des Arbres, historians think it more likely
that the claim was made with the political situation of the
time in mind rather than a strict regard for accuracy.

Elms, which form a notoriously difficult group botani-
cally, are the most numerous of the trees in Jersey in 1975,
though, depending on the severity of the attack of Dutch
elm disease, they may not remain so. Dr R. H. Richens has
studied them in detail and suggests that there are two main
kinds here, the small-leaved *Ulmus minor* and the larger-
leaved *U. minor x glabra*. The wych elm *U. glabra*, a more

northern tree, seems to occur in situations where it is
obviously planted specially, usually as a single tree, perhaps
to mark a place of importance. There is one record from the
past when an elm tree, of unspecified kind, is known to have
been so used. In 1707 the Seigneurial Court of the Fief des
Arbres in St Lawrence ordered Charles Le Brun to replace
an elm which he had felled, *'un certain orme appellé l'orme
du Conseil'* which marked the boundary of the fief.

Trees with an upright branching system, called the Jersey
elm or Guernsey elm *U. sarniensis* by horticulturalists,
have sometimes been planted as in the older parts of the
avenue outside St Ouen's Manor and along New Beaumont
Hill just above the Cannon. This type of elm, which Dr
Richens suggests is simply another form of *U. minor,* is
common in Guernsey but not in Jersey, and the name Jersey
elm as applied to it would appear to be a misnomer. Indeed
the name *sarniensis* suggests they are from Guernsey. If
from Jersey it would have been *caesariensis.* The normal
form of the small-leaved elm and the larger-leaved hybrid
make up a major part of Jersey's tree cover. Elm trees are
used to produce shelter belts for the fields. They are cut
back severely every few years with the result that they send
out side shoots which filter the wind and the canopy does
not become thick enough to shade the crop. This custom
calls forth many comments from tree lovers who do not
understand the farmers' reasons and who wish to see
specimen trees. The fact that elms are used in this way may
give a clue to the source of the hybrid here. It is known
that cider-apple orchards needed protection from the wind
and it is possible that elms might have been imported into
Jersey from Normandy at the same time as stocks and
new varieties of cider-apples.

The quantity of sweet chestnut is one of the features of
the Island. Trees of sufficient size and quality to produce
edible and roastable nuts occur on many côtils. During the
Occupation large numbers of trees were felled for fuel
even though the wood burns badly. The stools have now
grown again to maturity, each with several trunks.

The evergreen oak is considered to be native as far north as Brittany. When it spread to Jersey is unknown, but it is common here and regenerates freely. It is most often seen obviously planted round houses, rather than wild in woods, but stunted trees are to be found on some of the off-islets like La Grosse Tête and L'Ile au Guerdain and seedlings commonly occur on the cliffs. The sycamore is a comparative newcomer from central Europe and is now common on many of the inland côtils. It makes a beautiful tree when fully grown in isolation, but unfortunately it is more often seen invading woods and producing multitudes of weak saplings. Beech and ash, while not as common as the foregoing, are still widespread and can be found in most parts of the Island except the extreme west. Ash tends to be a single roadside or hedgerow tree, and so with beech, but several fine planted avenues of beech occur and saplings of both are found in woods.

Turkey oak, holly and hazel are frequent, but not as widely distributed as ash and beech. Single, planted trees of Turkey oak can be seen mainly in the south and east. Holly was also a favourite in the past for hedges and shrubberies, but it occurs in many wooded areas of the centre and east and seeds itself. Hazel occurred in enormous quantity thousands of years ago when the peat was laid down, and nuts can sometimes be found in the peat in St Ouen's Bay. Hazel trees now grow in the central valleys from Beaumont to Swiss Valley, usually along the streams. Some trees may be descendants of those of the far past, but I must admit that all I know look planted at some time. And so with alder trees. These were here in quantity at one stage in Jersey's archaeological history and many damp places scattered over the Island, except for the west, contain fine alders today.

The trees mentioned so far are the main constituents of most Jersey woods, but each area has its own individuality. In some, oak will predominate, in others sweet chestnut or elm, and there will be other species. In the woods of the National Trust for Jersey, the Don Powis and the Don Gaudin contain wild cherry, the Don Powis a few red oaks

and the Don Le Gallais hornbeam. A côtil above Dannemarche Reservoir in Waterworks Valley has a thriving copse
of snowy mespilus *Amelanchier lamarckiana*. Any area in
the north east is likely to contain medlar, for example,
the woods around the slip at Le Saie. The wood at the top
of the valley running down through the heart of Les Quennevais contains a few rowan trees and wild pears. All these
woodlands are of great interest and variety and well worth
investigating and exploring. It is to the maintenance and
re-stocking of these woods that the main tree-planting efforts
should be directed.

There is no tradition of charcoal burning in the Island,
yet charcoal was needed, for it was imported from England
and often appears in the accounts for Mont Orgueil. Nor
is there any evidence that the local woods were ever coppiced
even though the main ingredients of English coppices, hazel
and sweet chestnut, do occur here. It may be that the earth
banks below the actual hedges were so large there was no
demand for hurdles for fencing orchards or arable fields.
Animals were usually tethered or kept in bounds by walls.
Poingdestre stated in his *Caesarea* in 1682 that the hedges
were of hawthorn, blackthorn and willow, and he gave an
account of the construction of a hedgebank:

> The fences vsed in this Island are farre differing from
> those in other parts, being made of solid earth raised a
> good height, with a ditch on each side in ye manner of
> a bank or rampier, soe high that in some parts of ye
> Island a man with a staff in his hand three foot long can
> not reach to ye top . . . When they have raised it within
> a foot of its due height they take white thorne of two
> or three yeares old, which they haue of theire owne
> or buy it at easy rates, & lay it flat in a rowe upon ye
> top of ye fence crosswaye & that of both sides alike,
> each thorne distant not aboue foure or five inches
> from the other & then couer the roote with new earth
> from the bottom of ye ditch, a foot high, leauing of
> ye yong thorne but very little without; which they care-
> fully clipp euen with ye side of ye fence. This worke

is to be don in ye beginning of ye spring while it is yet
planting time, & it failes not to growe in few years into
a thicke hedge sufficient to keep any thing from breaking into ye ground within it. To produce that infinute
store of thornes wch is requisite for this vse, & wch is
made vse of yearly, they take about October or November of ye hawes or red berries growing plentifully upō
thornes one or two bushells, & lay drye three or four
foot deepe into the ground in a trodden place, first a
laye of hawes some two inches thicke, & then a lay of
earth & soe continuing lay after lay, till all ye hawes
be in. Then couering all with earth at least two foot
ouer them, they tred it so as ye raine may not pene-
trate through it, & soe leave them from Novemb (which
is ye moneth for this worke) till ye beginning of ye
spring not of ye next, but of ye other after, viz: about
sixteene moneths; & then they haue a care about ye
end of Febr. or beginning of March to obserue when ye
thorne begins to shoot. And yt is ye nick of time to take
it up; but then it begins to stirre & not before. It being
taken yp, they sowe it very thick into squares or beds
fittly prepared, & couer it with straw for ye birds: and
those are their nurseryes for thornes.

The remains of some of these hedges can still be seen
today in the northern parishes. They must have closely
resembled those in Normandy which the Americans found
so difficult to fight over in the battles behind the landing
beaches in 1944 that they call this part of the war, 'The
Battle of the Hedges'. Hawthorn, blackthorn and willow still
occur commonly in hedges and many blackthorn thickets
have arisen through the bushes spreading out over rough
uncultivated ground. Similarly an elm hedge is often backed
by a copse of elm trees formed by the original trees sucker-
ing. There is no layering of hedges, the lopping of the top,
whether the species involved is a tree or a shrub, taking
its place.

Willows seem strange plants to use for hedging in areas
not wet all the year round, but the native grey willow can

often be found away from water in lines obviously planted. This particular willow and also the other native species, creeping willow, which now occurs only on the wet parts of L'Ouaisné, are useless for basket work or lobster-pot making. For this purpose large quantities of other species were imported, particularly from the Nantes district of France, according to A. P. Laurent whose family has used willows for basket-work for years. Many were planted and the remains of willow beds for cutting can still be found. Laurent worked the one at the top of St Peter's Valley until recently, and Mrs J. Stevens tells me that besides willow occurring in field names in six parishes, there is a mention of *la saulsée ou taillis,* presumably a willow bed for cutting willows, in 1776. The planted species would be those which are pliable, specially the osier, which is now widespread, and Laurent also spoke highly· of purple willow which he had used from Handois. It still grows both near the mudpond there and in a hedge north-east of St Ouen's Pond. Branches of the white willow from Waterworks Valley were used for heavier work in the base of baskets.

Near the coast tamarisk and argentum or shrubby orache, *Atriplex halimus,* hedges flourish, the grey-leaved argentum being a superb foil for the pink feathery sprays of tamarisk. I have seen no seedlings of either of these species, and though the argentum sets seed it seems to increase only by layering itself in the ground. Euonymus, like tamarisk, seems to stay where planted and not to increase. We use its lovely fruiting sprays for Christmas decoration instead of holly, but in spite of some bushes bearing enormous quantities of fruit I have never seen a seedling. This hedging plant is *Euonymus japonicus* from Japan, not the European native species *Euonymus europaeus* the spindle. Euonymus has been used for hedging particularly near habitations in almost all parts of the Island. Some of it is so large and looks so well established it is difficult to believe it was only brought to England from Japan in 1804. After the vogue for euonymus, garden privet was used for hedging. This is not to be confused with our native wild privet which grows on Les

Quennevais and the Ile Agois. Another change in fashion, and probably availability, about 50 years ago brought Monterey cypress *Cupressus macrocarpa* in great quantity. Many hedges were left untrimmed, particularly during the Occupation, and bare trunks of gaunt trees now show where hedges used to be. Two other cypresses, Lawson's and Leyland's, have lately been planted in unsympathetic dark green lines, but more often round gardens than fields. It is difficult to say what the present hedging plant is for agricultural land. The old favourites previously mentioned are used occasionally and so is elder and flowering currant, but since the advent of the electric fence the need for substantial hedges has decreased.

Cover on the hedge banks increases from winter through spring until by the time of the *branchage* in July it is spilling over into the road. A second *branchage* is arranged in September so that the summer growth is also cut back. The interior hedgebanks carry the heaviest vegetation with red campion and green alkanet, which must be the bluest of all blue flowers, predominating in some parts. Arums do well, and both lords-and-ladies and its larger southern relative, the Italian lords-and-ladies are frequent, particularly in the south east. The leaves of the Italian lords-and-ladies, which come up in November and can then easily be seen among the sparse vegetation, are always pale-veined, but one sub-species has the most beautiful dark green leaves with pure white veins. Primroses and violets do grow on hedgebanks, but they are not as common as on the inland côtils and the cliffs. Parts of Grosnez Common were covered in sheets of flowering violets about 18 months after the great fire of 1969. On the other hand, greater stitchwort, which is absent from all the other Channel Islands, is extremely common along the inland lanes of Jersey. Very moist banks, shaded all year, are often covered with myriads of leaves of Cornish moneywort, a local plant confined to the west of Europe.

In 1852 Miss Julia Marett caused great excitement among fern botanists when she sent to London for identification a piece of a small very delicate fern from a hedgebank near

La Haule. It proved to be the annual fern *Anogramma leptophylla* which spreads up the west coast of Europe a short distance from the Mediterranean regions which are its normal home. It occurs in one place in Guernsey, but has not been found in the other Channel Islands or in the British Isles. Here it has been recorded from the roadside banks in most of the inland valleys running down to St Aubin's Bay, and a small patch flourishes on a vertical bank by the main path in St Andrew's Park. The banks where it grows are usually fairly moist in the early part of the year, and this is when it is at its best. By the time the heat of summer parches the soil, the Jersey fern, being annual, has already released its spores and disappeared.

Often the hedgebanks are built of large stones and soil. These tend to have a less lush vegetation. In the north and north west, where there are many such banks, purple stems of wild thyme trail over grey shale or pink granite. Silky-haired, black-glanded mouse-ear hawkweeds with large yellow flowers, particularly *Hieracium peleterianum,* flourish, together with dark green lanceolate spleenwort, whose fronds curl strangely backwards, and blue sheep's-bit, the only native member of the campanula family in Jersey now. Navel-wort is common on such banks and on most walls throughout the Island. Its peculiar round leaves are produced in spring and are almost over by June when the long spike which carries drooping whitish-green tubular flowers is fully grown.

Wet places in the inland valleys are so warm in summer they are full of the most luxuriant vegetation and are almost impassable. White umbels of hemlock water-dropwort and wild angelica compete for space, huge plants of the once rare great willowherb appear in quantity and massed spikes of purple-loosestrife are occasionally seen. Ragged-Robin, water forget-me-not, and yellow iris flourish among the lower marsh vegetation, with iris flowers sometimes forming a yellow ribbon along the sides of streams, as along the one which threads its way down St Peter's Valley. Many shallow wet areas will be bright blue with short spikes of the speed-well brooklime, and in late summer galingale, which belongs to the same family as the sedges, will be in flower. This plant, well-known as *han* in Jersey-French, is so strong when dried that, time past, it was extremely valuable, being used in place of hemp for cords and ropes. Matting for floors, tethers for cows, and halters and collars for horses were made of it. Les Hannièthes in St Ouen and La Hannièthe in St Martin are places where *han* grew, and indeed still grows today, but as Dr Le Maistre, looking at it from a farmer's point of view, writes in his *Dictionnaire: 'Y'a eune hannièthe là-bas; n'y'a pon grand patuthe'*.

Many species of roadsides and waste ground, i.e., of land disturbed by man, are those grown previously as crops or garden plants. They tend to persist for only a few years and then die out, but occasionally a species will compete success-fully with the native vegetation. The tens of thousands, or perhaps even hundreds of thousands, of feral daffodils and narcissi would seem to be a permanent reminder of the horticultural industry which began in a small way last century, increased just before the last war, and has been tremendously important since the 1950s. It is probably possible to find most of the varieties ever cultivated, growing feral somewhere and in artificial settings like the banks between fields they are a delight from January to May. But their method of increase is different from those of the truly wild species. The wild species sets seed freely and a new plant may grow wherever a seed falls, but the majority of feral daffodils seem to increase mainly by bulb offsets, so that though the clump may get bigger the plants remain *in situ* and do not spread over the intervening spaces. The result is that wild woodland deliberately planted out with cultivated species 'to naturalise' never again assumes a wild appearance but is always a somewhat distasteful hotchpotch.

The Jersey Agricultural and Horticultural Society, now the Royal Jersey Agricultural and Horticultural Society, experimented with new plant species from its foundation in 1833 hoping to improve the winter fodder of cattle and the quality of grassland for summer grazing. Some of the species they introduced are still in use today, and others, though no longer used, remain in the Island's wild flora. In the Report for 1834, an entry about crimson clover runs,

'The Visiting Committee saw, on 1st of last May, a crop of
this Clover, belonging to Mr. De Faye of Grouville, upwards
of three feet in height, rich, thick, succulent and in beautiful
flower; this crop had been sown in the previous September,
and cut in December, when after three months growth, it
was again fit to be cut. Can a finer crop be suggested to the
Jersey Farmer, who considers his cow the great object of
his care, and the great source of his profit?' This clover
is not in general use today, so presumably it did not live
up to expectations, but a few plants occasionally occur. The
flowers are so beautiful being a brilliant crimson with a
soft satiny sheen, that a whole field in full flower must
indeed have been a spectacular sight. Chicory was not
a success. It grew superbly, but according to Col. Le Couteur
it was too laxative. It would be interesting to know if any
of the chicory at present growing wild is a descendant of this
introduction. Col. Le Couteur also introduced a rough
comfrey '*Symphytum asperrimum*' which he said came from
the Caucasus. Some of our present comfreys may be derivatives from this introduction. The Committee experimented
with artificial grasses, and by 1837 a mixture of cock's-foot,
golden oat, rye grass, rough-stalked meadow grass, meadow
cat's-tail or Timothy, clover and sweet vernal grass, to use
the names of the time, was recommended for rotation
and a mixture of fox-tail, cock's-foot, rye grass, Italian
ryegrass, meadow fescue, rough-stalked meadow grass and
'Cow Grass—*true* trifolium pratenté perenné' were recommended for meadow lands. Of these golden oat, Timothy
and Italian ryegrass would be new species to the island.
Golden oat (yellow oat-grass) has not been seen here for
about 50 years, but Timothy and Italian ryegrass are still
used and are common.

In the past flax, good-King-Henry and hemp were reported
as escapes from cultivation. Today, potatoes and tomatoes
frequently appear. Tomato plants grow in the oddest places.
One, bearing ripe fruit, was growing out of a crack in the
pavement in St Helier. Isolated rocks out at sea often have
great numbers of them, presumably where tomato seeds
have been deposited in the droppings of gulls.

The mild climate of Jersey allows many garden plants to set good seed and if they have an efficient dispersal method they are likely to spread outside the garden. If they are infertile hybrids, or single-sex plants, thrown away as garden outcasts, they may well continue to grow *in situ* until again uprooted by man or covered by his next discarded plants. The huge clump of pampas-grass at St Catherine probably originated when someone threw away a load of garden rubbish. It is known to have been there at least 50 years. Among the larger garden escapes buddleja or butterfly-bush is probably here permanently. Its winged seeds may well germinate wherever they are blown, even high up on walls right in the centre of St Helier. The wind also distributes Mexican fleabane, the small pinky-white daisy-type flower which smothers some walls. Its seeds are topped with thistledown so they can drift away to new places in the slightest breeze.

Cottage gardens in the past often contained a gladiolus known as *êtchelles dé Jâcob* to a Jerseyman, Jack to a Cornishman, and *G. byzantinus* to a botanist. It seeds itself freely and plants appear frequently in the most unexpected places. For instance, one flowered on the Route de l'Eglise, St Ouen, at the foot of a roadside granite wall, and others have flowered on Green Island. In the gardens round Mount Bingham down by the harbour, large numbers grow, obviously where not intended. They must surely be some of the most beautiful weeds ever known and Jersey would also lose something of its history if they were to be weeded out.

In May, many roadsides are lined with the garden escape three-cornered leek which is often picked as white bluebells, but then thrown away when the smell from the cut stem or bruised leaves becomes noticeable. Bulbs can still be bought from nurserymen, though it has been part of the Island's flora since last century. Other garlics, some extremely beautiful, including honey bells *Nothoscordum inodorum*, which even has a pleasant scent, have escaped this century and are becoming well-established.

Another bulbous plant, winter daffodil *Sternbergia lutea*, flourishes on the south-east slopes outside the walls of

Gorey Castle. How it arrived is unknown, but it was well established more than 50 years ago. The large crocus-like flowers of brilliant gold come up in autumn before the leaves are in full growth. Normally they grow wild in the eastern Mediterranean, especially in biblical lands, and some authorities suggest that Christ was referring to them in his sermon on the Mount: 'And why take ye thought for raiment? Consider the lilies of the field, how they grow; they toil not, neither do they spin: And yet I say unto you, that even Solomon in all his glory was not arrayed like one of these'.

A climbing ragwort or groundsel, *Senecio mikanioides*, sometimes called German ivy, was found sprawling up and over hedges between Archirondel and Rozel in the mid-1920s. Since then it has spread to other parts of the Island. It is a tender, South African, climbing plant sometimes used to cover trellis. The leaves are ivy-shaped, but soft and palish-green and any superficial resemblance to ivy is shed at flowering time, late November, when it produces a typical groundsel head of small, yellow flowers.

Tree lupin from California is particularly common in the south west, not on the dunes, but on disturbed land of low agricultural value. Its origin is unknown though it probably came in as a garden flower. And so with the evening-primroses which glow with a yellow luminosity at dusk when moths are flying. Slender speedwell, now in many places in the eastern half of Jersey, undoubtedly came originally as a highly desirable rock-garden plant before the war. It blooms profusely, being covered with typical bright blue speedwell flowers for a good deal of the year, and it increases at what appears to be a highly satisfactory rate, until it takes over first the rock-garden, then the lawn and shrubbery, and finally goes through the hedge and down the road along the roadside bank. The lawns and borders of the Howard Davis farm gardens are full of it. Its original home was Asia Minor where it is no nuisance at all. It is difficult to imagine a tree as a weed, but if a weed is simply a plant growing in the wrong place then sycamore can be. Few trees are more majestic if well-grown, but, as mentioned earlier, too often they are to be found as weak saplings coming up in quantity in already established woodland and destroying the quality of that woodland. Its history in the Island is unknown but it is a tree of eastern Europe and is thought to have been in England for only about 400 years.

Some species have been deliberately introduced, particularly about the turn of the century, but most have not succeeded. For instance, in spite of repeated attempts to establish marsh marigolds in the wild, even single plants have rarely been seen in the last 50 years. A cultivated form grows in the ornamental pool in Rozel Manor grounds, and occasionally plants of this appear by the side of the stream flowing down to St Catherine. Few introductions have succeeded as well as the hare's tail sown by J. Piquet at St Ouen and his sweet flag still grows well in the pool on Noirmont where he planted it last century.

The composition of the weed flora of gardens and arable land is continually changing. Years ago, agricultural seed contained many impurities and cornfields or sown leys contained poppies, cornflowers and corncockle. There are few cornfields today and seed is much purer. Poppies remain but the cornflower and the corncockle have disappeared except as escapes from deliberate sowings in gardens. Some calcifuge species are scarcer because the States began giving a lime subsidy in the 1950s and fields which were once golden yellow with corn marigold now only have a few plants round the edges. Also weedkillers are used extensively in arable fields. Some species are less susceptible than others and as a result flourish in the absence of competition. In September I have seen scentless mayweed almost blotting out fields of tomatoes which were over and no longer being picked. There are some weeds which no weedkiller can yet destroy, principally the *Oxalis* group of which at least 10 different species are here now. Only one is native, the beautiful and entirely harmless wood-sorrel. A few of the others are reasonably decorative and not particularly damaging, but three species, *O. corymbosa*, *O. latifolia* and *O. tetraphylla* are some of the worst weeds known to man. They have leaves vaguely like clover leaves, but

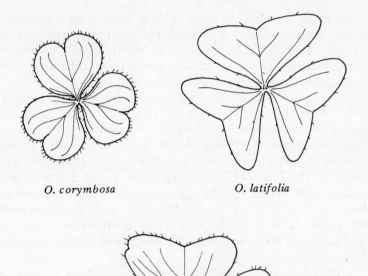

O. corymbosa   *O. latifolia*

O. tetraphylla
Leaves of three species of *Oxalis*, some of Jersey's most persistent weeds.

roots that look like white bulbs. One often hears that they came during the Occupation, but *O. tetraphylla* and *O. latifolia* were here before then, being recorded first in 1917/18 and 1925 respectively, though *O. corymbosa* was not recorded until 1956. Their spread is almost certainly due to a change in methods of tilling the soil. Ploughing or hand digging, as in the past, kept the soil and its contents more or less in one area, whereas the rotary cultivator now in use flings them far and wide, comparatively speaking. Oxalis bulbs and offsets could ask for nothing better and multiply exceedingly under this treatment.

But whatever the changes in large-scale agriculture and horticulture or small-scale gardening, some weeds have persisted down the ages. Common couch, field horsetail and bindweed are all as well-known here now as in the past, and as in the rest of Britain, but there are one or two specialities, mostly on light sandy soils of the coast. Crab grass or hairy finger-grass with an inflorescence like four or five fine fingers flourishes in many gardens. Its Latin name is *Digitaria sanguinalis* and the specific epithet comes from its colour if growing on parched ground and is not an expletive from generations of gardeners. *Pourpier, Portulaca oleracea,* also flourishes. This is a small yellow-flowered annual with shiny dark-green, rather thick leaves. Its cultivated variety var. *sativa* is sometimes grown as the pot herb purslane.

The lichen-covered granite walls are as characteristic of Jersey as its leafy inland lanes. The stones of the wall provide a foothold for the lichens, but the joints provide homes for innumerable other plants. Ivy and red valerian should be removed or they will dismember a wall. The roots of red valerian were found to be parting the massive granite slabs of the walls of Fort Regent when the States began the Fort Development scheme. Small species do little harm and many walls are known to have been covered for generations. Strangely, it is almost impossible deliberately to get wild plants to grown on a wall, yet, if conditions are right, they will eventually arrive unaided. Navelwort and Mexican fleabane are common, and so is ivy-leaved toadflax which bears masses of small purple-white snapdragon flowers. The seedhead shuns bright light so its stalk bends to push it into a dark recess in the wall. Cornsalad, which used to be eaten as a salad and was sold in the market until the last war, adorns many walls in spring with its small clusters of pinhead-size, pale blue flowers. Wall-rue and dwarf specimens of black spleenwort often grow, inextricably mixed, along the course lines of a wall, but the delicate maidenhair spleenwort tends more often to be on a wall by itself occupying every possible place over a small area. Rustyback, a fern which is green and silver on the upper surface of the leaf and totally covered with what appears to be rust on the back, used to be exceedingly rare, but has spread considerably in the last 20 years. It looks particularly beautiful growing among patches of the bright orange lichen *Xanthorium parietaria*.

Ferns were severely depleted during the amazing fern craze which was at its destructive height in the 1890s. Fortunately a sufficient number of plants of the much-sought-after species survived in inaccessible places, so Jersey, unlike some of the other Channel Islands, lost none completely. The huge majestic royal fern still grows on the cliffs and so does the small but exquisitely beautiful maidenhair fern with its leaves of paper-thin green triangles and its stems shining like fine black wire. In damp places in the interior, ferns abound, lady-fern, male-fern, broad buckler-fern, and soft shield-fern being the commonest. The National Trust for Jersey's property at Bouley Bay, the Don Ferey, called Le Grand Côtil de Bouley Bay, has a northern aspect and contains many of the larger species all growing superbly in the shade of the trees. Dark green, shaggy-stemmed fronds of the scaly male-fern, sometimes more than three feet high, can occasionally be seen in shadier places in the inland woods.

L. V. Lester-Garland, in the *Flora* of 1903, remarked on the wealth of clover species in the Island. More than 20 have been recorded at various times, of which 18 can be seen regularly. Some, like red clover, are common throughout western Europe; many, like fenugreek, are coastal with a somewhat southern distribution in Britain, and a few are decidedly rare in these latitudes. Long-headed clover, sometimes considered a sub-species of crimson clover, grows well on L'Ile au Guerdain, (Janvrin's Tomb), and very sparingly near Le Rouge Nez, St Mary, while twin-flowered clover grows among short turf in St Brelade. These two Lusitanian species are not found elsewhere in the Channel Islands and only on the Lizard peninsula, Cornwall, in the British Isles.

The clovers are almost all native, as indeed are the great majority of the legumes, but the wealth of species from abroad in other botanical families is sometimes remarkable. Among the Solanaceae, Apple of Peru *Nicandra physalloides* from Peru has been known from a field in St Ouen for upwards of 40 years and is a frequent casual elsewhere. The Duke of Argyll's teaplant *Lycium sp.* from Asia is naturalised as a windbreak along the south coast. Green nightshade, *Solanum sarrachoides* from Brazil, was first found in 1930 and is now a frequent weed in arable fields. Kangaroo apple *S. laciniatum* from Australia has been reported four times, once in quantity on a States compost heap. Thorn-apple *Datura stramonium* of uncertain origin, perhaps native, is frequent in light soil and has been found in nearly every parish, sometimes in abundance. Cape-gooseberry *Physallis alkengi* has been reported as a casual in the past and an edible *Physallis* was grown as a crop in Val de la Mare, St Peter, in 1973, while the potato *Solanum tuberosum* and the tomato *Lycopersicum esculentum*, both from South America, have been grown in vast quantities for years and are frequent escapes or outcasts. Bittersweet *S. dulcamara* and black nightshade *S. nigrum* which is often wrongly called deadly nightshade are common natives, but, strangely, the true deadly nightshade *Atropa belladonna* is absent, the one or two records from the distant past probably being of plants specially grown.

Orchids, both wild and cultivated, exert a fascination over many people which it is difficult to explain. Horticulturally they are often considered the ultimate in luxury and sophisticated living. This glamour seems to rub off on our native wild orchids to such an extent that whenever I illustrate a talk on wild flowers of Jersey with coloured slides it is almost always the orchids which elicit most surprise and most interest. The fact that the flowers of these native orchids are small, about bluebell size, and bunched together at the top of a stalk, rather than three or four inches across like those in a florist's shop, seems to make not a scrap of difference to the interest displayed. Wild orchids are declining generally, not only in Jersey. Many factors are involved, but one of them is this glamour which leads to their being picked. The following account is deliberately given in the hope that increasing knowledge will enable people to look at and admire a wild orchid and then leave it undisturbed to set seed for future years and future generations. Whether the orchid is a single specimen or one of a colony of several hundreds it should not be removed. You may be in the only viable colony in the Island. This applies not only to orchids but to all unusual flowers.

The first orchids of the year to flower are the early-purple and the green-winged orchids. The early-purple orchid is not as rare as it used to be, but it is still unusual. Of late years there has been a small population on Les Quennevais and a few elsewhere. The easiest places to see them are St Saviour's cemetery and Green Street cemetery, where they have flowered in April for many years. This is one of the commonest English orchids and it has innumerable English names including Shakespeare's Long Purples and Dead Men's Fingers in Ophelia's garlands. Unfortunately a certain amount of confusion is caused in Jersey because the green-winged also flowers early and is purple and at present is much commoner here than the true early-purple. Any purple or pinkish-purple orchid met with in Jersey in late April or early May is at present more likely to be the green-winged than the early-purple orchid. The flowers are slightly different, but the simplest way of distinguishing between them is that the leaves of the early-purple are black-spotted, whereas those of the green-winged are not. The green-winged occurs locally in the west in considerable quantity some years, but it dies after seeding, as does the early-purple. Large numbers flowering one year are therefore no guarantee that they will be equally high the next. Many years elapse before a seed produces a plant capable of flowering so a continuity of age-groups is necessary for the continuous flowering of a colony.

The green-winged orchid can be found on fairly dry heaths and dunes and also in damp meadows. Its flowering period overlaps that of another purple orchid of damp meadows, the Jersey or loose-flowered orchid which is normally at its best in late May, but this varies with the earliness or lateness of the season. The flowers of wild orchids are often set close to one another on the stem, but in the Jersey orchid they are spread out, enabling each flower of the spike to be seen as a separate entity. It is from this that its Latin name *Orchis laxiflora* comes and its other English name, the loose-flowered orchid, is a direct translation. The wetter low-lying parts of the south east, south and west of the Island used to be purple with sheets of it and in 1966 Mrs J. Brooks showed me an extensive area at St Clement where it was difficult to walk without crushing them underfoot. Unfortunately the area was by the Baudrette Brook and when this was channelled in the late 1960s the topsoil was removed and with it went the orchids. They are still present in the south east, and indeed they may return to their former glory there, but they are now at their best at St Ouen. It is a fairly common European orchid, which is unknown anywhere in the British Isles or the other Channel Islands, except Guernsey, where it grows in similar damp places. When news of its presence in Jersey as a native plant spread among British botanists last century there was a succession of visitors to see it, hence its name, the Jersey orchid, which is used in many British Floras, including the principal *Flora of the British Isles,* by Clapham, Tutin and Warburg. The usual height of a flowering spike is about 15 inches, but this varies with the height of the surrounding vegetation and may be as little as 10 inches in low turf. On the other hand among long grass and tall rushes in water meadows I have seen magnificent spikes nearly three feet high. Many fields, once its home, have been drained, and modern agriculture, if it is to be a commercial proposition, cannot maintain these old water-meadow pastures without improving them. The weeds, including the orchids, are then destroyed. Because the long-term prospects for the orchid were uncertain the National Trust for Jersey bought two of the best fields, Le Noir Pré and Le Clos du Seigneur, in St Ouen, in 1972 and it is hoped that with suitable management the Jersey orchid will continue to flourish in them.

Yet another pinkish-purple orchid, the southern marsh-orchid, comes into flower about the end of May and in June, and, as its name implies, it also likes damp meadows. By

the time it is in full flower the early-purple will have gone
and so will the green-winged. It often grows with the Jersey
orchid, but is easily distinguished by the numerous flowers
which are extremely tightly packed at the top of the spike
and by the long green bracts which protrude among the
flowers. In good growing conditions it also can be superb,
as can its hybrids with the next species to flower.

These are the two spotted orchids, the common spotted-
orchid and the heath spotted-orchid which come into flower
about the beginning of June and which together are probably
the most numerous of all the orchids in Jersey. Their flower
colour varies from a beautiful pale pink to white, and in June
they and their hybrids are the only orchids here with spotted
leaves. These spots give them their name. They occur here
and there on damp, heathy parts of the cliffs of the north,
in grassy meadows of inland valleys, in Grouville Marsh,
in the low-lying areas of St Clement and round St Ouen's
Pond, to name only a few places, but though they are
described as the most numerous orchid, this is only comparatively speaking and some of these areas may hold very few.
These hybridise with one another and with the marsh-orchid,
this cross in particular having great hybrid vigour and being
very fine. Another hybrid, again a beautiful one, occurs
between the Jersey orchid and the green-winged orchid.
As the Jersey orchid does not grow on the mainland of
Britain it follows automatically that neither does this
hybrid. T. W. Attenborough, the chemist, who had a
great love of orchids, first reported it in Jersey in 1914.
It was growing in the fields now owned by the National
Trust for Jersey, so that between mid-April and early
July these fields may, if the season is good and conditions
have been right, hold a succession of orchids: the green-
winged orchid, the Jersey orchid, the southern marsh-orchid,
the common spotted-orchid, and the heath spotted-orchid
together with some of their four hybrids.

Jersey was once the home of the summer Lady's-tresses,
an exceedingly rare orchid of wet places, but it vanished
about 50 years ago. Fortunately, autumnal Lady's-tresses
is still here in good quantity. It needs established turf like

the dunes, but any lawn which has been undisturbed for many years may, towards the end of summer, produce the short six-inch-high flowering spikes of this orchid. The flowers are very small, white, deliciously scented of almond, and arranged spirally down the top half of the stem, so that with imagination one might think of them as forming a ringlet. Hence the name autumnal Lady's-tresses, the Lady being the Virgin Mary. The time from a seed germinating to the production of the first leaf is about eight years and to the production of the first flower about 15 years. The reason for established turf now becomes clear, and a little thought will tell any Jerseyman the obvious places to search—the churchyards and cemeteries—and in most cases he will not be disappointed.

The pyramidal orchid occurs in June in turf where the soil has a high lime content. It used to be exceedingly rare but is increasing in some areas, though still scarce. As with autumnal Lady's-tresses there is a considerable time lag between a seed being shed and the new plant flowering. Most of the spikes of the recent increase survived to set their seed, that is, they were not picked, so we may perhaps have areas bright pink with pyramidal orchids in the 1980s.

Other orchids have occurred from time to time, and since the war both the marsh helleborine and the lizard orchid have flowered. The marsh helleborine field was ploughed, but the orchid may still survive in a vegetative state. Unfortunately, the lizard orchid colony was dug out during sand excavations. Nevertheless, the lizard orchid may well occur again as may others of earlier days: the common twayblade, the lesser butterfly-orchid, the bee orchid and the early spider orchid. The greater butterfly-orchid, the lady orchid and the man orchid have also been reported.

How many Jerseymen still call that small brilliant-red flower which only opens in good weather, *la baronmette ès pouorres gens*? To most people it is now scarlet pimpernel, the increase in use of the English name perhaps measuring a different atmosphere from in the past, a different pressure—the social pressure to conform. At one time

Jersey-French was the principal language of the Island, but as communication with the outside world became easier and the town of St Helier grew in importance, a knowledge of English became not only desirable commercially but a fashionable necessity.

Dr Le Maistre's *Dictionnaire,* in which close on 400 different wild plants are mentioned, some of them with more than a dozen names each, shows how rich the botanical knowledge of the people of Jersey was in the past. Few readers today will recognise both early hair-grass and silver hair-grass, two small common annual grasses of no agricultural value, which appear in spring and have usually vanished by early autumn, yet both have Jersey-French names. Early hair-grass is *sûthin,* and for silver hair-grass there is a choice of three, *barbe de lièvre, d'la finne hèrbe* and *de l'hèrbe ès anges.* And if, like me, you tend to be a doubting Thomas, then I can assure you that I have been brought both correctly labelled.

When a plant has several names, some are simple variations of one another depending on where the speaker lives in the Island. Osier is *osyi* in the west, but *osi* in the east because the east never says *y.* The primrose not only has variations on a theme as in *pip'sole, pip'solle, pip'thole, pip'role, pruenole, prunole, prunm'nole, prinm'thole, prînmerole, prînm'sole* and *pieunm'thole,* but also *pâqu'role* and *pâqu'thole* and the much-used *coucou.*

This name *coucou,* and also *iliet* and *violette,* are used for all sorts of flowers. *Coucou* by itself can be a primrose, bluebell, violet, sea campion, red campion, ragged-Robin, field pansy or cuckoo-flower, but often it is given a colour as in *du blianc coucou* sea campion, *du rouoge coucou* red campion, *du bliu coucou* violet, *du jaune coucou* cowslip, and sometimes it has other connections as in *coucou d'pré* ragged-Robin and *pain d'coucou* wood-sorrel.

Iliet is any small carnation-like flower, and there are at least five different ones: *iliet d'rotchi* sea campion, *iliet d'fôssé* red campion, *iliet d'falaise* thrift, *iliet d'mielle* Jersey thrift, and *iliet du dgiâble'ye* sheep's-bit. The names *iliet d'falaise* and *iliet d'mielle* again show how well people of old knew their flora. The common thrift does grow round the coast while the Jersey one is on the sandy area, *les mielles,* just inland. Oddly enough *violette* is not a violet except at La Moye. Elsewhere a violet is *du coucou* or *du bliu coucou*, yet there are plenty of flowers called *violette—violette dé pré* cuckoo-flower, *violette sauvage* and *violette d'hivé* wallflower, *violette d'été* stock and *violette dé mielle* sea stock.

Sometimes a species will have several unrelated names. Bindweed can be the descriptive *cannes à lait* or the fanciful *manchettes d'la Vierge* where *une manchette* is a white elbow-length sleeve, or it can involve some fact as in *des belles d'un jour* or simply be *des veil'ye* or *vêle* for no known reason. Stonecrop, as well as being known as *pêrche-pierre* and *hèrbe ès tuilles* is also called *pain à crapauds, corînthe à poules* and *hèrbe d'souothis.* Do toads, hens and mice really eat it?

Then there is a remarkable preoccupation with the devil. In some cases this may well be justified, e.g., in *pommyi du dgiâble'ye* thorn apple and *chrysanthème du dgiâble'ye* deadly nightshade, both of which contain highly poisonous alkaloids, but *verjùs au dgiâble'ye* for black nightshade seems rather strong and there may have been confusion with deadly nightshade. This may have happened in other cases, e.g., *iliet au dgiâbl'ye* is sheep's-bit, a member of the campanula family though it looks like a small blue scabious. The large blue flower *Succisa pratensis* is devil's-bit scabious in English or *mors du diable* in French. Legend says the root of this plant was bitten off by the devil to prevent it using its great healing powers, and the root does indeed stop suddenly as though it had been bitten off. The root of sheep's-bit does not do this, and I can think of no reason, other than confusion with devil's-bit scabious, why such a charming little flower which grows mainly on heaths and hedgebanks uncultivated by man should be called either *iliet au dgiâble'ye* or its only other Jersey-French name *flieur du dgiâble'ye. Cache-dgiâble'ye,* St John's-wort, was used to keep away the devil. *'Nou ramâssait du cache-dgiâble'ye aut'fais la sèrveille de la St Jean pouor pendre*

ès f'nêtre, pouor cachi les mauvais esprits et contre la fondre',
according to Dr Le Maistre, and this is entirely in keeping
with its use in other countries. But why should hedge woundwort, black horehound and white horehound all be *herbe
au dgiâble'ye*? And why, in Jersey only, should the devil
or the sorcerer use the fruits of storksbill as forks or needles—
fourtchettes au dgiâbl'ye or *épignes a chorchis*?

On the other hand there is remarkably little about the
Virgin Mary. In English there are many names in common
use like Lady's-tresses where the Lady is Our Lady, the
Virgin Mary, and the number is increased enormously as soon
as one starts looking at local names. Here, I can trace but
two, *les yeux d'la Vierge* forget-me-not, and *les manchettes
d'la Vierge* bindweed. Perhaps this reflects the religious history of the Island. Jerseymen embraced Calvinism in the 16th
century with the greatest of zeal and welcomed Huguenot
refugees with open arms. The Rev. G. R. Balleine suggests
that the Island may well have had folk songs and ballads
which it lost at this time. It may also be that flower names
connected with the Virgin Mary dropped out of use during
this period, but those connected with the devil remained.

Among the saints there is a bare mention only of St
Martin, St Jean and St George, though Jacob of the Old
Testament has four species named after him, *lermes dé
Jâcob* great quaking-grass, and the three garden escapes
plieurs dé Jâcob Solomon's seal and *etchelles dé Jâcob*
for both Jacks and montbretia. The argument is often put
forward that if a species has a Jersey-French name then it
must be an old-established resident of the Island with its
roots metaphorically away back in time. I have never been
able to agree with this as it involves the tacit assumption that
Jersey-French has always been a dying, or at least a static,
language. Until this century that was not true and as the
Island's flora changed, so would the Jersey-French language
to absorb the new species. There were three possible courses:
a new name could be invented, some foreign name could be
literally translated into Jersey-French, or if the new species
was vaguely like one already here, the name of this could
be used to cover both. If the words chosen were 'good'

Jersey-French then the history of the plant would be obscured. For instance, the actual words of *mergot ès pouochins* and *êtchelles dé Jâcob* cannot be faulted philologically, yet we know from the history of these species outside the Island that they cannot have been here long. *Mergot ès pouochins,* the small pinky-white daisy-like flower which grows in such profusion on granite walls that it looks like a native species, comes from Mexico, as its English name Mexican fleabane implies, and was probably introduced into Jersey late in the 19th century. But *êtchelles dé Jâcob* when applied to the now common montbretia *Crocosmia x crocosmiflora* is an even better example. Its flower was seen in 1880 for the first time by anyone anywhere only after a Frenchman, Victor Lemoine, had 'made' the species by crossing its two South African parents in his garden at Nancy. In view of this a Jersey-French name cannot be held to imply long residence here.

The religious festivals of Easter and Whitsuntide are commemorated in *des pâq'thole* used in the west for primrose and *des pentecôtes* for the three flowers lords-and-ladies, cuckoo-flower and the Jersey or loose-flowered orchid. These all flower at about the stated time, but one of the most beautiful names in the Jersey-French language, *les clioches dé Carême,* has surely gone astray? Carême is Lent and I am assured that this is one of the names for bluebell, yet Lent is sometimes so early that not a single *clioche dé Carême* will be standing ready to ring even when Lent ends. This may be connected with the change from the Julian to the Gregorian Calendar.

Few names indicate a medicinal use of the plant. The orange juice from the stem of the greater celandine is reputed to cure warts in both France and England, and its Jersey name *hèrbe à véthues* means 'herb for warts'. But petty spurge and sun spurge are called *hèrbe à chorchi* as well as *hèrbe à véthues* so it may mean that warts could be charmed away rather than cured by some healing power of the plants. *Tchèrpentchiéthe* or *hèrbe au tchèrpentchi* is the carpenter's herb, yarrow, used to staunch bleeding according to Le Maistre: '*Faithe servi d'la tch`erpentchiéthe pouor êtantchi l'sang d'eune cope . . .*'.

Names with animal and bird connections abound: *coue d'rat, coue d'cat* and *coue dé r'nard* for horsetail, osier and spotted-orchid; *pid-d'ouâisé, pid-d'alouette* and *pid-d'co* for hedge mustard, hairy finger-grass and cock's-foot; *ouothelle dé souothis, ouothelle dé brébis, ouothelle d'âne* and *ouothelle dé lapîn* for mouse-ear, foxglove, burdock and ribwort plaintain. Knapweed is like a bee, *bourdonniéthe*, but the oddest of all is *la vaque enraigie*. This is another name for *la chue,* hemlock water-dropwort, though a cow which had eaten the tubers would be more than *enraigie.* It would be dead. And so, according to some reports, would rabbits be after they had eaten a different *la chue,* hemlock, which is therefore sometimes called *le tue lapîn.* Certainly our local wild rabbits never eat it though it sometimes occurs so abundantly along the roadsides that its smell of mice fills the air in damp weather.

All mosses, liverworts and lichens were lumped together as *la mousse*, which is a little surprising considering the richness of the Jersey-French language in other sectors. Lichens are indicators of air pollution in that they die in a polluted atmosphere. Judging by their size and quantity, air pollution does not seem to exist in the countryside of Jersey or in coastal areas away from the town. Ursula Duncan in her *Guide to the Study of Lichens* comments that a few areas in Great Britain and Ireland possess a large number of rare species and gives the Channel Islands as one such locality. The British Lichen Society visited Jersey in 1966 to study the Island's lichens generally and to search in particular for *Umbilicus murinum* a lichen unknown in the British Isles but collected from maritime rocks at Beauport first in 1786 and again in 1860. Such has been the unchanging nature of much of Jersey's coast that it was still there in 1966. Will it still be there in 1986 let alone 2066? Old apple trees and elms are good lichen-hunting country and so are rocky outcrops and walls in damp valleys. Les Quennevais is rich in species which grow on the surface of the soil, many being rare and some of the plants being of very great age. Few lichens have English names, one exception being reindeer moss *Cladonia rangiferina*. This arctic species obviously does not grow in Jersey, but the closely-related lichen *C. rangiformis,* sometimes called false reindeer moss, is common on the dunes. It is only an inch or two high, greyish-white and the whole plant is much branched, each branch forking into two parts almost immediately. Large quantities of it are blown about by the wind on the surface of the dunes in winter.

The Island's liverworts and mosses, the bryophytes, have recently been studied by Miss E. H. du Feu, who listed nearly 100 liverworts and over 200 mosses in *A Bryophyte Flora of Jersey,* published by the Société Jersiaise in 1966 and in a *Supplement* to it, with Mrs J. Paton, in 1972. Most people associate these only with areas permanently damp, like the inland valleys and the north coast streams, and these are perhaps the most productive areas, but Miss du Feu tells of a thread-moss between paving stones in town and of feather-like mosses over boulders, mosses which remain almost invisible until a shower of rain, when they suddenly become pale shining green or a rich bronze. One moss can be found growing in the spray zone of the coast with thrift and sea campion. Some appear after a fire has swept through an area and others, many not more than a millimetre high, grow in arable fields. The oddest place I remember being shown one was in the darkness far down the entrance to a rabbit burrow on the côtils of Val de la Mare reservoir. Green specks of *Schistostega pennata* were glowing and glinting like emeralds in the roof.

The great majority of fungi are difficult for an amateur to name correctly. The larger commoner ones, with easily identifiable characters, are straightforward enough, but the vast range of smaller species and the multitudes of similar-looking ones require a trained mycologist. The Island has been fortunate in that Dr H. Phillips and M. E. Upstone, both working at the Howard Davis farm on the rusts, etc., of agricultural crops, have been personally interested in the Island's fungi generally, including those of no commercial importance. The expert reader is referred to their papers for details of all species so far recorded, but, as Upstone comments, these lists represent only a fraction of the total number which occur.

No one, walking round the Island in autumn, can fail to notice the enormous numbers, and when one's 'eye is in', for other than the edible ones, fungi will be seen at all seasons of the year, and in the most unlikely places. Of the larger, more obvious and better-known fungi, the horse mushroom is at least locally common as are three other *Agarics*, the edible field mushroom, the inadvisable yellow staining mushroom and one, *A. sub-peronatus*, which seems to be without an English name, but makes superb eating. Many of the filled-in and finished rubbish tips have later produced literally tens of thousands of shaggy ink caps which grow on rotting wood in soil. Eaten young, before they begin their auto-ingestion and drip black ink, they are considered delicious by many people, and so are parasol mushrooms, which sometimes grow in abundance on grassy areas, as in the autumn of 1972 at Les Landes. Giant puff-balls elicit comment wherever they appear and so does the lattice stinkhorn fungus *Clathrus ruber*. This is like an

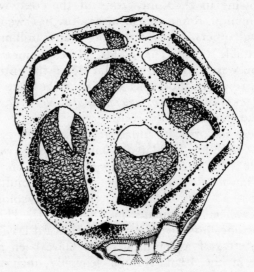

Lattice stinkhorn *Clathrus ruber*, an orange-red fungus not uncommon in Jersey. Height 3-10 in.

orange-red bath sponge with large holes in it and a hollow interior. Though rare in England it occurs here fairly frequently. Its foetid smell when ripe is so appalling that one householder called the public health authorities, thinking that the drains had gone wrong.

Few fungi are deadly poisonous. Among them is the fly agaric, the bright red, white-spotted toadstool of fairy stories. This occurs here only rarely, but every mushroom picker should familiarise himself with the death cap which some years is locally common. Honey fungus *Armillaria mellis,* sometimes called root rot, kills many trees every year in Jersey and Upstone lists apple, cherry, elm, euonymus, oak, peach, privet, rhododendron, rose, and walnut among the casualties.

As I write this, one of the smaller fungi *Ceratocystis ulmi,* which is responsible for Dutch elm disease, may be changing the face of the Island. In July 1974, W. K. Vinson drew my attention to some elm trees on Mont Matthieu which he considered were suffering from the disease. The States' plant pathologist of the Department of Agriculture removed samples the same day, confirmed the disease, and sent them to the mainland for more detailed analysis. There have been one or two cases in the past, but all minor and caused by a mild form. This outbreak was identified as caused by the particularly virulent strain which is killing off vast numbers of elm trees in England. Since then, the Department of Agriculture and the Department of Public Works have co-operated in an effort to stop its spread, but the severity of the attack can be judged from the fact that, by the end of September 1974, more than 5,500 infected trees had been found and marked for felling and burning. It is thought that the disease began in the west of the Island near the airport and was here in 1973. Elms provide most of the shelter for farmland. Their roots are a nuisance, but the species which form the bulk of the elm population here do not suddenly drop their branches like the wych elm does. To the elm's credit, the leaves filter bright sunlight giving a dappled effect without the deep shade of trees like sycamore. Also, elm leaves rot down to produce a fertile soil where they fall, whereas the needles of conifers do not. Though the thousands of elms so far affected still form only a small proportion of the number of elms here, even they will be difficult to replace satisfactorily.

3

MAMMALS

'Wee haue in Jersey an infinite store of them euery where...'
Poingdestre,
Caesarea 1682

THE COUNTRYSIDE OF JERSEY still contains enormous quantities of mammals, rabbit-size or less, as it has done for hundreds of years. No population survey, even over a restricted area, has been carried out on any species so it is impossible to hazard a guess as to the actual numbers. It is usually assumed that they have decreased, the reason given being the expansion of man's activities into the countryside for purposes other than farming, but, in the absence of quantitative measurements, even this may not be true except for certain species.

Man himself has changed his mode of life. At one time he would go for a walk in the country for the sheer pleasure of it. Now he seldom does. He would frequently walk home in the dark from work or from meeting friends. Now he drives home, seeing nothing but what appears for a brief instant in the car headlights. The result is that the great majority of people who live here today have not seen more than half of Jersey's mammals living naturally in their chosen habitat.

Eleven species of mammals are known to be living wild here now, excluding the water vole and the black rat, the status of both of which is doubtful, bats, about which very little is known, and escaped oddments like mink and polecat x ferret. They include four insectivores: the hedgehog, the common shrew, the lesser white-toothed shrew, and the mole; one member of the order Lagomorpha: the rabbit; five rodents: the red squirrel, the bank vole, the wood mouse, the house mouse, and the brown rat, and one carnivore: the stoat. Unfortunately, some of these are most active at night and are therefore seldom seen. The wood mouse is almost entirely nocturnal, even preferring moonless nights. The house mouse is mainly nocturnal as many householders will know. The hedgehog, the rabbit, and the brown rat can often be seen at dusk or dawn, but night is their main feeding time.

The number of dead hedgehogs on the roads in the morning
testifies to this. The stoat works chiefly by night, but it also
hunts by day, perhaps depending on its hunger. The two
shrews, the mole and the bank vole, are active day and night,
but moles are usually underground, though not always, and
shrews and bank voles are usually in leaf litter or cover of
some sort. The red squirrel regularly keeps the same hours as
man does and it can be seen feeding in the early morning and
sometimes at midday and towards evening. In theory this
seems as though the red squirrel is the only animal which can
be seen in Jersey during normal hours, but in practice most
of them move about a little during the day in the open. The
trouble is that we do not stay still enough, long enough, for
them to get accustomed to our presence. As well as these 11,
the black rat, the brown hare, and the red fox have established themselves for long periods and have bred freely, so
that at one stage last century, 14 species, excluding bats,
were living wild here together, and 15 if the water vole
records are correct.

Over the years there has been much discussion as to how
these species arrived. The problem of getting across an open
stretch of sea is much more difficult for a mammal than an
insect, a bird, or even a plant. In an effort to sort out what
part man has played, deliberately or accidentally, in shaping
the mammal fauna of the Island, historical records and
documents going back to the 12th century have been
searched. G. F. B. de Gruchy states in *Medieval Land Tenures
in Jersey* that, 'one does not hear of deer in Jersey, nor any
of the savage forest laws to protect them, nor can I find a
medieval allusion to the hare, fox, and red-legged partridge,
all three surviving in my lifetime though now extinct'.
Working independently, I also have found no early mention
of any of these. Details concerning individual species are
given later, but I consider that the rabbit, the black rat,
the brown hare, the brown rat, the red fox, the hedgehog,
and the red squirrel were all introduced by man, deliberately
or accidentally and roughly in that order, between the 12th
or 13th century and the 19th. And has he added mink and
polecat x ferret in the 20th?

Date A.D.	1100 1200 1300 1400 1500 1600 1700 1800 1900 2000
Rabbit	
Black Rat	
Brown Hare	
Brown Rat	
Red Fox	
Hedgehog	
Red Squirrel	
Polecat x ferret	
Mink	

Approximate dates of introduction and extinction in Jersey of those species which arrived with the accidental or deliberate aid of man.

It may be that some of these were here earlier and died out before historical records began, but there is little satisfactory archaeological evidence for them. Small pieces of bone of a hare-like or rabbit-like animal were found at La Cotte de St Brelade. In later work bones of the blue hare were identified positively. One jaw bone of *'Canis vulpes'* was also found at La Cotte. This name could cover many species or forms of fox other than the red fox which was present in the Island last century.

This leaves the wood mouse, the house mouse, the two shrews, the stoat, the mole, the bank vole, and, perhaps, the water vole as having arrived at some unknown time with or without the aid of man. Until recently island naturalists have tried to attribute the distribution of the mammals within the Channel Islands mainly to the order in which the islands were split off from the Continent. Any land mammals which were spreading across Europe during the time that Guernsey was detached, but Jersey was still part of the Continent, would obviously be able to reach Jersey on foot, but not Guernsey. It is essential to know from independent evidence when the individual islands were split off from the Continent, and from one another, and to know when each species of mammal spread across Europe so that the two can be correlated. The common shrew and bank vole are thought to have crossed Europe after Guernsey was an island, and therefore to have been able to reach

Jersey only, and the bank vole then proceeded to oust any field voles which were here. If this is true, why are there no voles of any kind on Alderney, Sark or Herm?

But trouble really begins with the rest: the wood mouse is in all the islands; the house mouse in all but Herm; Jersey has, and Guernsey may still have, the stoat; Jersey and Alderney have the mole; Jersey and Sark have the lesser white-toothed shrew and Guernsey, Alderney and Herm have the white-toothed shrew. In view of this, the date of isolation cannot be the only answer. Another agency must also have been at work. Man, accidentally and unknown to himself?

When Sark was colonised in 1565 by Helier de Carteret, Seigneur of St Ouen, the island lay desolate according to contemporary accounts. The first settlers who joined him were all from Jersey, many, from their names, being St Ouennais. They took with them material to construct houses, trees for shelter, and fruit trees for their gardens. Boats taking all this would probably leave from somewhere in St Ouen, the most likely place being Grève de Lecq. There were no piers and transport would be from beach on Jersey to beach on Sark. Lesser white-toothed shrews feed among the stones and pebbles of the beach and we know that these shrews were in the north west at Crabbé, St Mary, in the 17th century. If the stores destined for Sark were left on the beach, any lesser white-toothed shrew, exploring them, might well be transported to Sark and released in the same habitat. In the early 1960s a neighbour of ours had a plague of mice in her house. She went to Alderney by air on holiday and a mouse jumped out as she opened her suitcase. When this can happen, any mammal rat-size or less can be transported anywhere among the Islands. Examples of this accidental transport to islands are known elsewhere. The house mouse population of Skokholm is the result of the chance introduction of some in sacks of potatoes in the 1890s, and it has been suggested that the wood mouse populations of the Scottish islands were chance introductions from Viking times not more than 1,200 years ago.

There can be no single, simple explanation for the differences in the fauna of the Islands. The wonder is perhaps

3.–Maps showing distribution of mammal species in the Channel Islands

Key: A and B

● species seen in 1960 or later and believed still present
o extinct
●? or o? status probably as indicated but see text
? status unknown

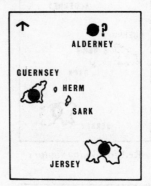

Hedgehog *Erinaceus europaeus*

Mole *Talpa europaea*

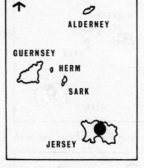

Common shrew *Sorex araneus*

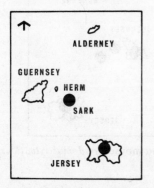

Lesser white-toothed shrew
Crocidura suaveolens

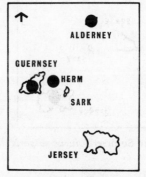

White-toothed shrew
Crocidura russula

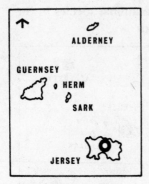

Red fox *Vulpes vulpes*

Stoat *Mustela erminea*

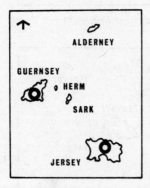

Brown Hare *Lepus capensis*

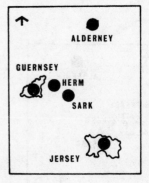

Rabbit *Oryctolagus cuniculus*

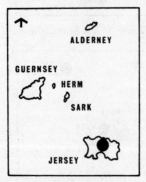

Red Squirrel *Sciurus vulgaris*

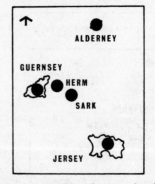

Wood mouse *Apodemus sylvaticus*

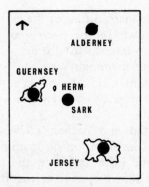

House mouse *Mus musculus*

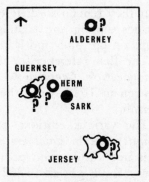

Black rat *Rattus rattus*

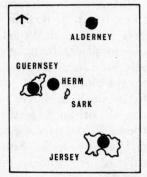

Brown rat *Rattus norvegicus*

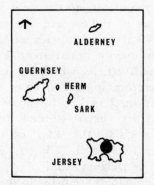

Bank vole *Clethrionomys glareolus*

Water vole *Arvicola terrestris*

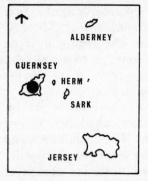

Field vole *Microtus arvalis*

that they remain so different. The distribution of the various
species among the Islands is shown in the accompanying
maps on pp. 63-5 and is also given later in list form.

The first reference to the small mammals seems to be in
Poingdestre's *Caesarea* which, from internal evidence, was
written in 1682. Until then they were covered by the word
'vermin'.

The various editions of Ansted and Latham's *Channel
Islands* contain small amounts of information on mammals.
It is not known who provided the information in the first
and second editions 1862 and 1865, but that in the third
edition 1893 was provided by J. Sinel. The main accounts
of mammals are by Sinel in the 1908 *Report and Transactions* of the Société Guernesiaise and by H. J. Baal in the
1949 *Annual Bulletin* of the Société Jersiaise. Baal's article
was mainly descriptive, few dates and places being given.
Sinel's article, which was extensively used by Baal, contains
therefore in several cases the last available detailed information. Jersey is fortunate in that its small mammals have
recently been studied by some of Britain's foremost
zoologists,. the Earl of Cranbrook, P. Crowcroft, and
Mrs Crowcroft (Gillian Godfrey), and by I. R. Bishop,
M. J. Delaney, and M. J. R. Healy in their student days.
Their papers are listed in the bibliography.

These small mammals are not easy for a non-specialist
to separate, and the first writers would have few, if any,
reference books whereas today there are many excellent
ones. The reader is referred to them for full descriptions,
but one or two simple points to help towards identifying
those likely to be encountered in Jersey are: shrews have
long pointed noses; the tips of the teeth of the common or
red-toothed shrew are black-red, while those of the lesser
white-toothed are white; both shrews are covered with
short fur, including along the tail, but in a good light the
lesser white-toothed will be seen to have some long white
hairs projecting almost at right angles here and there, particularly along the tail; the house mouse has a tail the same
colour above and below, whereas the wood mouse's tail is
dark above and pale below; the bank vole is a somewhat

bigger, stubbier-faced animal with small ears and a short
tail about half the length of its body. Young rats can be
confused with mice.

DISTRIBUTION OF SPECIES OF MAMMALS IN THE CHANNEL ISLANDS

(J=species seen in 1960 or later and believed still present in Jersey; j=extinct in
Jersey; J? or j?= status probably as indicated; ?= status or species uncertain.
Similarly: G, g, Guernsey; A, a, Alderney; S, s, Sark; H, h, Herm.)

	J	G	A	S	H
Hedgehog *Erinaceus europaeus*	J	G	?		
Mole *Talpa europaea*	J		A		
Common shrew *Sorex araneus*	J				
Lesser white-toothed shrew *Crocidura suaveolens*	J			S	
White-toothed shrew *Crocidura russula*		G	A		H
Greater Horseshoe Bat *Rhinolophus ferrum-equinum*	J	G	?	?	?
Pipistrelle *Pipistrellus pipistrellus*	J	G	?	?	?
Grey long-eared bat *Plecotus austriacus*	J	G?	?	?	?
Red fox *Vulpes vulpes*	j				
Stoat *Mustela erminea*	J	G?			
Polecat x ferret *Mustela putorius x M. p. furo* ..	J				
American mink *Mustela vison*	J				
Brown hare *Lepus capensis*	j	g			
Rabbit *Oryctolagus cuniculus*	J	G	A	S	H
Red squirrel *Sciurus vulgaris*	J				
Wood mouse *Apodemus sylvaticus*	J	G	A	S	H
House mouse *Mus musculus*	J	G	A	S	
Black rat *Rattus rattus*	j?	g?	a?	S	h?
Brown rat *Rattus norvegicus*	J	G	A		H
Bank vole *Clethrionomys glareolus*	J				
Water vole *Arvicola terrestris*	j?	g?			
Field vole *Microtus arvalis*		G			

The Hedgehog

The hedgehog was almost certainly introduced last century. In 1893, when Sinel wrote the mammal section for
the third edition of Ansted and Latham's *The Channel
Islands*, he considered that hedgehogs had increased considerably in the previous 20 years, so that by then they
were common, especially in the east of the Island. He knew
of no record before the 1850s.

In February 1895 the Executive Committee of the
Société Jersiaise also discussed the tremendous increase of
the hedgehog, saying that it had multiplied in an extraordinary manner. They thought it had been introduced
about 30 years previously and suspected Sinel of having
introduced it. However, at their next meeting, in March
1895, G. C. Godfray said his father had introduced hedgehogs in 1857, the year that the service between Weymouth
and Jersey was established. In 1908 Sinel stated that many
hedgehogs had been brought in as pets from both France
and England, and suggested that the Island stock was derived
from them.

That they are not indigenous is supported by Poingdestre
not mentioning them in his *Caesarea* in 1682. He would
surely have discussed them in his chapter 'Of things Detrimentall' if only to defend them. He insisted that toads,
shrews and lizards did no harm, and he argued this from
personal observation. Had there been hedgehogs in the
Island he would surely have watched such fascinating
creatures and felt bound to try to dispel the inevitable false
rumours which would surround them. And rumours there
certainly were later, because the belief that a hedgehog could
milk a cow dry during the night was so firmly held by the
islanders in Sinel's time that when he was 64 years old he
was moved to write, 'I used to argue the matter with my
country friends but have now abandoned the effort owing
to failing health'.

There is also some evidence from philology to support
the theory that the hedgehog is a comparatively recent
introduction. Standard French for hedgehog is *hérisson*
and Jersey-French is identical. Had there been hedgehogs
in the Island for centuries, in the quantity they are today,
the word would have been in constant use and might well
have differed from present-day French.

Hedgehogs are now spread across the entire Island, being
reported from such diverse areas as the dry sun-baked areas
of St Ouen's Bay, the water meadows of St Peter's Valley
and the back gardens of town. A letter to the *Jersey Evening
Post* told of one which recently appeared unexpectedly in

a reader's garden in Drury Lane, St Helier, and there are many reports of them from the areas in and around the town which have been left undisturbed. These are usually areas too steep to be developed or the semi-wild large gardens which still exist behind some of the older houses. It is not generally known that hedgehogs climb well, so that a rough wall is no obstacle. They usually feed at night but can sometimes be seen in the early evening. Their diet consists principally of slugs, snails, worms and insects. Slugs and snails often emerge when a shower of rain ends a long dry spell of weather, and then hedgehogs will feed on them during the day. No estimate of their numbers is possible, but they are the commonest wild creatures now found dead on the roads, replacing toads for that grisly distinction. Their increase so closely parallels the toad's decrease that there may be a connection.

Hedgehogs were also introduced into Guernsey last century and are now common. Alderney had none until the early 1960s when some were introduced. Young were seen in 1973. There are no records from Sark or Herm.

The Mole

Jersey's farmers and gardeners have been plagued by moles for centuries and they still are. In the 17th century the nuisance from moles was such that the *Cour d'Héritage* set up a committee to look into the matter. Certain recommendations were put forward and these were embodied in an Act of the States in 1675. The principle was simple: each person was to get rid of the moles on his own land. This was not left to the individual's conscience, and each person was to declare how much land he owned. Those with enclosed land had to produce one mole for every vergée, while those with land *'en campagne'*, unenclosed, had only to produce one mole for every two vergées. Houses with less than one vergée of land round them still had to produce one mole. Half the necessary number of moles was to be produced between 6 May 1675 and Christmas Day, and the other half between then and 15 May 1676. Any person short of the right number had to pay a fine for each one missing.

Six years later, Poingdestre was writing that their numbers were beyond belief so the campaign cannot have been a success though he thought moles were not entirely harmful. They might be bad for corn and grass, but he considered they did fruit trees good by letting water through the soil. Falle confirms that the campaign was useless, for in 1694 he also complained they were a nuisance. Nevertheless, a century later the States tried again, and in 1785 they set up another committee to advise them on how to get rid of *'Le nombre infini de Taupes, qui infestent le Pais'*.

In 1792 yet another committee was formed consisting of two Juré-justiciers, three Rectors and three Constables. Perhaps as a result of the deliberations of this committee, the States decided on 2 May 1796 that the best way to get rid of moles was by a concerted attack on them by the whole population, so they ordered that:

1. The Vingteniers would hold themselves in readiness to receive moles from their Vingtaine and they would be given two *liards* per mole.

2. The Vingteniers would give two *sous,* French money, for each mole; they would immediately cut off the tail to make sure it was not produced again. They were to keep a register of the names of people and the number of moles paid for; and to do this they would give their time, in a place to be announced, every Monday and Thursday, between eight o'clock and nine in the morning, and they would watch to see that no one tried to commit a fraud.

3. The Vingteniers would keep the tails and produce them to a parish committee formed specially for this, which would meet once a month, the tails then to be counted and destroyed in the presence of the Constable.

4. In order that the Vingteniers would be able to make payments, the Constable of each parish would, from time to time, give them the money they needed, following the report of the committee.

5. These rules would come into force on 9 May and would continue 'en vigeur' to the last day of October when the Vingteniers and Constables would send their accounts to the Defence Committee of the Island which would divide the cost among the parishes according to their proportion of the public rate, before submitting the whole to the States.

The same orders were given on 2 February the following year, 1797, but the season for collecting was lengthened, being from 6 February to 30 November, and the price rose to three *sous* per tail. Not content with two years, moles were collected yet again in 1798. The same rules applied, but the dates are not known.

The numbers of moles destroyed and the cost to the Island were:

Date	Numbers	Cost in French money
9 May–31 Oct. 1796	24,074	3,009 livres 6 sous
6 Feb.–30 Nov. 1797	49,932	8,741 livres 10 sous 6 deniers
? – ? 1798	36,248	6,348 livres 8 sous
	110,254	18,099 livres 4 sous 6 deniers

It is impossible to relate this to present-day money, but it is worth comparing it with the price of 200 livres de France paid in 1797 to Isaac Renouf for eight perches of land for a road to Le Havre at Fliquet. At this rate, the money spent destroying the moles would have bought 18 vergées of land.

Whether this figure of more than 100,000 moles killed in three years was accurate or not is open to question. In spite of the precautions taken against fraud, it is highly likely that fake tails were somehow included in the counts. Elsewhere, tails for which bounties were paid have been made from the animal's fur and included. It is also unlikely, even if the figures were correct, that it made much difference to the mole population. With an abundant food supply and almost no natural enemies, the population would increase as soon as the campaign stopped and all available areas would be colonised again. On the other hand, the number of men offering themselves as Vingteniers might well diminish. And indeed this campaign appears to have been no more successful than those in the past, for Plees in 1817 considered moles and stoats to be the 'principal noxious animals' there being 'immense numbers of moles, which have been called Jersey ploughmen'.

To be a mole-catcher was reckoned an honourable and worthwhile occupation and in no way unusual. Dr Le Maistre in his *Dictionnaire* writes *Mess Le Merquand taupîn* would be used to distinguish Mr Le Marquand the mole-catcher from, say, Mr Le Marquand the baker, or Mr Le Marquand the butcher. Sir John Le Couteur paid his molecatcher 19s. a year in the 1850s, but by the end of the century the occupation had almost died out. It would not be through lack of moles, for there are still untold numbers, but the price of moleskins probably dropped so low that it was not worth trapping them. Perhaps the States were not fierce enough with their legislation, for Larkin, working in England in 1948, estimated that there were eight moles per acre in summer and four in winter. At that rate the States should have demanded considerably more in their 1675/6 campaign. The mole is *la taupe* in Jersey-French, and if someone was in *Le Rouoyaume des taupes* it meant they were interred. 'Pushing up daisies', would be the equivalent English expression.

In 1975 moles are plentiful in every type of habitat throughout the Island, except pure sand. They are in gardens, cultivated fields, woodland and meadows, some of which can be surprisingly wet. They can be found in thin soil over rocky headlands and on the grassy areas here and there down the cliff side until the cliff drops vertically into the sea. The beach is free of them and so are the pure sand parts, the blowouts, on Les Quennevais dune system, but elsewhere moles are present in the lightest of soils. Their runs have even been seen across the floor of a recently worked-out sandpit.

In Sinel's time, a cream-white form occurred sparingly in several parts of Jersey chiefly in St Lawrence and St Martin. It would be interesting to know if it still occurs.

Moles are common in Alderney but are not present in Guernsey, Sark or Herm.

The Shrews

The first mention of shrews is by Poingdestre in 1682. He calls them field mice, but that was the custom of the time:

> The 3d. sort [of field mouse] is not halfe soe bigg as any of the former sorts, being scarce worthy of that name, though the Latins call it *Mus-araneus* & agreeth exactly to Dioscorides his description of *Mygale*. This word *Mus-araneus* is compos'd of a mouse & a spider; not that it participates of ye shape of ye Spider, but of his poisonous quality. Wee haue in Jersey an infinite store of them euery where, but those which heretofore were taken notice of as a rare Singularity proper to vs were those onely found neere ye sea upon Beaches among ye pebles, whose excrement is perfect muske, from whence it is called Musquine, as if one should say a Musk-mouse, of a dun colour euery where but vnder the belly, where it is white. The places most frequented by them are about St Heleryes mont, both neere ye Towne & towards Haure des Pas, whither ye Boyes doe vsually repaire to seeke ye sayd Musk among ye pebles, where it is both easily discerned from other filth, for ye cleanelinesse of ye place, & is alsoe purer & better sented; because there is nothing there which can corrupt ye smell. There are also other places about ye Island abounding with them, especially one in St. Maryes Parish called Crabec. But those in inland parts of the Countrey were neuer, that I knowe, taken notice of to haue the same propriety, but were esteemed a differing kind, & were not called Musquines, but Besaraignes or Musaraignes, for distinction; till very lately, that some hauing flead one of them for curiosity, they found the skinne to haue ye sent of a perfumed gloue . . . Though the ancients haue held them for venemous, it was neuer obserued that any

of those with vs were soe; nor is it likely that hauing ben
soe often handled without any harme, & yeelding soe
sweete a perfume, they should be soe. . . .

Fashions seem to have changed in scent as much as in
other ways if the scents of shrews could be admired. Sinel
simply gives 'shrew' in his 1893 list, but by 1908 he

Lesser white-toothed shrew *Crocidura suaveolens*.
(Head and body approx. 70mm.; tail approx. 40mm.)

separated the red-toothed Genus *Sorex* from the white-
toothed Genus *Crocidura*. The common shrew *Sorex
araneus* he recorded as abundant in Jersey, but not found
in the other islands, while the white-toothed shrew *Crocidura
russula* he considered plentiful in Guernsey but rare in
Jersey. The white-toothed shrew of Jersey was accepted as
C. russula until the Earl of Cranbrook found that a shrew
skull from Sark was nearer those from the Isles of Scilly
than those from Guernsey. He and Crowcroft (1958) then
examined white-toothed shrew skulls from all the Channel
Islands and found that those from Guernsey, Alderney and
Herm were the white-toothed shrew *C. russula* but those
of Jersey and Sark were the lesser white-toothed shrew,
C. suaveolens.

The white-toothed shrew of Guernsey, Alderney and
Herm occurs throughout France, including the coast opposite
the Channel Islands, but it does not occur elsewhere in the

	Red-toothed Shrew	Lesser White-toothed Shrew	White-toothed Shrew
Jersey	*	*	—
Guernsey	—	—	*
Alderney	—	—	*
Sark	—	*	—
Herm	—	—	*

British Isles. The Jersey and Sark lesser white-toothed shrew is the same as those on islands off the west coast of France, and in France itself, though not until about a hundred or two miles to the south and east of the Channel Islands: it is missing from northern France and from the French coast immediately opposite the Channel Islands. It does not occur in Britain except in the Isles of Scilly, where it is slightly different from the type and is given sub-specific rank *C. suaveolens cassiteridum.*

The common shrew in Jersey was determined as the sub-species *S. araneus fretalis* by Miller, and lately it has been shown to have the same chromosome number as French common shrews.

Shrews in general are sometimes called *les démouaîselles* in Jersey-French, probably because of their smallness, with the common shrew, the less musky, being either *les besaraignes* or *les musaraignes*, and the lesser white-toothed, the really musky ones, *les musquines* or *les mustchinnes*.

In 1960–61 Bishop and Delaney, trapping in St Lawrence, captured very few shrews, only seven common and two lesser white-toothed out of 248 animals. And in 1963 Rostron only caught 11 common shrews out of 72 animals in St Ouen's Bay. In spite of these low numbers I think the common shrew is, in fact, common, and the Longworth traps, as used by Bishop and Delaney and Rostron, have not caught a representative section of the small mammals of Jersey. I see common shrews frequently on our own côtil; they form a high proportion of almost every barn owl's prey; I am frequently given them by friends whose cats have killed, but not eaten, them, and if an empty bottle has been left in a semi-upright position where a small animal can crawl into it, and not get out, the chances are high that there will be a dead shrew in it, sometimes five or more. Twenty-two in a champagne magnum is the present Jersey record.

Common shrews are not confined to inland areas. At Le Pulec one was trapped right down on the edge of the coast within reach of the spray. In the gully just north of Le Pulec, in an apparently identical situation, the shrew trapped (and also released) was the lesser white-toothed. This question of coastal distribution is interesting. For some time in the island, there was a legend that the lesser white-toothed shrew was only to be found on the coast of the south west. Earlier records had been forgotten, but then Bishop and Delaney caught two at the foot of Waterworks Valley. Rostron caught one by hand on the high tide line below the Watersplash in St Ouen's Bay. D. Clennett found them to the north of St Ouen's Pond and also among the reeds at the inner edge of the pond on an area where the reeds were growing through clear water. There were a few dry tussocks of great fen-sedge, and it is possible that these and some small bramble bushes gave them shelter. Poingdestre earlier had mentioned several places in the Island where his musk shrew occurred, and in the 1930s their remains had been found in owl pellets in St Peter and St Martin as well as in St Brelade. An appeal was therefore made for recent records. The map shows where lesser white-toothed shrews have been found, dead or alive, since 1965 and under what conditions, i.e., trapped *in situ*, caught by cat or dead in bottle, so that due allowance can be made. It will be noticed that the records are not confined to the south west or to the coast. Neither this map, nor the one showing the known distribution of the common shrew, is complete, and readers may care to enter more records.

The two shrews at Le Pulec may not have ranged over the same territory, but two shrews, one of each species, were feeding within a yard of one another, and of me, when I was weeding in our garden in Val de la Mare in 1971. At one time shrews were supposed to be prone to die from

4.—Common shrew *Sorex araneus*

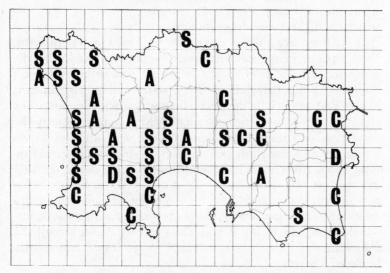

Lesser white-toothed shrew *Crocidura suaveolens*

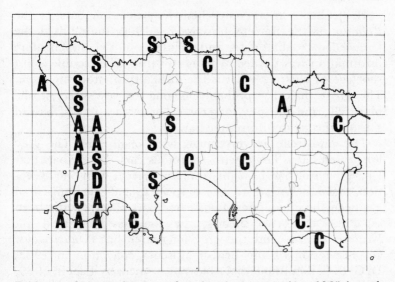

Evidence of shrews has been found at least once since 1965 in each of the marked squares. A=alive; S=skull in bottle; C=caught by cat; D=found dead.

shock. It is now known that they have a very short life
span, those being born one summer living through the
winter and the following summer, but dying in the autumn,
that is, they live only a complete year plus a few months.
That one, at least, was not prone to shock is shown by the
following story. A milk bottle thrown away in St Ouen's
Bay was found half full of dirty water and green slime. It
was tipped out. Half the green slime was a dead decomposing
common shrew, but the other half, which looked exactly the
same revolting mess, was seen to move very slightly. It was
brought home, the slime was washed off under lukewarm running water, and a bedraggled small animal, more dead than alive
emerged. It was dried on an old piece of towel before being
put in front of an electric blow heater. Within minutes, a
lesser white-toothed shrew, none the worse for its experience,
was looking for food. It was fed every few hours until the
following day when it was released where found, apparently
in perfect health.

The Bats

H. J. Baal, in a comprehensive article on bats in the
Bulletin of the Société Jersiaise for 1950, summarised the
knowledge to that date, and pointed out that much more
information was needed. This is still true. The trouble is not
shortage of bats; rather it is the difficulty of studying them.
The great majority probably belong to two species, the
pipistrelle and the grey long-eared bat, with a few of a third
species, the greater horseshoe bat.

The pipistrelle is very small with small ears. The grey
long-eared bat is larger with enormous ears. All the bats that
I have seen or had brought to me in Jersey, with one exception, have belonged to these species, and the long-eared
has been the commoner. Long-eared bats have recently been
separated into two species, the common long-eared bat
Plecotus auritus and the grey long-eared bat *P. austriacus*.
On inspection of the British Museum collection in 1963,
Dr G. B. Corbet found that a bat sent to them by Baal in 1939,
and at that time labelled the long-eared, was according to
new knowledge, the grey long-eared. Since that time every

'long-eared bat' which has come to hand in Jersey, about 10, has been checked, and all have been found to be the grey long-eared. The fur is slightly different in colour, but the essential point is that the tragus, or inner ear, is broader in the grey long-eared than in the common long-eared. The question now arises as to whether or not only the grey long-eared is present. If so, this would not be unexpected as it is a continental species, whereas the common long-eared is more a British species.

Sinel recorded both the pipistrelle and the 'long-eared bat' as abundant, and this is still true. They can be seen, not merely on summer evenings, but on any mild night in any month of the year.

The third species known to be present is the greater horseshoe bat. Baal records one taken at Belle Hougue Cave at Trinity, but gives no date, and it is thought that the unlabelled specimen in the collection of the Société Jersiaise is this one. A second was caught at St Ouen's Pond in 1959. Baal also records one at Portelet but, from the information given, it might equally well have been a grey long-eared. Nevertheless, the greater horseshoe bat may exist in larger numbers than the records indicate.

The status of the following species, recorded in Jersey only once, is unknown. Sinel reported that a serotine taken at Georgetown in 1895 was in Dr A. C. Godfray's collection. G. F. B. de Gruchy, Seigneur of Noirmont, found a Natterer's bat some years previous to 1950, in the outbuildings at the Manor, according to Baal who saw it only in flight, and there is a specimen with no data in the collection of the Société Jersiaise. Baal identified a bat found in a chute at St Brelade's church as a Leisler's bat because it had a wing span of about 10 inches and hair under the forearm. Crallan reported several large bats flying fast and high at dusk on 4 October 1921 and thought they were noctules. He gave no other information in his note in the Société *Bulletin* for 1922.

Jersey is also within the geographical range of the lesser horseshoe bat, Daubenton's bat, the whiskered bat, Geoffroy's bat, the large mouse-eared bat and the barbastelle. Anyone who finds a bat is asked to get in touch with any of the Island's naturalists.

The pipistrelle, the greater horseshoe bat and a long-eared which has not yet been specifically determined have also been recorded for Guernsey, and bats are also present in Alderney, Sark and Herm.

The Red Fox

There were no foxes in Jersey in 1694 according to Falle, and there are none now in 1975, but at some point in between they were introduced, and for a time they flourished. Even if Falle had not stated that there were none, a perusal of social and economic records of earlier days would have forced one to the same conclusion. With the exception of one unsigned, unlocalised hand-written note, there is no mention in any of the available literature up to the 19th century of foxes being present here, yet the Island's records are full of references to rabbits and poultry which are their obvious prey. When orders were given that the King's rabbits were to be guarded carefully, men were often charged with stealing them and foxes never blamed. In early days when *poulage* was due in kind from every householder to his Seigneur, one would expect excuses that foxes had stolen the fowls, chickens, capons, geese, or eggs which constituted the *poulage*, yet there is no such excuse.

Thomas Read in *The English Traveller* (1749) stated that there were no foxes here, but his other comments are often so like Falle's that he may simply have been repeating Falle's remark. Durell, in his 1837 edition of Falle's book, said he hoped foxes were not introduced, which implied he thought there were none then in the Island. He was perhaps too late, for a hand-written entry in a copy of Le Lievre's 1861 *Guide to Jersey* in Mrs D. L. Le Quesne's possession, says one was killed in 1788. This may, or may not, be correct and there is no indication of whose note it is or where the fox was killed. In the *Jersey Times* of October 1848 there was the news: 'A fine fox was shot at Noirmont a few days since'. This may well be one of those which, according

to Le Lievre in this 1861 *Guide,* had been 'stealthily introduced of late into the island'. About this time there were
several records. *'Un magnifique renard, un des plus forts,
dit-on, que l'on avait vu dans cette île'* was shot at Sorel
according to the *Chronique de Jersey* on 2 August 1862.
Another hand-written entry in Mrs Le Quesne's Le Lievre's
Guide reported that five were killed in 1862.

Sinel, in 1908, thought that they had been numerous up
to 1860 or 1862, breeding as near town as Surville and
Samarès, but from that period they rapidly became scarce.
The last one he remembered seeing was killed at St Brelade
in 1870 and was 'very probably the last of its race'.

A meticulous search through local newspapers of last
century would probably yield several other records, but
later ones may well be from further introductions, for
instance, the one shot at Bouley Bay in 1896 was thought
by the *Evening Post* to be one of a pair released near there.

In 1969 a French couple who went to live in Norfolk
were found to have taken a fox cub with them. The Norfolk
police believed their story that they had spent a few days
in Jersey on the way to England, had found the cub on the
roadside at Grève de Lecq Hill, had picked it up, and shortly
afterwards, when they went to England, had taken it with
them. There are no quarantine regulations between Jersey
and England, so no offence had been committed, but if it
had come from France where rabies is increasing, particularly
among foxes, a serious charge would have been brought
against them. If the Norfolk police were right to accept the
story, then the question arises as to how a fox cub came to
be found in Jersey where there have been no foxes for the
greater part, if not all, of this century. It, or its very near
forebears, must have been introduced, but from where?
After an episode in 1973 when a woman smuggled a dog
from the Far East into Jersey to avoid quarantine regulations,
there is greater vigilance to prevent the illegal bringing into
Jersey of animals from outside Britain. When Philip
Dumaresq wrote his *Survey of ye Island of Jersey* in 1685
he could claim: '. . . it was never known that a Dog grew
mad, tho very numerous in the neighbouring provinces of

France, where 'tis said our dogs, when transported, to be free from that'. The States have regulations which should be rigorously enforced to ensure that Jersey remains free of rabies.

A search of the woods in Grève de Lecq revealed no traces of foxes or their earths. In 1970 the *Jersey Evening Post* carried a story that a visitor had seen foxes near Bellozanne, but this was eventually proved to be incorrect. There are no records of foxes in any other Channel Island.

The Stoat

On 26 April 1599 the *Cour d'Héritage* told the constables to give a demi-reall to anyone who brought them a dead *martre* because *'les martres et la vermyne de tell espece sont dammagables tant au gibier . . .'*.

Fifty years later, on 21 September 1649, the States ordered the Constables again to pay a demi-reall for '*Martes ou bjen aucuns Corbeaulx'* and to keep a well-guarded bin in good order for the vermin. The reason given was that *'la Quantjté de Martes ou Bellettes qui sont grandement multjpliee en ceste Jsle ruyne, et gástent le Gybjer'* and there was an urgent need to preserve game for the King. (Charles II was proclaimed King in 1649 immediately on the death of his father. Jersey was staunchly royalist and did not come under the rule of the Parliamentarians until 1651.)

Control measures of this type are expensive and rarely work as the States were to find out both then and when they tried the same method with moles. If the States were right in saying that the stoat population had increased greatly then a predator might have been removed or there might have been an increase in their food supply. It is difficult to think of any natural predator which at any time could have kept the stoat population in check. There were almost certainly no larger predatory mammals on the Island, so hawks and owls would be their only natural enemies. Man would be their chief predator, and it is of interest that it was during the late 16th and early 17th centuries that the islanders turned from farming to knitting as their main employment, and there were complaints that the land was being neglected. The threat to food supplies was such that laws were passed limiting the amount of time workers could spend knitting so that they had to help cultivate the fields. It may be that with loss of interest in labouring on the farms, the heart went out of man's fight against the stoat.

If it were not the removal of a predator which caused the great increase could it have been an increase in food supply? Stoats will eat almost any living thing smaller than themselves, including mammals, fish, reptiles, amphibians or birds. Later in the 17th century we know there were enormous numbers of some of these, but there is no information on their populations earlier, except that there was a plague of black rats at Elizabeth Castle in 1645. And in the absence of such information it is impossible to say whether the large number of stoats in the late 16th century was because there was an abundant food supply, or whether the 'scarce credible' numbers of small animals in the 17th century was the result of these measures taken earlier against their main predator, the stoat.

On the other hand there may not have been an actual decrease in the amount of game in the Island. It may simply have been that, particularly about 1649, far more was required than at any time in the past and that demand exceeded supply Charles II had a large retinue with him, and he and his followers would live very differently from the ordinary islanders. Game would be required to feed them and the pursuit of game would be an end in itself as a pastime. The Order of the States was not put into effect until 4 April 1650, but no information is available as to how well it worked.

If the stoat population was reduced at all it was only a temporary decrease, for when the States ordered the Constables to collect moles from their parishioners in 1675 (one per vergée on enclosed land and one per two vergées on unenclosed) they stipulated that one *belette* should count as four moles. This again was no use, for only a few years later, in 1682, Poingdestre commented on the unbelievable number of stoats.

**5.—Stoats have been recorded at least once since 1965
in each of the marked squares.**

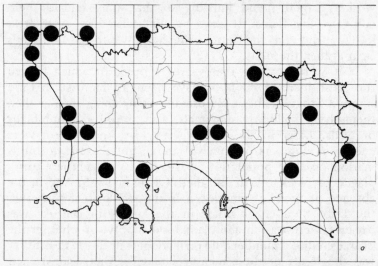

The *Cour d'Héritage* and the States seem confused as to
the name of the animals they were trying to destroy, calling
them *marthres, martres ou bellettes* and *bellettes* on different
occasions, and this confusion has continued down the centuries. The animal itself is not in question. It is the stoat,
Poingdestre being the first to name it so. Martens and weasels
do not exist in Jersey today, and almost certainly have not
since records began. Three distinct animals require three
distinct names:

English					Standard-French today
marten	..	..	..	..	*martre*
weasel	..	..	..	..	*belette*
stoat	..	..	..	..	*hermine d'été*

Jersey has only one of these animals, the stoat, *l'hermine
d'été*, but, unfortunately, in the past it was given the name
of either of the others, and to this day is known in Jersey-
French as *la belette* or *la b'lette* causing infinite confusion.

Plees classed them with moles as the 'principal noxious
animals' of Jersey in 1817. Sinel reported them as fairly

common and widely distributed in 1908. Most people living in the Island today have not seen one, but nevertheless they still exist in country districts, particularly on wild cliff land. Their number is difficult to estimate and has obviously declined, but the population is still viable and the stoat is not nearing extinction in Jersey. More information is necessary before the stoat's present distribution over the Island can be worked out. Meanwhile a map is given showing all recorded sightings since 1965.

In more northern latitudes the stoat moults its brown summer fur late in the year and has a white coat in winter, except for its tail which is always black tipped. Its winter fur is the white ermine of the fur trade. In Jersey a change in colour sometimes takes place. I have never seen a very pale or off-white one, but in 1949 Baal wrote that he had once seen a normal-coloured one and a white one on the same winter's day at St Ouen, and there are three recent records of white specimens: Mrs B. Getlif of Haut de la Garenne has the pelt of one she found shot in Rozel Woods; A. Rolland of La Tombette Carnation Nurseries saw one near the Devil's Hole, and R. Burrow one north of St Ouen's Pond. These localities are widely separated across the Island, east, north and west. If the colour change is genetically determined it would appear that the genes producing it occur in individuals throughout the Island population, and not just in one isolated pocket. Unfortunately, the exact year when these near-white or white animals were seen, is not known so that it is not possible to attempt to correlate their incidence with low temperatures in the preceding winters or summers.

For those unfamiliar with the animal my experience is that it suddenly appears, unexpectedly, crossing the road or threading its way over rocks or across heathland. Its short legs move so quickly, its body is so long and thin and so close to the ground that it gives the impression of a piece of brown ribbon moving at high speed. If anything like this is seen, look quickly at the end of its tail. It should have a black tip. At low tide in September 1973 my family and I saw one appear on rocks on the shore at L'Etacq, St Ouen. It was returning to the land from an area of rock pools and gullies which would be covered at high tide. These pools and gullies were not on any short cut that the stoat might have been taking from one land mass to another, and it must have made a special journey there. No fresh water occurs on that particular part of the beach, so it could not have been drinking. When first seen, water was dripping off it so it may have been catching food in the rock pools, but it was carrying nothing. We watched it as it came ashore and until it disappeared about a hundred yards away.

In Guernsey, stoats were very rare on the south coast cliffs in the 1950s, and Jee commented in 1967 that any small stoat-like animal was more likely to be an escaped ferret. This is not true in Jersey. Brehaut, writing in 1974, gave the last record in Guernsey as 1960. None had been recorded in Alderney, Sark, or Herm.

Ferret, Polecat x Ferret, Polecat, American Mink

Stray ferrets are occasionally found, but they are always obviously only recently out of captivity and there has never been any suggestion that they might be breeding in the wild.

Polecat ferret crosses, some looking very close to polecats, established themselves in the late 1960s in the west of the Island and some still survive. These animals are the size of cats; their faces are pale with dark masks; legs and tail dark, almost black; body pale with longer dark hairs. Between 1969 and 1972 there were 14 sight records along the foothills of St Ouen's Bay from Mont à la Brune in St Brelade to Route du Marais in St Ouen. Of five dead ones examined, all the teeth were intact, i.e., none had been filed down or extracted. There were several records in 1974 near St Ouen's Pond and one on Mont à la Brune. In 1975 one was found dead on the road near Kempt Tower, and another was caught at the foot of Jubilee Hill.

In Ansted and Latham's *Channel Islands* of 1893, Sinel tentatively suggested that some animals which he had not been able to examine closely might be pine martens, but in his later paper he omitted them. There is a possibility that these were also polecats x ferret derivatives.

In June 1970 P. Gould reported two strange animals among the rocks of Icho Tower. His description of them fitted American mink and this was what they proved to be. Both animals were seen again on Icho rocks and one was caught. A mink farm was established at Gorey just after the war. Later two more were established, one at St Peter and one at Fauvic. Now there is only the one at Fauvic. The mink farmers at first denied that any of their animals had escaped, but later, on checking, found they were two short. Icho Tower may seem a strange place for mink, but they swim well, are fond of fish and eggs, and have been found on Valencia Island several hundred yards off the coast of Eire. Mink are now an established pest along many waterways in England, where they are reported to be apppallingly destructive of other wild life. They are extremely secretive, in one place in England 11 being trapped when only two were suspected. If two mink escaped, unknown to their owners, how many others have? Are there more at large?

The Grey Seal

No seal breeding colonies exist at present in the Bailiwick of Jersey, but grey seals *Halichoerus grypus* are occasionally seen. Some years single animals will spend a few months near Les Ecréhous or Icho Tower. Archaeological excavations on Les Minquiers have shown that at two periods of time in the past, one about 2,000 years ago, and the other yet earlier, grey seals were abundant on La Maîtresse Ile, and men went there to hunt them. It is thought that a rise in sea level on each occasion destroyed the habitat.

The Brown Hare

On 20 October 1649, six months after Charles II was proclaimed King in Jersey, he issued a proclamation forbidding anyone to shoot partridges or hares, or carry fowling pieces. In previous centuries the sovereign possessed, or had at some time claimed to possess, almost everything of value within the Island and the seas around it. Only his right to the four 'Princely things', gold not worked, silk not worked, scarlet cloth whole, and cloaks without fastenings, had gone unchallenged. Every other claim, and there were many, including rights concerned with wreck from the sea, whales, porpoises, dolphins, rabbit warrens, stray animals, the drying of congers, and the keeping of pigeons, to name but a few, were hotly contested by the islanders. Among all these claims by succeeding kings there does not seem to have been one specifically for hares until this by Charles II in 1649. It seems unlikely, when so much fuss was made about rabbits, that other four-footed animals, bearing good quality meat, should be loose on the Island in Norman and Plantagenet times without their being named somewhere or without their being the jealously-guarded property of someone. Jean Chevalier notes the proclamation in his diary which he kept from 1643 to 1651, yet, in the two years following 1649, he makes no mention of any complaint against it. Considering the Jerseyman's readiness to object if he thought his rights were being removed, this lack of protest is out of character unless none of them had ever had rights over hares. Had hares perhaps not been in the Island in earlier days? Had they not, until Tudor or Stuart days, been part of the game so often mentioned? It may be that when more records from the previous centuries are available this will be made clear. They were in Guernsey, where Marquand considered they were intro- duced, by 1548, for the hunting of hares as well as rabbits was then restricted by law to a few people. Poingdestre does not mention them in either his *Lois et Coutumes de l'Ile de Jersey* or in his *Caesarea,* so they cannot have been an important part of the Jersey scene, though, only a little later, Falle in 1694 commented that hares and rabbits were 'the only constant game'. Plees in 1817 reported seeing them occasionally, but Durell thought there were very few left by 1837. They must have increased again, for Le Lievre in his *Guide to Jersey* in 1861 stated that they were more numerous than partridges.

According to Sinel, they were plentiful round about 1870 or 1880, so much so that rows of tails could be seen decorat- ing kitchens. He stated that from time to time the numbers were reinforced by imported stock, so perhaps the increase during the mid-19th century was not from those hares already in the Island. It is difficult to pinpoint when the decline, which eventually led to the hare's disappearance from Jersey, began. The hare was still given as common by Sinel in 1893, but in 1908 he reported that it was on the verge of extinction and the only note of interest concerning hares after this is a negative one from G. F. B. de Gruchy that in 1917 there was none on Noirmont warren.

I have seen one or two undated preserved specimens said to have been shot in Jersey, and all have been brown hares *Lepus capensis (L. europaeus)* which is the species on the Continent opposite and over most of England.

Bones of the blue hare *L. timidus* were found in La Cotte de St Brelade. This is the hare of northern Europe and the Arctic and it presumably roamed the area that is now Jersey when the climate was cold.

Belgian hares, which are rabbits, are occasionally kept as pets and sometimes escape.

Hares died out in Guernsey towards the end of last century. There is no information about them in Alderney or Sark.

The Rabbit

Rabbits are so common in the country parishes today that it may require a considerable effort of mind to accept the fact that they were unknown in the Island until Norman or Plantagenet times. The first Jersey record of them is on 23 April 1253, when Richard de Grey, custodian of the Isles, was told by Henry III to guard the royal warrens and rabbit holes well as was done in the time of the previous Kings of England. The document commanding him to do this is in the *Lettres Closes* in the Public Record Office in London. The importance attached to guarding the King's rabbits can be judged not merely by the fact that they were mentioned at all, at a time when correspondence must have been difficult, but by this document seeming to rank equal in importance with others commanding Richard de Grey to hold assizes and keep the fortifications of Jersey in good repair.

Rabbits were originally introduced into north-west Europe from the south by the Normans for food, providing a good supply of fresh meat during the winter months. The first

English record is from the Isles of Scilly in 1176. Warrens began to increase on the mainland of England in the mid-13th century, so that Jersey would appear to have had rabbits introduced at approximately the same time as other parts of the King's realm.

In the *Extente* of 1274 of Edward I there were complaints that evil men were taking the King's rabbits, but it was not stated from where. The King himself had two rabbit warrens, one round the *Chateau* (i.e., Gorey Castle), and another on the cliffs at La Moye, but he pointed out that he had a right to any rabbit anywhere in the Island. Were they perhaps already beginning to escape, for there could be no rabbits in the Island other than from introduced stock, and in theory the King alone had warrens? If so, this is paralleled in England where there were complaints in Somerset in 1254-7 about their destructive habits. At this time it was thought there were about 500 rabbits on Sark and 300 on Alderney.

On 28 May 1282 there were again orders from Edward I that his warrens were to be guarded and no one allowed in them for rabbit hunting. By 1299 he had decided that further action was required. Powerful landowners were also keeping warrens, so at the Assizes of 1299 various people were asked by what right they kept a warren on their land. Drogo de Barentin of Rozel Manor claimed that he had all the privileges which belonged to the manor and that these privileges had been enjoyed by all the previous owners from time immemorial. While this might have been true of some of the other privileges, the keeping of rabbits at Rozel would stretch back very little beyond living memory, if at all. That the warren was important to him is shown by him having a servant called William the Warrener, though it must be admitted that William's duties were more than just guarding a warren, for Drogo was heavily fined at the same Assizes for making his warrener exact a toll from owners of all animals which passed Rozel on the King's highway.

Also at these Assizes of 1299, Peter de Saumarès was asked to explain why he claimed right of wreckage, free rabbit hunting, and various other privileges, not only within his Samarès boundaries but right up to the old course of the stream west of St Helier where he held no land whatever.

In reply, Peter de Saumarès claimed that when his predecessors conferred the site of the town of St Helier on the Priory of the Islet they kept, among other rights, that 'of free hunting of rabbits through the whole Mount of St Helier with dogs, ferrets, nets and sticks where no one else except the Lord King can hunt in this manner'.

Reginald de Carteret of St Ouen's manor and the Abbot (of Mont St Michel) of St Clement's manor also had warrens about which questions were asked.

In 1309, in Edward II's reign, they were still having to explain at the Assizes why they claimed the right to keep a warren, but they were now joined by others: John de Carteret in St Ouen, Philip de Cheny in St John, and William des Augrey in Trinity; and the Abbot of Mont St Michel had added another one at Noirmont. The King himself seems to have had at least one other warren besides Gorey and La Moye, for Robert l'Eveque and John Falu were found by night with nets in the warren of the King at Le Mourier. Rabbit-stealing seems to have been rampant. William Ranulph was imprisoned in the Castle (Gorey) for chasing 'conies of the Lord the King', but later 'abjured the islands', as did Gregory de la Vergee, who first fled to St Lawrence church after stealing conies.

In 1329 John de Roches, who kept accounts for King Edward III, paid out money for the upkeep of three warrens, one of which was still at La Moye, but in 1331, according to the *Extente* of that year, it was no longer worth keeping a warrener there because his wages exceeded the profit. The warren round Gorey Castle was also beginning to be a problem, for the rabbits themselves were not worth much and after they had eaten what they needed, the vegetation which was sold for fuel, was not worth much either. Nevertheless, the King still kept his warrens *'aux landes de Lestac'* in St Ouen and also in St John, where the tenants of the various pieces of land nearby had a duty to keep a ferret, night and day, at their expense. Was this to help keep the rabbits within bounds?

No records can be found for the next two centuries in Jersey, but it seems a fair assumption that the numbers of rabbits continued to increase as they did elsewhere in the

Channel Islands. In 1540 on Leland's map of the Channel
Islands *ubi cuniculi multi* is written against Burhou, the
small island to the west of Alderney, and *cuniculorum fer-
tilissimum* against Sark. These two islands, and indeed the
whole of Guernsey also, seem to have been farmed each as
one big rabbit warren for the King rather than as in Jersey,
where areas were kept specially for his rabbits. The taking of
rabbits in Guernsey was not completely illegal, but was
carefully regulated so that the King had most. A jury ruled
in 1309 that people be fined for taking rabbits 'out of the
the customary season, viz., from the month of September
to the month of February' and laid down a strict order of
precedence for hunting rabbits: the King and his officers
went first, then the Abbot and Nicholas de Cheny, then
Philip de Cheny and others, and so on until presumably
the close season had arrived and only enough rabbits were
left to provide a breeding stock. In spite of this concession
individual landholders continued to claim free warren on
their land.

In 1600 the Governor of Jersey appointed Charles Hamelin
to be *Maître de la Chasse* because of the number of 'lazy
vagabonds' in the Island. It was forbidden to take nets or
snares or *'hacbusze arbeleste'* into fields without permission,
but there is no mention of what the so-called lazy vagabonds
were trying to catch. Game birds? Rabbits? In 1642 Elie
Dumaresq of La Haule went to the trouble of getting six
pounds of twine specially from St. Malo to make nets to
catch rabbits. That they were still an important asset to a
landowner is evident from the fact that in 1643 when Sir
George Carteret was, in Letters Patent, granted the fiefs
and manors of Melesches, Grainville and Noirmont; he was
also given 'all that warren of conies lying and being in or near
the parish of St Helier in the said Island of Jersey with all
the rights of the said warren belonging and appertaining'.

In his book *Lois et Coutumes de l'Ile de Jersey,* Jean
Poingdestre who was bailiff of Jersey from 1668 to 1676
discussed the *droict de chasse* and the *droict de Franche
garenne,* i.e., the right to hunt and the right to keep a warren.
He concluded that anyone had the right of chase, but only
over his own land not over anyone else's, and he cited, as an

example of the right to keep a warren, that kept by the Seigneur of Samarès on Mont de la Ville, presumably the one claimed by Peter de Saumarès at the Assizes of 1299. He pointed out that though the inhabitants of St Helier owned Le Mont de la Ville, it was not theirs to dispose of, or use, as they wished, for the *droict de garenne* of the Seigneur of Samarès must always be protected. If rabbits were found outside the precincts of Le Mont, i.e., outside the warren which was the whole of Le Mont, then they belonged to the owners of the properties on which they were found and still not to the inhabitants of St Helier. It is of interest that when the right of free warren on Le Mont de la Ville was actually claimed in 1674 it was ruled in 1677, after much argument, that the right had lapsed through lack of use. This was hotly disputed and the matter was only settled by the owner of the right voluntarily relinquishing it.

Poingdestre also considered that anyone had the right to set up a warren on his own land, but there was one essential condition: that the rabbits should be kept inside and should not be allowed to damage the oats and other crops of neighbours. He reiterated this when dealing with the right to keep a fishpond: '. . . *il y a bien de la différence entre le poisson enfermé en un Estang & le Conil qui s'escarte quand il veut la Garenne et qui va à la pasture non pas jour, comme les autres animaux, mais de nuict quand il ne peut estre empesché ou preuenu par aucune diligence'*.

In 1694 Falle stated that hares and rabbits were 'the only constant game'. They must still have been valuable, for in 1704 Philip Pipon, Seigneur of Noirmont, took a gun away from a tenant's son who was shooting rabbits on the land his father rented. Pipon claimed that he alone had shooting rights over his seigneurial land, but the Privy Council ruled otherwise. Later that century an article of the Code of Laws of 1771 restricted *la chasse* and made it an offence to dig out rabbit holes but, as might have been predicted, the States soon decided this was a nuisance and contrary to the public good. In 1792 they therefore voted to repeal it and to permit anyone to take what measures he thought fit to destroy rabbits and all other species of game on his land. One wonders what the other species of game were. Hare, but

what else? In 1817 Plees commented that the rabbit was
the only useful wild animal which, in view of the damage
it could have done, seems to indicate that its numbers were
being kept in check.

It may be that as standards of living rose so the rabbit
declined in popularity as an article of food and that without
rigorous hunting its numbers began to increase. In 1908
Sinel thought they were common, and certainly in the 1950s
they were common, if not abundant, until myxomatosis
struck. It had already been raging on the British mainland
for some years when the first reports of rabbits suffering
from it here began to circulate. The exact date is difficult
to pin down. Rumour followed counter-rumour for some
time, then, suddenly in 1958 and 1959, the disease erupted
and no longer was it possible to doubt its existence. Dead
and dying rabbits were a common sight over most of the
Island, though parts of the east seemed to escape. It has not
been possible to find out how it came to Jersey but man is
suspected of having introduced it deliberately into the south
west of the Island. This is simple to do and man did deliberately introduce it later into Herm and Jethou.

Since that time rabbits have fluctuated in numbers. In the
early morning, in times of plenty, it is possible to see a score
or more from the windows of our house at Val de la Mare,
St Ouen, this in spite of the whole area being shot over
frequently. Spring 1974 was such a time, but then a wave
of myxomatosis swept through them and by September 1974
only an occasional one could be found. This seems to happen
whenever they reach plague proportions, but they have never
been wiped out, not even in the first, the most virulent wave
of myxomatosis, as they were in many areas of similar size
in England. Myxomatosis is carried by rabbit fleas so rabbits
living in close contact in large warrens are at much greater
risk than those living in isolation. I was walking through Les
Marais at St Ouen in 1970 with three schoolboys when one
of them, William Le Marquand, suddenly stooped down to
a tussock of purple moor-grass and brought out a young
rabbit, only a few days old and with its eyes still closed,
from a fur-lined nest of dry grass inside the tussock. To
human eyes the nest looked invitingly warm and cosy and

extremely beautiful. Le Marquand said he often found such nests, that this was no happy accident. In Le Marais tussocks like this would be chosen because they were dry shelters among the wet marshland and it may be that enough rabbits live above ground in Jersey, or in some way apart from one another, to escape the disease and be able to recolonise the Island within a year or two of each outbreak.

Man and his dogs and cats are the main predators of the rabbit today. When stoats were common they would take a considerable number, but in those days rabbits were not a problem. At times they were even an asset to a land-owner. Now there are not enough stoats to make much difference to the rabbit population. Owls, ravens, crows and great black-backed gulls which are predators elsewhere are also not in sufficient numbers. The occasional escaped ferret must live principally off rabbits and so must polecats or polecat ferret crosses.

The Red Squirrel

No early writer mentioned the red squirrel; neither Poing-destre nor Falle, nor even Sinel in his 1893 list. Surely an animal so appealing to man would have been mentioned had it occurred wild? Or did its popular appeal not begin until much later, after Beatrix Potter had written Squirrel Nutkin? There are two vague unsubstantiated records which refer back to the late 18th century and the beginning of the 19th. Sinel was told when a boy by one of the 'oldest inhabitants' that he and his friends when young had often chased squirrels where St Luke's church now stands. Sinel put this as the last quarter of the 18th century. Nevertheless, he was not convinced that squirrels were native. The second early record is from the unedited handwritten *Procès Verbaux* of the Société Jersiaise for March 1895. P. A. Aubin told the Committee that in 1810 there were squirrels living free at Plaisaunce, St Saviour. This information is not in the published version, so it may or may not have been accepted.

Monica Shorten and A. D. Middleton, in their monographs on squirrels, both give 1885 as the date of introduction of the red squirrel to Jersey. This is based on information in

6.—Red squirrels have been recorded at least once since 1965 in each of the marked squares.

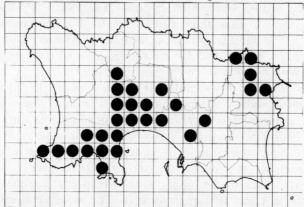

a letter from G. F. B. de Gruchy, a well-known Island naturalist and later Seigneur of Noirmont, to A. D. Middleton in the 1920s. Mrs Dixon, G. F. B. de Gruchy's daughter, has searched her father's diaries for any mention of the red squirrel about 1885 but can find none.

According to the published *Procès Verbaux* for February 1895 red squirrels were seen in the summer of 1894 at La Hague Manor, La Moie House and St Ouen's Manor. This disclosure brought the information from Mr Le Brocq of La Hougue Boëte, St John, that he had introduced some into Jersey in the spring of 1894. They came from the estate of Sir Walter Phillimore in the south of England. Young were later seen at La Hougue Boëte, and in May 1895 there were reports of them at La Pouquelaye, St Helier and Patier, St Saviour. The interest displayed by the Committee of the Société in 1895 in reports of these sightings suggests that squirrels in the wild were new to Jersey. In 1908 Sinel stated without details that, to his knowledge, numbers had been brought from France and liberated on several occasions within the last 20 years.

Knowledge of the year of successful introduction is perhaps of no great importance, it being sufficient that two much-respected Island naturalists, J. Sinel, who lived from 1844 to 1929, and G. F. B. Gruchy, who lived from 1869 to 1940, i.e., over the critical years, both considered that red squirrels were successfully introduced here towards the end of the 19th century.

C. L. Gruchy, the States veterinary surgeon, tells me that his father used to see them about 1900 near Rozel. By 1908 Sinel assessed them as fairly numerous in the north and north west, and said they were spreading towards the centre, some having been seen as close to town as Vallée des Vaux.

Baal, in his Société article in 1949, wrote of the red squirrel, 'Although indigenous in Jersey, many have, within the past fifty years, been brought from England and France and released, so that our present Squirrels do not differ in any marked degree from type . . . At one time only in the west of the Island, they have now spread to almost all parts'. He gives no reason for stating that they are indigenous and quotes no sources; the type red squirrel is Scandinavian and the last sentence gives a somewhat different picture of their early distribution from Sinel's.

In the late 1940s when Baal stated that they were widespread, there were records, among others, from places as far apart as the centre of St Helier (the Royal Square and Snow Hill Bus Station), St Ouen's Manor and Le Mourier Valley, St Mary, all areas which today seem to hold none. My records and all I have been given, post 1965, are spread out diagonally across the Island as can be seen in the distribution map. Red squirrels are sufficiently plentiful in the south west for most people who have wooded gardens there to be able to see them frequently. They can also be seen regularly in Rozel woods. Sightings in areas between suggest that the red squirrel population is one unit.

In 1450 Regnaud de Carteret of Longueville used a seal with a crest showing a squirrel holding a nut. This is still the family crest of the de Carteret and Pipon families, but there is no reason why the choice of this design should imply there were then squirrels in Jersey. There are no records of red squirrels from any other Channel Island.

Grey squirrels do not occur in Jersey and it is an offence to introduce them. In late summer or early autumn there are sometimes reports that grey squirrels have been seen. As far as possible such reports are investigated in case some

have been illegally released by people ignorant of the damage
grey squirrels may do to other wild life. Fortunately, such
fears have so far proved groundless. The red squirrel which is
a good handsome red in summer, changes in autumn to a
grey-brown coat not unlike a grey squirrel's. This is perhaps
where the confusion arises, but any suspicions that grey
squirrels have been introduced should continue to be
investigated.

The Wood or Long-tailed Field Mouse

In my experience most of the small mammals which are
found in houses and outbuildings in the country in winter
are wood mice, not house mice. Wood mice are also found
in gardens, hedgebanks, woodlands and coastal areas, but,
being largely nocturnal, they escape notice unless they interfere with man's crops. Nine, of which at least six were
different animals, were caught in 11 trap-nights on the Ile
Agois in 1974. A powerful searchlight suddenly shone over
a meadow at night will usually reveal some. They will not
scurry to the nearest shelter but will leap, with body arched
and tail erect, over grassy tussocks in a mad attempt to
escape from the light.

Mice have been in the Island in quantity since at least
Poingdestre's time. Sinel listed the long-tailed field mouse,
now usually known as the wood mouse, in 1893, and again
in 1908. He thought the inland ones were darker than those
on the coast.

The wood mouse and the closely-related, but larger and
differently coloured yellow-necked mouse, occur in Britain
and on the Continent opposite. The form in the Channel
Islands is intermediate in size and slightly different from
both in colour. In Ellerman and Scott's 1951 *Checklist of
Palaearctic and Indian Mammals* it is given as the yellow-
necked mouse, but, from examination of the teeth and skull,
the Earl of Cranbrook (1957) suggested it was nearer the
wood mouse. Delaney and Healy confirmed this in 1966 and
considered that it was not sufficiently different from the
typical wood mouse to be given sub-specific rank. It is of
interest that Hinton said he found no signs of the wood
mouse in the rodent bed excavated at the archaeological
site at La Cotte.

The House Mouse

Poingdestre's 'domestick' mice of 1682 were probably house mice, but they do not seem to be mentioned again until Sinel stated that they were abundant in 1908. He mentions a strikingly different form at Dancaster's Farm which was north of La Crabière, St Ouen's Bay, but he himself did not see it so the identification must be in doubt. Baal in 1949 said that when the house mouse does not live in houses or barns it is not always recognised. While this is true, he implies that the house mouse is common by saying that 'The owl pellets often give a proportion of 33 and one-third per cent. of house mouse skulls as compared with those of the wood mouse in the same district'. Apart from the fact that there are too many variables in owls and their prey for us to be able to deduce, from owl pellets, the comparative frequencies on the ground of small mammals, he has only used part of the published information on owl pellets. True, at St. Peter's House there were 11 house mice and 34 wood mice in a group of pellets, but he ignores the records from other places where 0, 3, 0, 1, 0 house mice and 25, 36, 17, 7, 10 wood mice were found respectively in owl pellets. There has been no house mouse skull in any owl pellets which I have teased apart.

It has been pointed out under shrews that Longworth small mammal traps do not seem to catch a representative selection of the small mammals of a region, but it should perhaps be mentioned that when Bishop caught 248 small mammals in Longworth traps in Waterworks Valley in 1960–61, some at a farm and others in woodland and meadows, not one was a house mouse. Similarly Rostron caught 72 small mammals in St Ouen's Bay in 1963, and not one was a house mouse. I find it impossible to hazard a guess as to their numbers in the countryside. I myself have only seen one in the country, here in Val de la Mare. Single specimens have been shown to me from near Gorey, Victoria Village, Five Oaks, above Bonne Nuit, St Brelade, La Haule and Le Hocq. Most of these are areas which have been inhabited for many years. In St Helier there is no doubt about their quantity. In the early 1970s a plague of house mice was so bad in parts of the town that at times people temporarily left their homes, and a sweet shop was forced out of business.

The Rats

There are, or more probably were, two species of rat in the Island, the black rat and the brown rat. Neither is native, but it is not known exactly when they came. The Island would still be free of them when William, Duke of Normandy, became King of England, and for some time after that. Black rats are known to have arrived in western Europe from the East during the 13th century, perhaps being brought back in the ships of the Crusaders, and they probably arrived in Jersey about that time. The Black Death, bubonic plague, which is carried by rats, raged in Jersey in 1348, and so many people died that Edward III, unable to collect his fishing dues, waived them. The plague may have been brought by people fleeing from the Continent, where it raged a little earlier in 1348. Balleine states that 100,000 corpses were buried in four months in Rouen alone. Equally the plague may have been brought by infected rats.

The foregoing is simply a reasoned guess as to when black rats arrived, putting Jersey in the geographical/time scale. The first mention of rats by name is about 300 years later in Jean Chevalier's diary. He reported that the Lieutenant-Governor and his family were forced to leave Elizabeth Castle on 9 December 1645 because of the large quantity of rats which had come from patrol vessels stationed there, and the prizes of war. Grain, originally belonging to those who had fled the Island because they were on the Parliamentarians' side, was stored at the Castle, and there were wheat granaries holding the Castle's provisions. This was an ideal situation for the rats, but not for the Lieutenant-Governor, and he moved out until the poison which was put down took effect. He returned on 23 January.

These must have been black rats because brown rats had not yet arrived in western Europe. Like the black rat, the brown, or Norway, rat arrived out of the east, but along a northern route, and was in the British Isles in the early 18th century. It also is carried in the holds of ships. Vessels of sufficient size were plying constantly between Jersey and England, and Jersey and the Continent, so there is no reason to suppose that Jersey escaped when the brown rat colonised this part of Europe and, as soon as it arrived in Jersey, the black rat which had previously been at least locally abundant would probably begin to decline in numbers. This happened elsewhere and again there is no reason to suspect that the two species behaved differently in Jersey from elsewhere.

Its status this century is difficult to determine. Sinel in his 1908 article gave a general undated comment, including that the black rat of Herm was larger and more robust than that of Sark and Jersey. He also said it was probably extinct in Guernsey. In the absence of any such comment about Jersey, did Sinel think the black rat was still here when he was writing? Baal used to tell me in the early 1950s that one had not been seen for many years. In his article in the 1949 *Bulletin* of the Société Jersiaise he follows Sinel (1893 and 1908) so closely in his description of the two colour forms of the black rat in Jersey and of its haunts that it is difficult to decide how much is from personal observation. Again no dates or localities are given so the last known record remains that in the Societe's *Procès Verbaux* of 26 February 1895 when it was stated that the black rat, which had almost disappeared from the Island, had been found again at 'Hautrée', St Saviour, and in a store in Commercial Street. It may be that the black rat had disappeared by the turn of the century; on the other hand it may survive in an isolated pocket. The brown rat is common.

The Bank Vole

Poingdestre described various mice in 1682, one of which was probably the bank vole, and Sinel mentioned a short-tailed mouse in 1893. Sinel's was almost certainly the bank vole, two of which were collected by Barrett-Hamilton (1896) in St Helier and identified as such for the first time. The bank vole of Jersey does not exactly match those of either the British mainland or the Continent. Crowcroft and Godfrey did considerable work on it in the late 1950s and showed that compared with the bank vole in Britain it was consistently larger and heavier, and a variation of the teeth was more often present. It is regarded as being sufficiently different to be named as a sub-species *Clethrionomys glareolus caesarius* (Miller), and Jersey is the only place in the world where this sub-species exists. There are no bank voles on any other Channel Island, but isolated groups exist on islands elsewhere round Britain. Those on Skomer and Raasay are also sufficiently different from the type to be given sub-specific rank, and those on Mull may be.

Their life span is short like that of other small mammals. Bishop and Delaney in the early 1960s found that the first young animals appear in June and become numerous by August. If they live out their life span they survive the first winter and some old ones can be found as late as January of the second winter. This means most live not more than about 20 months, and it may be less, as those still alive the second January may have been the last ones born in their year group.

To Crowcroft and Godfrey the bank vole appeared to be the most numerous of Jersey's small mammals. There is no other species of vole so, perhaps because of the absence of

Bank vole *Clethrionomys glareolus.*
(Head and body approx. 110-120mm.)

competition for territory, it is in both the woodlands and hedgebanks of the interior as well as rough grassland and gorse of the coast. While it is true that there are large numbers of bank voles, those of wood mice must run them at least a close second.

Dr M. A. C. Hinton who worked about 60 years ago on the rodent beds at the archaeological site, La Cotte de St Brelade, stated that he had searched in vain for remains of the bank vole. On the other hand there were many examples which he referred to as the *Microtus 'arvalis'* group. This is particularly interesting because though no field vole *Microtus arvalis* occurs now in Jersey it is common in Guernsey. Its distribution in western Europe is strange. There are no records of it from Brittany or the British Isles except for five islands or groups of islands, Guernsey, the Orkney mainland, Sanday and Westray Islands, South Ronaldshay and Rousay Island, in each of which the form is sufficiently different from the type to be given sub-specific rank, Guernsey's field vole being named *M. a. sarnius*.

History, Mystery, Water Voles and Water Shrews

Poingdestre in 1682 described three different species of animals-

> Of field mice wee haue three kinds: ye comon sort differing nothing from domestick ones, but onely in biggnesse; ye second kind differing both in bignesse collour & parts, being of a midle size betweene a rat & a mouse, of a gray not dunne colour, & of a deeper haire. They haue but foure teeth, two belowe & two aboue, but those belowe twice as long as ye vppermost; theire eyes are very litle & scarce discernable: but that which is most remarquable, when you looke vpon them you shall perceiue noe eares, till with yor finger you remoue the shagg that hides them; and then will appeare the eares large as to the size of ye beast, round and open, & very like those of a man, naked of either haire or downe, of a thinne substance, much like that of a bladder. Unto ye which, because that creature was to liue in ye earth, nature hath prouided ye said shelter, as well as to ye eyes, that it might not recieue iniury by ye fall of some hurtfull thing into them'.

His third sort were the shrews and his description of those has already been given. But here, presuming, perhaps wrongly, that the house mouse, the wood mouse and the bank vole were all in Jersey at the time, were his 'domestick' ones house mice and was he first describing the wood mouse followed by the bank vole? This is thought unlikely, for while the wood mouse is large in Jersey so is the house mouse, and I doubt if anyone today would say they differed only in 'bignesse'. Most people confuse them. Also the description of the second does not exactly fit a bank vole. Or has he lumped wood mouse with house mouse in the 'domestick' ones, as indeed a lot of them are in winter? In that case was it the bank vole which differed 'onely in biggnesse' and, if so, what was his second kind? Water vole? But that it lives near water is not mentioned, and Poingdestre's animal is too small. The water vole of Britain *Arvicola terrestris amphibius* is about the size of the black rat which would in theory be the only rat present in Jersey in 1682. Or were Poingdestre's second kind a continental race or species of *Arvicola*?

Sinel in 1893 listed the water vole, without comment, among the Island's mammals. In 1908 he again included it, but saying that it was not nearly as common as formerly. He could not account for this as he thought conditions had in no way altered. He may, in his youth, have been confusing a swimming brown rat with a water vole. This is considered unlikely and in support of the record it should be pointed out that, before the low-lying coastal plains were drained, there were plenty of marshes with slow-flowing streams which are ideal habitat for water voles. And though Sinel thought conditions had remained the same it was during his lifetime that most of these marshes were drained. Baal in 1949 stated that it had gone and blamed the brown rat for ousting it. There is no specimen, in spite of Sinel being a keen collector, and several students have searched for it recently without success. All reported sightings, capable of being checked, have proved to be brown rats.

The water vole was first reported in Guernsey in 1895 when, according to the *Reports and Transactions* of the Société Guernesiaise for 13 May 1895, 'The appearance of the Long-tailed Field Mouse and Water Vole was also noted; the latter was found in the stream at Grande Mare. This latter is new to the Guernsey list of mammals'. The Grande Mare, like some of Jersey's low-lying areas, would be a suitable place for water voles, but it seems strange that this should be the first sighting and was it the last? R. H. Bunting suggested to the Société Guernesiaise in 1909 that the water vole 'might turn up if such localities as the marshes at Rocquaine and Vazon Bays were trapped'. Jee comments in 1967 that reports of water rats usually turn out to be brown rats near water.

Were there ever water voles in the Channel Islands, and, if so, do they still exist? I have been unable satisfactorily to answer these questions.

In 1949 Baal claimed that the water shrew used to be fairly numerous in Jersey valleys but had disappeared. I can find no basis for this claim unless he was taking Poingdestre's second kind to be water shrews, but the description, even on a quick inspection, is wrong. No one else has mentioned water shrews and no specimen exists.

The difficulties experienced in identifying these small mammals are reflected in the way the Jersey-French word *mulot* is used. It can, according to Dr Le Maistre, be applied to a bank vole, field vole, field mouse, or water vole in spite of a field mouse being *souothis d'clios* or *southis d'fôssé* and a water vole *rat dg'ieau.* I have also heard a young rat called a *mulot* in Alderney.

4

BIRDS

The many hedges in this Island breed and afford shelter to
an infinite number of small Birds, who chant it merrily all
Spring and Summer-long, and delight the Traveller with
their pretty Melody . . .

Rev Philip Falle
An Account of the Island of Jersey, 1694

JERSEY HAS ABOUT 130 different species of birds which
live here permanently or are regular visitors at certain times of
the year. About another 200 species have been seen, some
fairly frequently, some infrequently, this century. While it
is always pleasing to see an extreme rarity, it is the normal
birds of an area, including how they have varied over the
years, which hold most interest, and in the account which
follows more attention has been given to them than to the
rarities. They can be divided roughly into five groups:

1. residents which are here all year round;
2. summer visitors which nest here but leave for the south
   on the approach of cold weather, and do not return
   until the following spring;
3. winter visitors which arrive with the onset of cold
   weather in autumn, but depart for their nesting areas
   further north or perhaps east as the weather improves
   the following spring;
4. passage migrants which do not stay in Jersey but merely
   use it as a stage on their journey, generally northwards,
   in spring and again on their return journey southwards
   in autumn; and finally
5. casuals or vagrants which do not normally visit Jersey
   but for some reason are off course.

These categories merge into one another, and different
individuals of the same species may belong to different
groups. A house martin may be either a summer visitor or
a passage migrant, but never either a winter visitor or a

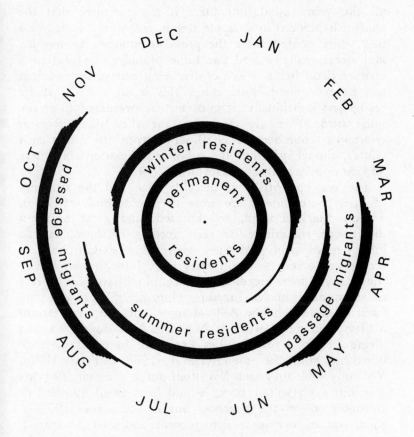

Diagram showing status of birds in Jersey at different times of the year.

permanent resident. Likewise with the other hirundines and some of the warblers. On the other hand brent geese are winter visitors with perhaps a few passage migrants and only captive or weak birds will stay in summer in Jersey. House sparrows are unusual in that they seem to be residents only. The species which seem the simplest are sometimes the most complicated. Chaffinches are with us all the year round, but there is no guarantee that the chaffinch perched in an apple tree in mid-winter is one of a pair which nested there the previous summer. It may be, and occasionally a bird has some plumage variation or a characteristic habit or a peculiar song phrase by which it can be recognised. But, unless this is so and it can be recognised individually, it must not be presumed to be the same bird. There is evidence that the Island receives enormous numbers of chaffinches from the north each winter, though whether the summer population stays here all year or goes south is not known.

The sea just offshore, the tide edge and the stretches of open water inland are areas of intense bird activity in winter. Black-throated, red-throated, and great northern divers can sometimes be seen feeding offshore, as can black-necked and Slavonian grebe and exceptionally a red-necked grebe. Normally they leave Jersey waters before they assume their breeding plumage, but I have seen a great northern diver in full breeding plumage in April preening itself in the sea below Belle Hougue, and the same month a Slavonian grebe, with its ear tufts fully developed, was diving for food just off Les Ecréhous. In my experience divers and grebes became rarer in the 1960s and early 1970s. Not only were they seen less often out at sea than 20 years ago, but each winter fewer would be washed up oiled or storm-blown on the beaches. But in the winter 1973/74 there was an increase in sight records, and after the storms, one of which was near hurricane force on a high spring tide, in January and February 1974, grebes, particularly Slavonian, and divers were again recorded in many of the counts of beached birds. Most of the grebes and all the divers nest some considerable distance to the north or east of Jersey, but Jersey is well within the breeding range of the great crested grebe. These occur in fair numbers in winter, often near St Aubin's Fort, but have shown no sign of staying to nest. The little grebe is occasionally seen out at sea, but is normally on the reservoirs or St Ouen's Pond. A few pairs now nest each year. If a small bird submerges on one of the reservoirs as soon as it is seen, the chances are it is a little grebe. It will probably emerge well out of sight.

Fulmars had been seen regularly off Alderney since the early 1950s, but it was still with a certain amount of surprise that K. and F. Le Cocq and I saw one flying along the cliffs near Le Grand Becquet, St Ouen, in Jersey in April 1955. From that date, there were sightings along the north coast cliffs in most years until by 1970/71, if one waited on Le Grand Becquet, a fulmar would eventually fly past. In 1974 W. B. Barker and P. Jones found a colony of four pairs and five individual birds sitting on narrow ledges on the vertical face of a cliff on the wildest stretch of the St Ouen coast line. In 1975 one young was reared.

Manx shearwaters were also at one time reckoned an extreme rarity, but Advocate F. C. Hamon has shown that, at times of stormy weather with strong westerly gales in summer and autumn, they can be seen half a mile or more off the north coast. They fly low, moving ever westerly into the wind, showing first black, then white, as they careen at wave-top height. Any of the headlands from Belle Hougue to Grosnez will serve as an observation point. This is almost certainly not a change in the range of Manx shearwaters. Rather they have probably always been offshore like this, but have previously gone unnoticed. Grosnez in particular is proving an excellent look-out post. Anyone prepared to walk down to the lighthouse there and brave a full autumn gale, preferably near hurricane force, from the west or north west, with driving rain, may well see, besides Manx shearwaters, sooty shearwaters, arctic skuas, great skuas, gannets, kittiwakes, black terns, white-winged black terns, scoters, and several other possible rarities not as yet satisfactorily identified.

Storm petrels, Mother Carey's chickens, are regular breeders on a few of the offshore islands and may well be on more. For instance, though no nest has been found on Les Minquiers, an addled egg was found there in 1959 and two birds flew overhead at night in July 1973. Except when they are incubating their one egg or brooding the chick, storm petrels spend their entire lives at sea. There seems to be a certain amount of movement between colonies well apart, an adult ringed in July 1966 on Burhou, off Alderney, being caught at its nest site on a rock off Jersey in July 1969. Leach's petrel has been found three times only at long intervals: 1895, 1916 and 1952, two of them at least being storm casualties.

Gannets nest on rocks off Alderney and on Les Sept Iles, Côtes du Nord, France. It is therefore not surprising that watchers on the cliffs, particularly at Grosnez, often report gannets well out to sea. Sometimes the gannets are flying singly, but occasionally there are also milling, circling groups from which individuals peel off to dive vertically into the water for food.

Cormorants and shags can be seen all the year round. By local tradition they all seem to be called cormorants, which is a pity as the cormorant is much the less common. Shags nest in quantity on all the cliffs and offshore islets, whereas cormorants have never been known to nest on the mainland of Jersey, only on the outlying reefs. Shags' nests are usually in shelter of some sort: under a boulder, tucked in hard against the cliffs under a slight overhang, or inside a derelict hut, as on Les Minquiers. Cormorants' nests tend to be larger, higher structures built out in the open. I have only seen them in three places: the high flat-topped rock at the south-west end of La Maîtresse Ile at Les Minquiers, Les Maisons at Les Minquiers, and on a wide ledge beside the landing place on La Maître Ile at Les Ecréhous. In the distance shags and cormorants may look similar, but a shag has a crest which is visible at close range or through binoculars, and a cormorant has a white patch on its chin. The patch is well defined and entirely different from the diffused white throat patch of a young shag. In the breeding season, cormorants also have a conspicuous white patch on their flanks. They tend to come on to fresh water more often than shags, and perhaps one of the easiest places to see a cormorant is St Ouen's Pond where there is often one fishing. After feeding, or if disturbed, it will fly back to the sea in St Ouen's Bay.

7.–Map showing possible routes of brent geese between their breeding grounds in the high Arctic and Jersey. Dark-bellied, the commoner form, come from the Russian Arctic, while the pale-bellied come from the Canadian Arctic.

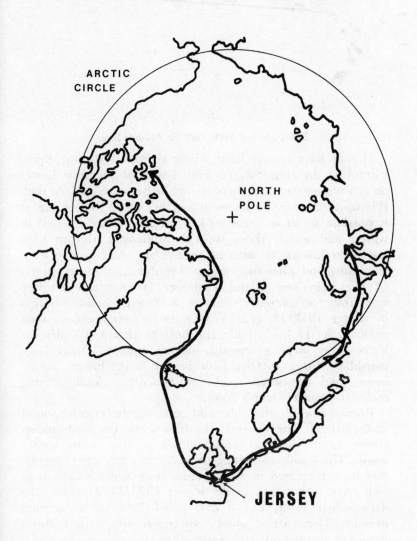

Brent geese at West Park, St Aubin's Bay.

Herons have always been winter visitors. Walk out, being careful of the tide, towards Icho Tower or Seymour Tower on any winter day, and there should be herons about. At high tide up to 20 may be gathered together on La Rousse, and it is possible to sit in a car parked on the south-east coast in winter and watch them through binoculars. Herons have not been known to nest in Jersey, but their numbers are increasing and each succeeding year there are more reports of them being seen inland in summer. Twenty years ago they were only occasional visitors to St Ouen's Pond, whereas in winter 1972/73 and 1973/74 up to four could be seen regularly in the back fields, and both there and in Vallée des Vaux there were a few sightings in summer. Other large marshland birds, bittern, little bittern, night heron, purple heron and spoonbill occur infrequently, usually being recorded from St Ouen's Pond.

Brent geese are the only wild geese regularly to be found in the Island. They nest in the high arctic on the boulder-strewn tundra and, as winter closes in, they move southwards. The numbers coming to St Aubin's Bay and Grouville Bay have increased in recent years from some hundreds to well over a thousand in the winter 1973/74. Most are the dark-bellied form, but a few pale-bellied are sometimes present. They arrive about November and depart about April, so throughout the winter they are one of the sights of Jersey, not in some remote corner where they have to be sought out and carefully approached, but close inshore, hard against the most populated parts of the Island. The historian Falle mentioned them first in 1694, 'Here are to be seen the famous Sorland Geese . . . We call them Bernacles, and they are only seen about the sea, and in very cold weather'. But they may have been coming as long as man himself, and many Jersey people still call them 'Bernacles' which leads to confusion since the name 'Barnacle' is applied to a different species of goose in Britain.

They are vegetable feeders and the principal attraction of St Aubin's Bay and Grouville Bay is the small eel-grass, *Zostera nana* which grows about half-tide mark. It is possible to stand on West Park slip, St Helier, and have these magnificent geese from the far north feeding within a few yards. When the sea is calm and the tide sufficiently high completely to cover the walls of the bathing pool at West Park by an inch or two, the geese often stand on top of the wall waiting for the tide to ebb. The sight is remarkable. No visible sign exists of the wall so the geese appear to be standing in a semi-circle on the surface of the sea more than a hundred yards out.

The larger ornamental, privately-owned pools have often had mute swans put on them. Of late the numbers have increased and the swans occasionally move to the reservoirs or to wild areas like St Ouen's Pond. There have been several attempts to breed on Town Mills Pond in recent years, the first successful attempt being in 1969 when N. Le Brocq reported one cygnet was reared. Seven were reared in 1974. Genuinely wild mute swans sometimes arrive, as in January of the exceptionally cold 1962/3 winter when up to 10 were seen together off the south-east coast.

Mallard nest regularly, most of the larger stretches of open water having a few pairs. The numbers are increased by migrants in winter, and then they are not so restricted to inland waters, but can be seen sitting out at sea just beyond where the waves break. Other species of duck also arrive in winter, particularly if there is hard weather on the Continent, teal, wigeon, pochard, tufted duck, and shoveler being regular visitors in small but increasing numbers. They come principally to the reservoirs and St Ouen's Pond, but some

reservoirs are more favoured than others. Grands Vaux is
easily the best from an ornithologist's point of view and has
been since it was filled in 1952/3. On the other hand, Val
de la Mare reservoir seldom has any duck on it, even now,
about 15 years after its construction. This may be because
Val de la Mare has steeper cotils running down to it than
Grands Vaux, which lies much more open, but it is more
likely that the attraction at Grands Vaux is a better food
supply. Whether the water level is high or low, Grands
Vaux supports a varied community of plant and animal
life along its banks and in the water, while Val de la Mare
reservoir has steep sides of loose shale, and many of them
still appear to be sterile. The older reservoirs have their
resident mallard and a few migrant duck during the winter
months.

A walk across wet marshland in winter may put up some
teal, perhaps a hundred or more, and a few wigeon. They
will settle on open water inland and, like mallard, they are
often out at sea. Pochard and tufted duck, being diving
ducks, feed on the reservoirs and St Ouen's Pond. Tufted
duck in particular have increased slightly in the last few years
and so have shoveler, which at one time were a decided
rarity. For the last few years there has been a flock of
shoveler up to 30 or more strong on St Ouen's Pond, and
each year some have been paired and indulging in courtship
display before leaving. Hopes have been high that they would
stay to nest and they may have done so in 1974. The first
gadwall was reported only in 1968, but a few have appeared
on St Ouen's Pond every winter since then. Common scoters
used to be frequent out at sea, often off Elizabeth Castle,
but they seem to have decreased. Red-breasted mergansers
are also round the coast in winter, particularly off the east
and south east. A careful count can reveal as many as 300,
not in large flocks like the brent geese, but singly, or in small
parties only.

Every winter a varying selection of rare or unusual geese
or ducks arrives. The following species have been recorded
this century, some only once, others more often, but none
with any regularity in their appearance here: barnacle,
greylag, white-fronted, bean and pink-footed geese, shelduck,

pintail, garganey, scaup, eider, velvet scoter, long-tailed duck, goldeneye, smew and goosander.

Birds of prey were affected in Jersey, as elsewhere, during the 1950s and 1960s when organo-chloro pesticides like aldrin, dieldrin and DDT were used indiscriminately. Both the sparrowhawk and the peregrine disappeared as breeding species during this time, but the kestrel remained. Any bird hovering overhead, or airborne on outspread wings yet motionless, is almost certain to be a kestrel. It will be facing into the wind with head bent down and eyes searching the ground for shrews, voles, mice, beetles, and so on. The cliffs of the coast and the open land of the west are the best places to see them, but they also occur inland. Peregrines used to be on the coastal cliffs. Dobson records G. F. B. de Gruchy as finding a peregrine's eyrie on the north coast in 1922, and this eyrie was in use from time to time until the eventual disappearance of the peregrine as a breeding bird from the Island. Dobson also tells of how he himself, in the course of spending many hours watching peregrines, found about a dozen eyries along the north, west and south cliffs. These eyries were not occupied every year and he thought there were never more than four resident pairs. I knew three occupied eyries on the north coast in the early 1950s, but I cannot say whether there were any on the west or south cliffs. By 1958 only one pair was left and, though eggs were laid, no young were reared. Since then very few birds have been seen. Elsewhere the decline in numbers may have been halted, and though there is not yet an increase, we may eventually see the return of the peregrine to Jersey as a regular breeding bird. The north coast cliffs seem empty without them. Writing of the years 1934 to 1947 Dobson says 'The sparrow-hawk is generally distributed throughout the island and most woods of any size contain a pair of these birds'. They were becoming scarce about 1950 and since the mid-1950s very few have been seen. The last nest I know of was about 60 feet up in a macrocarpa tree in the wood on the rocky outcrop separating L'Ouaisné from St Brelade. It had four eggs in it, one of them broken, on 5 June 1954.

Other birds of prey have been recorded over the years.
Some, like buzzards, marsh harriers and merlins, may be
regular migrants in very small numbers, while ospreys, red
kites, goshawks, rough-legged buzzards, hen and Montagu's
harriers, Greenland falcons and hobbies are probably only
accidentals.

Red-legged partridges were present by the 17th century,
and when Charles II proclaimed in 1649 that they were not
to be shot there were no objections. This suggests that they
were fairly recent introductions and no one else had rights
over them. At times they were in sufficient quantity to be
exported to London, where, according to R. R. Marett, they
were called 'Jerseymen'. They declined in the 19th century
and were not seen after the 1870s. Attempts were made in
the early 1970s to introduce pheasants, but they seem to
have died out. It is now fashionable to keep waterfowl on
artificial ponds, and many escape. Most are seen only for
a short time, but a pair of mandarin ducks bred in the south-
east in the early 1960s.

Quail nested here in fair quantity last century. They
then began to decrease over most of western Europe, including Jersey. No nest has been found for many years, but they
still come to the Island on migration and their unmistakable
three-syllable call 'Wet-my-lips', repeated over and over
again, was heard in St Ouen in 1961. Flocks of migrating
cranes flying high in V formation have long excited people's
imagination. Normally the routes are well to the east of the
Channel Islands, but 17 were seen over Guernsey on the
afternoon of 31 October 1963, and an hour later E. D. H.
and G. F. Johnson saw them flying down St Ouen's Bay.
Halfway along the Bay the flock turned and flew inland
over the Island. The last records of another huge bird, the
great bustard, were about a century ago when some arrived
in fields at St Clement and, as was the custom of the age,
were promptly shot. There is little chance of such enormous
birds being seen again, though attempts are now being made
to re-establish them near Salisbury Plain in England. Little
bustards, vagrants from south Europe, were recorded three
times in the early years of this century.

Like the quail, the corncrake also used to be fairly common, but now it is only an irregular passage migrant. It seems to become strangely tired on its journeys, as most records are of birds found so exhausted as to allow themselves to be picked up. Dobson reports Baal as having had 18 taken to him in 1938. Among the places where corncrakes have been picked up since the war are Pitt Street in St Helier, the Gasworks Yard in Tunnell Street, a cornstore along the Esplanade, the veranda of a house in Queen's Valley and Val de la Mare, St Ouen, where one was found walking up the drive to our house. All seem to recover after being rested for a few hours. In spite of being seldom seen or heard now in the British Isles, the corncrake or land rail is a bird well-known by name. Nothing like so well-known is its close relative the water rail. Most people have never heard of it, yet Dobson described it as not uncommon in Jersey and this is still true today. It frequents marshy areas and wet ditches throughout the Island in winter. Though shy and skulking, it seems peculiarly accident-prone, some being found dead or injured each winter. It is extremely secretive and so far no nest has been found, or any indication of nesting other than the presence of the adult birds occasionally in the breeding season. In early summer 1972, 1973 and 1974, for instance, C. E. Buxton reported adult water rails present in Vallée des Vaux in exactly the right habitat for nesting.

The spotted crake, another marshland bird, is perhaps even more skulking than the water rail. It is thought to be a very scarce autumn migrant at St Ouen's Pond and Grouville Marsh from where there are recent records, but it has a long history in both these areas and many may escape notice. J. Romeril who once shot 15 in a season claimed they used to be common in Grouville Marsh.

Coot and moorhen nest regularly in small numbers, moorhen by any area of open water, but coot chiefly on St Ouen's Pond. In autumn there is an influx from the north with the numbers of moorhen increasing gradually, but those of coot sometimes increasing with spectacular suddenness. Occasionally Gorey Harbour or the North Canal at St Ouen will be full of coot, which arrive in these large flocks if there is a sudden spell of severe weather in Europe. From returns of birds ringed in Jersey there would appear to be a movement of coot and moorhen from Holland and the Baltic region in summer to the French Atlantic coast in winter, with Jersey an intermediate calling point on the way. Some stay here and go no further. The furthest travelled is a coot ringed in March 1954 at St Ouen's Pond which was found dead on the shore of a lake near Stockholm, Sweden, 1,720km. away, in August the same year.

The coastal stretches of the Island are the feeding grounds of flocks of waders, usually smallish birds which feed at the edge of the tide. When disturbed, they fly in tightly-packed formation, twisting and turning in unison, showing first one side and then the other, dark, then light. The best places to see them are not the beaches of pure dry sand beloved by holidaymakers. These hold little food and are therefore lacking in interest to birds. Waders prefer the wetter parts of the shore, particularly the muddier areas or the seaweed-strewn gullies of the south east where there is a rich abundance of plant and animal life on which they can feed. The best place in St Aubin's Bay, for instance, is between the Albert Pier and West Park Slip, an area neglected by all but fishermen who dig there for bait. Other good places are La Rocque Harbour, by some of the slips along the south east, particularly Mary Ann Le Vesconte's, L'Etacq and many places where fresh water runs down the beach.

At low tide in winter, waders will be spread out over all the feeding areas, but as the tide rises, they are forced to move up the beach with it or perch on rocks not as yet submerged. On a neap tide of about 28 feet a fair amount of beach is still uncovered and heads of rock remain projecting above the sea, but on a spring tide, particularly in autumn or spring, when it can be as high as 39 feet, there is almost nowhere left on the beach or at sea for the birds to perch, especially if the tide is rough. Spectacular numbers of waders can then be seen milling round the few remaining areas or perched on ledges of rocks projecting into the sea from the cliffs.

Throughout the winter, flocks of small waders will usually consist of ringed plover, turnstone, dunlin and sanderling

Head of a snipe. Bill 60-70 mm.

with turnstone having a preference for the rockier shores
and sanderling for sandier ones, as their names imply. Larger
black and white waders, often seen flying offshore in flocks
of a few hundred or more, will be oyster-catchers. At close
range, their long orange beaks and pink legs are unmistakable.
Curlew and redshank will also be present in fair number,
sometimes in large groups, but more often singly or in small
parties. The five-inch-long thin curved bill of the curlew,
and the long delicate-looking orange-red legs of the redshank
are diagnostic. Of recent years purple sandpipers have been
recorded regularly at several places: L'Etacq, Le Petit Port,
La Rocque, where they had probably been overlooked
previously. They feed on the seaward side within reach
of the spray where the tide is breaking against rocks, and
seldom move to the more sheltered land side. Their
purple-brown sober colouring gives them perfect camouflage against the granite or shale so that, except at high tide
when they are restricted to the limited uncovered areas,
they are difficult to see. A few bar-tailed godwit and grey
plover, both of which used to be rarities, or at least were
rarely recorded, are now to be seen daily in winter.

Inland, up to a hundred snipe can sometimes be found
at Grouville Marsh, the meadows near La Becquetterie,
St Clement, or behind St Ouen's Pond, and smaller numbers
can be put up from almost any other inland marshy area.

As with other winter visitors, the numbers depend to a great extent on the weather elsewhere. None stay to breed. Sometimes snipe will get up as soon as they see an observer, and at other times they will wait until he is only a few yards away. When they do get up, they give a raucous call and fly off with remarkably quick wing beats on a zigzag flight track, settling again only in the far distance, if at all. Jack snipe, and there are a few in the island each winter in similar places to snipe, behave differently. They wait until almost trodden on, then get up without a call, fly with less quick wing beats on a straighter path and usually settle again a short distance away. Woodcock may also get up from almost under an observer's feet, but they will rise with enormous commotion, and from drier areas like the scrub and bracken-covered hillsides of the north coast or the hillsides of Portelet and L'Ouaisné. They are decidedly scarcer than snipe.

The open fields contain varying numbers of lapwing, sometimes called peewits or green plover. During mild weather there are very few, but colder weather, or even its prospect, immediately brings them. They seem to begin arriving about 24 hours before the full onslaught of any bad weather in Britain. Flock after flock of birds with slow, unhurried flight, comes in from the north. Many pass straight over the Island, but others land. Certain areas, though not usually particular fields as in the case of the golden plover, seem more favoured feeding grounds than others: the high land of St Mary, St John and Trinity, the area round La Hougue Bie and the open undeveloped expanses behind Grouville and St Ouen's Bay. On 8 January 1967 the weather deteriorated all day. Lapwing began arriving in quantity just after midday and landing in the field at St Peter known as Les Trois Roches. This went on all afternoon, unceasingly, until just before dusk the field was black with them, standing shoulder to shoulder, and the field, which is 24 vergées in area, could physically hold no more. Later arrivals circled many times, but finally had to settle in adjacent fields. There must have been tens of thousands of lapwing in Les Trois Roches that night. The weather improved quickly the next day, and with equal suddenness they left, but whether to continue their journey south or return north is not known. Small parties of lapwing are sometimes seen in summer, but they never stay long, and there are no breeding records. When flocks of lapwing begin moving down St Ouen's Bay at the onset of cold weather, a few flocks of golden plover usually come with them. Their flight is quicker, less leisurely-looking than a lapwing's. They are regular winter visitors, but never in such numbers, and they have certain curiously restricted feeding grounds, particular fields, which they use year after year. Some of these are near La Hougue Bie, others are round the airport, and the only beach they use regularly is Le Petit Port, St Brelade.

Common sandpiper and whimbrel are the only other waders occurring in sufficient numbers to be seen regularly on passage. In spring and autumn common sandpipers feed by the reservoirs and St Ouen's Pond or on the grubs and flies in vraic thrown up on rocky shores. Some years non-breeding birds have stayed most of the summer by Grands Vaux reservoir. Whimbrel breed in Scotland and beyond, but winter off Africa and Ceylon. Only a few are seen on autumn passage to Africa, their migration route apparently lying to the east of Jersey, but in late April and May many small groups pass through Jersey each year as they return to their breeding grounds in the north. It is usually their four- or seven-note call which attracts attention. Similarly other species of waders sometimes pass through Jersey on their long migrations. Exactly which of these will visit the Island in any given year is not predictable. Some may come regularly, but in such small numbers that whether they are recorded or not may depend on an observer being in the right place at the right time. Other species may be here simply through some accident like being blown off their normal course. Late summer or autumn is when most of these unusual species are here, with a few records in winter. Greenshank and green sandpiper are the most likely to be encountered; little stint, curlew sandpiper, knot, ruff, spotted redshank, black-tailed godwit, and grey phalarope are less likely, and very rarely will one see little ringed plover, dotterel, wood sandpiper, avocet, red-necked phalarope, or stone curlew.

Curlew, turnstone and redshank can usually be found throughout the summer, but these do not breed. The only wader which still does nest in Jersey is the oyster-catcher, and most offshore islets and stretches of cliff hold at least one pair. Their agitated piping shatters the peace the moment an intruder approaches. Kentish plover used to nest in St Aubin's Bay, and at the north end of St Ouen's Bay, but they disappeared after the building of the sea walls changed the habitat.

Waders found here bearing rings from abroad, or recoveries elsewhere of those ringed in Jersey, are now beginning to tell us something of their movements. Two lapwing ringed as nestlings, one near Inverness, Scotland, the other near Stavanger in Norway, were found dead in St John in winter about 18 months later. An oyster-catcher from Aviemore, Scotland, and another from the Faroe Islands, were picked up dead at La Rocque. Other species so far have come from a more north-easterly part of Europe, but obviously far more recoveries are needed before any conclusions can be drawn. Nevertheless, the following are of interest. A ringed plover from Amagar in Denmark was found dead at La Pulente. Another ringed as a nestling in Heligoland in 1965 was caught on 12 December 1968 on the beach at La Haule by D. Steventon, and he caught the same bird on the same date the following year. Four dunlin from near the south-east tip of Sweden were found in Jersey, three in St Aubin's Bay, and one in St Saviour. Snipe recoveries are from yet further away and by 1972 there had been sixteen. Most were to the north, but a few were to the south, indicating that Jersey is merely a port of call and not the final winter destination for some of them. One bird ringed in September 1968 at Samarès was shot at the Lago di Lesina, Foggia, Italy, 1,600km. away, six months later. Those recovered to the north were mainly spread out in an east-north-east direction: Northern France, Belgium, Holland, Denmark, north Germany, and Russia, the furthest being two from Petrokropost and Volkhov, near Leningrad,

2,400km. and 2,500km. away. None was from Norway or Sweden, and only one from Scotland. An adult turnstone, ringed on 2 September 1973 by R. Burrow at Le Pulec, St Ouen, was recovered on 15 October, the same year, 4,500km. away at Ilheu do Rei, Guinea Bissau, formerly Portuguese Guinea.

Herring gulls are here in quantity all year round. They are scavengers and until recently would find most of their food on the beaches or floating in the sea, and only occasionally would they feed inland. But of late they have had two new sources of food. I write this in 1975 when the affluent society of the last decade or so has meant the establishment of huge rubbish tips which have provided food for thousands of herring gulls. If disturbed, enormous white clouds of wheeling, screaming gulls will rise from these dumps. Also people have begun to feed gulls, not just by throwing kitchen scraps over the sea wall as has been done for many years, but unnecessarily in their gardens. This has resulted to a certain extent in a change of where herring gulls look for food and of their choice of nest site. The very great majority, several thousand, still nest in colonies on the cliffs and offshore islands, but a few are now nesting on roofs of houses to the great inconvenience of the inhabitants. Great black-backed gulls and lesser black-backed gulls also nest here, but until recently, almost entirely on the offshore islets. Both are increasing, and a few now nest regularly on the mainland of Jersey itself. Lesser black-backed gulls nest in the same situations as herring gulls, but great black-backs tend to choose isolated stacs out at sea or rocky outcrops, and one pair will nest on the top of each. Both species occur in larger numbers in winter, the lesser black-back usually being mixed with herring gulls, but flocks of great black-backs only, sometimes up to 200 strong, are occasionally seen in St Ouen's Bay.

In theory black-headed gulls are winter visitors, but in practice they are here for all but a very short period, roughly May and June, when they are at their nesting grounds in the north or east. By July some can always be found again, and those that return first usually have the

chocolate-brown head, which is so dark as to look black
at a distance and gives them their name. Later this 'black'
head becomes mainly white and remains so throughout
the winter. It re-develops as the birds come into breeding
condition, so many are again 'black'-headed before they
leave in April or May. They feed more inland than the other
gulls and the majority of those following the plough are
this species. Almost every morning there are some feeding
on the Lower Park at West Park, 'paddling' on the grass to
make worms and insects move. Many have flown great
distances from northern or eastern Europe to get here. They
bear rings from as far away as Sweden, Poland, Russia and
Czechoslovakia, and one ringed by F. R. Lawrence on board
the *L'Espérance* in St Helier Harbour in February 1969,
was picked up 2,200km. away in Jeppa, Baasa, Finland,
in May 1971.

Common gulls are extremely rare, but there is often one,
and it may well be the only one in the island, on Gorey
Slip. In the mid-1950s there were occasionally small flocks
elsewhere, and I remember rowing out to a duck trap on
St Ouen's Pond at dusk on 26 February 1956. As we
approached, the trap was seen to be full of common gulls
which regurgitated seahorses in their agitation at being
approached. There were 23 common gulls, and they brought
up so many seahorses that the bottom of the trap, 4ft. by
6ft., was covered with them. Some of the gulls were ringed
and released, but not having enough rings, we left to get
more. When we returned about a quarter of an hour later,
the seahorses had been swallowed again, and this time they
were not regurgitated. R. F. Le Sueur, the marine biologist,
pointed out that there had been an exceptionally low tide
late that afternoon. He suggested that the common gulls
had found a shoal of seahorses trapped in a pool at low
water. Two of the common gulls were later recovered, one
nearly two years later in the Gulf of Finland, and the other
five years later on the Baltic shore of Germany. Kittiwakes
used to be considered rare, storm-tossed visitors, a few
sometimes being found exhausted on the beach, but
F. C. Hamon has shown that in bad weather they can often

be seen close inshore below Grosnez, apparently enjoying the gales. They have never been known to breed on Jersey's cliffs though they do on Ortac and have, in the past, on Les Etacs off Alderney and on Sark. Three other gulls, the little, the Iceland and the glaucous have been seen but rarely.

Common terns and sandwich terns are summer visitors, common terns nesting on islets off the south coast. Some of the low rocks where they have attempted to breed are just offshore and, unfortunately, the colonies are much disturbed by vandals. Terns are particularly beautiful and graceful birds which dive vertically into shallow water in search of minute marine life. If allowed to breed without interference, as they should be under the *Protection of Birds (Jersey) Law,* 1963, they would be visible throughout the summer from some of the coast roads and beaches of the south east and would delight both islanders and holidaymakers. Even the colonies on the outlying reefs are disturbed from time to time. The one on Les Ecréhous is sometimes on Marmoutier or Blanc Ile, and sometimes on La Maître Ile. If terns are on Les Minquiers, they are on La Maîtresse Ile only. Sandwich terns occasionally nest, but have not done so for many years, though they can be seen in summer. The black tern and the little tern have both been seen on a few occasions and are probably regular migrants in very small numbers, whereas the white-winged black tern has only been recorded twice and the arctic tern once.

Puffins and razorbills still nest in small numbers along the north coast from roughly Douet de la Mer to Plémont. They depart for more open waters in August and for the last few years ornithologists have watched anxiously each spring to see if they would return. Numbers of auks, the family of birds to which puffins and razorbills belong, are decreasing along the whole coast of Europe, partly through oil pollution at sea, but this is not the only cause, and other unknown factors may be involved. So far a few have always returned. The best time to see them is in early morning in May or June, just after dawn, when they sit about a hundred yards out at sea occasionally doing a ritual swim together. Later in the day, one bird will be brooding the egg in a burrow on the

cliff, and the other will be away at sea feeding so a visit to
the area will be useless. For many years 'Oscar Puffin',
the puffin on Channel Independent Television, has been a
great children's favourite. Every Jersey child should see a real
live one in its natural surroundings lest shortly it be too late.
Guillemots used to nest here, but have not recently. They
are still about in winter because each year one or two come
ashore oiled. Little auks and black guillemots are exceedingly
rare winter visitors, little auks usually turning up as
casualties on the beach after violent storms at sea.

The cliffs on which these auks live are still much the
same as they were 300 years ago when Poingdestre wrote:
'Those high Clifes, which wee call Falaises, haue in some
places deepe hollowe dens, which the sea hath made,
frequented by Cormorants & other wild sea fowle· which
harbour there; & a kind of wild pigeons, which nestle there
in great numbers'. The wild pigeons were probably rock
doves and it was from the same species that the pigeons
of the seigneurial colombiers were descended. These
pigeons, these domesticated rock doves, caused trouble
throughout the years, and they are still a nuisance.

In the Rolls of the Assizes for 1309 in St Helier it is
recorded that 'The same Ralph [Lemprière] long ago
erected a dove-cote & he was ordered in the previous assizes
to pull it down &c. And Ralph now comes & gives to the
lord the King the rent of one lb. of pepper to be taken
every year for ever, so that he and his heirs may enjoy that
dove-cote, saving the right of each. And it is allowed because
it is not to the prejudice of the lord the King'. It might. not
matter to the King, but it was greatly to the detriment of
the tenants of the land round about. There were complaints
of hordes of pigeons from the dove-cotes feeding in cornfields and the farmers not allowed by law to drive them off.
The colombiers are extraordinary constructions in stone.
The Longueville Manor colombier belongs to the National
Trust for Jersey and is well worth visiting. Descendants
of these pigeons are now in the Royal Square causing
trouble. On the coast true rock doves have interbred with
feral pigeons and though they are still the same species, rock

dove, their colours now vary from white or pale brown to grey.

Woodpigeons are not in sufficient numbers to make them the nuisance that they are on farmland in Britain, but they are common residents and so now are collared doves. These were unknown in western Europe until they began to spread spectacularly north-westwards from Asia Minor during this century. They nested successfully in Grouville in 1961 and since then have spread to nearly all the inhabited parts of the Island. They are an urban or suburban bird preferring gardens and the company of people to the open countryside or natural woodland. Shortly after arriving they could be seen regularly in the Royal Square. Nesting is not confined to spring and early summer as was shown by a bird feeding young in a nest in one of the chestnut trees in the Royal Square in December 1967. This nest was built in a traditional site of traditional materials, twigs, and so on, on the branch of a tree, but they are prepared to use any modern substitute. R. Long found one made entirely of pieces of wire and built high up on the metal crossbars of a pole carrying telephone wires along Tunnell Street to the Gas Works. Turtle doves are summer visitors, not usually arriving until May and departing for their winter quarters in Africa in August or September. They require a habitat slightly different from either a woodpigeon's or a collared dove's: one with lower trees and bushes than a woodpigeon's, and preferably not so close to people as a collared dove's. Dobson often saw turtle doves on the ground in country lanes, and this is where I also see them frequently. Stock doves are recorded by the older ornithologists, but Dobson saw none, and they were not recorded again until the 1960s. Since then small flocks have been seen regularly in the Val de la Mare region and they nested in 1966 in a tree on one of the wooded côtils of the reservoir.

Readers of the local newspaper, the *Jersey Evening Post,* vie with one another to be the first to hear the cuckoo each spring. Since the arrival of the collared dove which calls all the year, these dates have become earlier and earlier, and confusion is suspected. Cuckoos winter in tropical Africa and do not normally arrive in these latitudes until April. Many pass through the Island each year and the numbers which stay vary, 1973 being a particularly good year, at least at St Ouen. I see and hear them more often near the coast than inland, but again this may be because I live near the coast. So far only three hosts are known, the meadow pipit, rock pipit and robin, with the reed warbler being long suspected but never proved.

The only resident owl is the barn owl and C. G. Pile, who did a good deal of work on it in the 1950s, estimated that there were about 35 pairs. He found that the same next sites tended to be used over and over again if there was no disturbance, one in St Peter then having been in constant use for at least 71 years. The barn owls of Jersey are strangely silent, seldom being heard calling, so that many people are unaware that there are owls here until they see one at night in the headlights of a car. Also, Jersey's barn owls are hardly ever seen during daytime or when the light is just beginning to fade. They tend to feed when dusk is well advanced or at night. Twenty-five pellets picked up in April 1973 underneath a barn owl roost near La Corbière contained a total of 44 small mammals and six birds, the mammals being 16 wood mice, 12 common shrews, six lesser white-toothed shrews, and 10 Jersey bank voles. The barn owl of Britain is white-breasted, but as one crosses Europe, the dark-breasted form begins to appear until in eastern Europe the dark-breasted alone occurs. Jersey has a mixture of white and dark-breasted with more dark-breasted than her geographical position in relation to the cline seems to warrant. Short-eared owls are occasionally seen on heathland during the day. There is probably a small but regular passage of them through the Island in autumn. Long-eared, little and tawny owls have very seldom been heard or seen.

Last century the nightjar was a very common summer resident here, as it was in parts of Great Britain. For some unknown reason it has all but disappeared from this part of its range. Dobson noted that the records this century had

come from the Noirmont—La Moye area and this is still substantially true, the last record being of a bird heard churring
in the breeding season in exactly the right habitat at La
Moye in 1972. Swifts nest in the cliffs and old buildings,
Gorey Castle and Fort Regent being favourite places.
Hundreds of screaming swifts sometimes circle in the air over
the Fort on a June evening. In 1968 a pair of kingfishers
stayed throughout the summer and bred in one of the inland
valleys. Normally they leave in late spring and return in
July to spend the winter feeding in the rock pools of the
coast. There are also often kingfishers at Grouville Marsh
and St Ouen's Pond. A kingfisher held in the hand is so
brightly coloured it almost hurts the eyes, emerald and
sapphire above, coppery chestnut below, yet as soon as
one settles against a granite rock on the coast it blends in
so well that it vanishes from sight. They fared badly in
the 1962/3 frosts, the rock pools of the coast being frozen,
and it was several years before their winter numbers were
back to normal. Hoopoes are seen occasionally in spring
and autumn, usually on short grass, often on a lawn, near
the coast. The presence of nearby buildings does not disturb
them, and one fed on a lawn at the old Power Station,
Queen's Road, for several days, and another on the lawn in
the Newgate Street Prison, St Helier. They have never been
known to stay long enough to nest, which is surprising since
they do in Normandy and Brittany. On the other hand the
roller, an exotic-looking bird seen at Belcroute in 1935, was
not expected to stay, being a stray vagrant, an accidental
visitor from south or east Europe.

From ornithological accounts of last century wrynecks
would appear to have been as common in summer then
as wrens and dunnocks are now. By the beginning of this
century they had declined considerably, and they continued
to do so until by the 1920s, if not earlier, they had ceased
to nest here. Since then there have been a few records of
single birds only. On 8 August 1954 I watched one in a
garden at St Brelade where it was feeding on ants. Whenever
an ant walked within range the wryneck would shoot out
its sticky tongue and pick it up. To see the ants, it would

twist its neck in the most alarming way: hence its name wryneck. Its colouring was very beautiful, mainly in muted shades of grey and brown in a vermiculated pattern except for a conspicuous 'V' in a dark velvety brown down its back.

It has, or perhaps had, a great variety of Jersey-French names, and it is fortunate that Dr Le Maistre began *Le Dictionnaire* when the names were still available, for few people living in the island today will know this once extremely common bird. It was called *tui-tui* from its call, *teurt-co* from the way it twisted its neck, *ouaîsé du printemps* and *ouaîsé du r'nouvé* because it arrived in spring, *ouaîsé du coucou* and *ouaîsé a maq'thé* because it came with the cuckoo and with the mackerel. No other bird has so many different names in Jersey-French, though dunnocks which are in every garden and every hedge are *mouésson a p'tit-bé* sparrow with a small beak, *mouésson d'fôssé* sparrow of the hedge, *p'it jerriais* a small Jerseyman, and *vèrdreu*, which according to Le Maistre means green egg. This I do not understand since dunnock's eggs are clear sky blue with no trace of green. The pied wagtail also has a number of different names, perhaps because it is so conspicuous during the winter ploughing and at potato planting time: *p'tit labouotheux*, small labourer in the fields; *gliaineux*, gleaner; *craulant-coue* or *craulant-tchu*, tail wagger; and *s'meux*, which again I do not understand because it is connected with seed-sowing, whereas wagtails are essentially insect eaters. Comparatively speaking, there are fewer Jersey-French names for birds than for flowers. The variety is not so great and they tend to be nearer the French. Dobson gives most of them, together with the English and French, and there are a few extra in *Le Dictionnaire*.

The great spotted woodpecker was almost unknown in the Island until a pair was heard drumming in Rozel Manor woods in 1952, and an occupied nest hole was found in a rotting tree. Since then it has bred in several inland valleys and has fed at bird tables during the winter. In the same way that the wryneck has decreased in western Europe, so the great spotted woodpecker has increased and Jersey's colonisation about that time, was to be expected.

Skylarks are still common residents, as they have been for many centuries and they are the first small birds I can find mentioned in old records. In 1299 William the Warrener of Rozel was summoned to appear at the Assizes to answer a charge of assaulting Richard des Vaux, servant of the parson of St Martin. Richard had been at out at night trying to catch larks with cloak, fire and nets, and the said William did not deny that he struck him so he was put *'in misericordia'*. Almost seven centuries later people are again out at night catching larks with lights and nets. In the old days, the larks would be for the pot. Now they are being ringed and released unharmed, for study purposes. Woodlarks have been recorded, but rarely, and usually in winter, though a pair bred in 1940, and a shorelark appropriately spent a fortnight on the shore at St Ouen in November 1957.

Swallows are common throughout the summer, nesting in all parishes, and large numbers pass through on migration. They congregate in huge flocks wherever midges and small flies are abundant. Returns of ringed swallows seem to indicate that those passing through Jersey are not bound principally for north east or east Europe like the black-headed gulls, but are on a more north-westerly route to Britain and Ireland. A map of recoveries to 1974 is given. House martins rarely used to nest, but of late years their numbers have increased. Many farms and houses now have colonies, and house martins are often seen feeding over the reservoirs and ponds in summer as well as on spring and autumn migration. On some farms they have physically ousted swallows from the barns and outbuildings which they have used for generations. In particular a colony of swallows had been in continuous occupation of a set of outbuildings at a farm in St Lawrence for at least 70 years until driven out by the house martins in the early 1970s. Swallows remain on the farm, but not in their original first-choice nest sites. Sand martins are one of the first birds to return in spring. They spend the winter south of the Sahara and never stay in Europe. The first sand martin of the year is therefore, to many birdwatchers, the first positive sign that a new year has begun. Sand martins have been

8.–Map showing migration of swallows.

Swallows ringed or recovered in Jersey up to 1974 either came from the marked places or were recovered there, not necessarily in the same year. Seven records are from England and six from Ireland in summer. The remaining records are of individual birds, the South African ones being in winter.

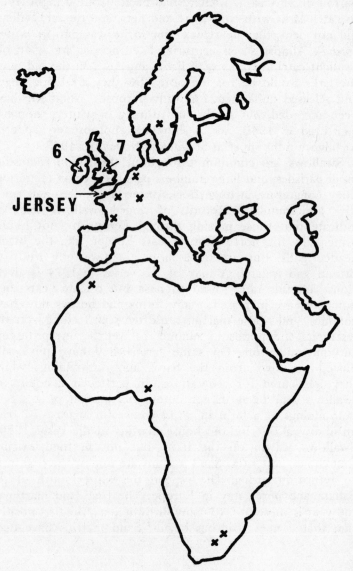

seen hawking flies over St Ouen's Pond as early as 6 March
and the only other returning migrant likely to be back so
soon is the wheatear. Most of the thousands of sand martins
which come through in April and May are migrants going
on further north. The numbers staying to nest depend on the
availability of nest sites. They need a vertical bank of fairly
hard sand or sandy soil, and this is not often present in
Jersey. The pure sand of most of Les Blanches Banques
would collapse before they finished excavating a nest burrow.

Meadow pipits and rock pipits are both here in good
quantity all the year round. Meadow pipits frequent open
ground and consequently are commoner near the coast than
inland because this happens to be where most of the wilder
land occurs now. Rock pipits, on the other hand, feed
entirely on the shore, so they are confined to the coastal
strips. They nest in some small recess against a rock face,
often behind a piece of vegetation, but they are not restricted
to the cliffs. Walls by the coast will do just as well, and I
have been shown nests in some of the busiest parts of St
Helier harbour.

There has only been one record of a tree pipit since the
Occupation, but water pipits, which are the mountain form
of rock pipits, have been recorded in several recent winters.
This may not be an extension of range, but simply that they
previously went unrecognised.

Three species of wagtail, the pied, the grey and the yellow,
have nested since the Occupation, but all very rarely. The
pied is usually more a winter visitor and can often be seen
feeding on the shore or on newly-turned earth inland. They
tend to gather at night in communal roosts using the same
ones year after year. Up to 200 are sometimes together in
a small area of the reed-bed at St Ouen's Pond, and others
congregate in the reeds at Grouville and L'Ouaisné. More
and more watercourses are being culverted, particularly those
which run down the side of roads or country lanes. In the
recent past grey wagtails, elegant birds with blue-grey backs,
bright yellow rumps and underparts, and long black and
white tails, would often be feeding by these streams in
winter. To see one get up and fly off, perhaps to land a short

distance further along the roadside stream, was one of the delights of a country walk. They are still here, but have to be sought out in places yet unaffected by the present craze for flattening, straightening and draining. Yellow wagtails are not in Jersey in winter, but arrive back in April or May, most staying only a few days before flying further north. The plumage of the male at this time is magnificent, rivalling the dandelions which are usually in full flower in the fields or on the dunes where the yellow wagtails feed. The blue-headed wagtail and the white wagtail which are closely related to the yellow and pied, respectively, are sometimes recorded.

Apart from a great grey shrike which was recorded for the first time in November 1974, no shrikes have been seen during the last 10 years, but three other species, the red-backed, woodchat, and lesser grey have been recorded, rarely, in the past. The woodchat shrike was the most likely to be encountered in the 1950s. Waxwings, nesting birds of the far north east of Europe, move where conditions are slightly less harsh in winter. Occasionally a population explosion of some kind occurs, and in the autumn waxwings spread right across Europe. In these irruptions, waxwings may reach Jersey, and in the winter of 1965/6 up to 16 birds were seen on Trinity Hill, in Vallée des Vaux, in Bath Street, and in St Clement. They stayed from November to January, feeding mainly on berries in gardens, cotoneasters being specially favoured. One was recorded in 1971 feeding on hawthorn berries.

Wrens and dunnocks (hedge sparrows) are the commonest birds of the Island, probably because neither needs a specialised habitat and will thrive just as well on the coast as inland and in the town as in the country. As long as there is sufficient cover to provide a nest site these species will be present.

In summer, the copses, hedgerows, gorselands and reed-beds contain nesting warblers. Dartford warblers and Cetti's warblers stay here all year round, but, except for a few chiffchaffs and a smaller number of blackcaps and perhaps garden warblers, all warblers depart for the south in the

Dartford warbler on gorse.

late summer or autumn. Dartford warblers inhabit the gorse-covered headlands, hillsides and commons from Noirmont to La Corbière and La Pulente, along the foothills of St Ouen's Bay to L'Etacq and Grosnez and along the north coast to almost the Tour de Rozel. It was from near Grève de Lecq that the visiting zoologist Harvie-Brown first recorded them in 1869. I have never seen one in the east or in the inland valleys, but Mrs M. L. Long has recently seen one in winter in the north of St Lawrence, and in summer 1975 a Dartford was reported feeding young, out of the nest, at Archirondel. During the winter they move about more and are not so restricted to gorse or heather as in the breeding season. Young birds, colour-ringed as nestlings, on Ouaisné Common were seen later at La Moye, presumably having crossed the built-up area of St Brelade's Bay. Morning, on a calm fine day, is the best time to see them. The temperature does not seem to matter, but it is no use looking for them in damp weather or rain. As soon as the worst of the snow and ice had gone in the winter of 1962/3 my husband and I drove to Les Landes to see how the Dartford warblers had fared. Within minutes we saw some in the gorse near Grosnez Farm so we went to above L'Etacq and there again saw some almost without waiting. We were forced to the conclusion that snow on top of the gorse had acted like a blanket, insulating feeding areas inside the bushes underneath. Dobson considered that gorse fires, by removing nesting sites, were an important control of Dartford warblers in Jersey, and my own observations over 25 years support this. But the control that a gorse fire exercises is two-fold. Tall, leggy gorse holds no place where Dartford warblers can nest, and its replacement by young growth from time to time is essential. Dartford warblers prefer the gorse to be not more than about two feet six inches or three feet high, and the nest is usually about 18 inches from the ground near the edge of the gorse bush. In my experience it is invariably near a clearing or a path. In spring and early summer the male does a characteristic song flight over his territory, but not so well-known is the beautiful little subsong delivered from inside a gorse bush in autumn. In winter the simplest way to find a Dartford warbler among gorse is to look for a male stonechat. Stonechats are fairly common in Jersey and there will probably be one perched on the top of a gorse spray. Make the stonechat move across a clearing, and the chances are that, a few seconds after he has moved to the top of a gorse bush on the other side, a Dartford warbler will cross the clearing at a lower level and go into the middle of the bush. There will probably be a pair of stonechats, but it is the male which is followed and, as far as I can tell, there is no communication of any kind between him and the Dartford warbler. He leads, feeding at random over the gorse common, and the Dartford warbler tags along, well behind. I have never seen this association mentioned, but it is so frequent in winter that it provides a method of finding one of the most elusive of birds.

At one time the call notes of the Dartford warbler might be confused with those of the whitethroat which used to be a common summer visitor, nesting in low undergowth, particularly bramble bushes. Since 1969 there has unhappily been almost no chance of confusion. The large numbers of whitethroats in the island in 1968 departed as usual in the late summer and autumn for their winter quarters somewhere in Africa, south of the Sahara, and simply did not return. In 1969 to say there were half a dozen pairs of whitethroats here might be an exaggeration. I myself have seen four since 1969 and two of these were not until August 1974. They may be slowly increasing again, but even if they are, it was still possible in the summer of 1974 to spend an afternoon walking across what used to be good whitethroat country and not see or hear a single bird. A crash of such magnitude in the numbers of a natural population has attracted a good deal of attention from scientists. The crash was not confined to Jersey but affected whitethroats throughout most of Europe. The probable, but not certain, cause seems to be the drying-up of watering or feeding places on their migration across the Sahara Desert. Lesser whitethroats have always been rare, and still are, though they are increasing slightly and at least one pair bred in 1972.

Chiffchaffs can be heard singing in mild weather most winters and their repeated call *chiff-chaff, chiff-chaff, chiff-chaff* . . . fills copses, gardens and scrubland in late March and April as enormous numbers come through on migration. Many stay to nest. The willow warbler also comes through in quantity on migration. Its plaintive song with a beautiful descending cadence is usually the first indication of its presence and one of the best places to hear one in summer is the Railway Walk to La Corbière. A few stay to nest, but not in numbers like the chiffchaff. Wood warblers are scarce, irregular migrants. Blackcaps and garden warblers, both uncommon summer visitors, can be heard singing in the woods or scrub on overgrown côtils in inland valleys, and I once saw a group of male blackcaps in a hedge bordering the main Corbière Road. Each winter since the Occupation there have been a few reports of blackcaps feeding at bird tables. Dobson was puzzled by G. F. B. de Gruchy's many sight records of melodious warblers in autumn at Noirmont, a bird no one else had reported this century, but in August 1975 one was trapped in a mist net at Le Feugeral House, La Moye.

The marshes and reed-beds contain reed, sedge, aquatic and Cetti's warblers, species which do not occur in the drier areas. In the same way that the first sight of a sand martin or wheatear means to many birdwatchers that spring is here, so the first song of a reed warbler or sedge warbler from the middle of a dense reed-bed means that the long hot days of summer are on the way. Reed warblers return to the Island from tropical Africa in late April. Many pass through on their way further north, but most reed-beds of any size contain nesting pairs in summer. The ringing of birds is usually considered primarily as a means of finding out something about their movements, but equally important information on other aspects of their lives can be obtained. Reed warblers have been ringed for many years at St Ouen's Pond, and we are now learning how long some of them live. One bird ringed as an adult in 1952 was recaptured in several following years, and finally in 1963. By this time it must have been at least 12 years old, and as reed warblers spend the winter some 4,000 miles away to the south it must have travelled not less than 96,000 miles on migration alone. Another ringed in 1953 was also recaptured in 1963. Reed warblers weigh only 12 or 13 gm., about half an ounce. Twelve years and 11 years are remarkable ages for such small birds in the wild, and they are among the longest known. One great reed warbler was caught and ringed in 1956. The first sedge warblers tend to arrive just a day or two before the first reed warblers, but none were thought to stay to breed until one was seen feeding young just out of the nest in 1957, and since then a few other pairs have· stayed. Aquatic warblers were unknown in the Island until one was caught at St Ouen's Pond in 1953. It is now thought to be a regular autumn migrant in very small numbers at both St Ouen's Pond and Grouville Marsh.

Cetti's warbler, previously a sedentary bird of south Europe, has spread slowly northwards this century. This extension of range has not been spectacular like that of the collared dove. Also, the collared dove, a conspicuous bird, lives close to man and is immediately noticed, whereas Cetti's warbler, a small brown bird, is often heard in or near reed-beds, but is seldom seen and has probably gone unnoticed in Jersey by all but a few birdwatchers since it was first recorded here in 1960. The same has happened elsewhere.

The bird is extremely secretive in the breeding season. It probably bred in the early 1970s, but the first nest was not found until 1973. This nest was removed later in the season long after the young had successfully flown. In 1974 the same bird built a nest within a few inches of the first site, deep in the middle of a large bramble bush. In 1975 a different male held the territory, and in it he had at least two nesting females, probably three. The broods flew within a few days of one another and all went to the heart of the male's territory so that the area was full of the sound of young Cetti's warblers. Cetti's warbler would now seem to be an established resident.

A delicate nest, unbelievably fragile-looking, of moss, spiders' webs and feathers slung underneath the outer end of the branch of a conifer will belong to a goldcrest, the smallest British bird. Some goldcrests remain in the Island all year, but their numbers are greatly increased in winter, and some migrate through the Island. I remember standing on the far end of St Catherine's Breakwater one autumn day and hearing very high-pitched call notes. A flock of minute goldcrests came flying along the Breakwater and continued straight on out to sea towards France. Firecrests also arrive in winter and likewise some pass through on migration. Of late years the numbers have increased, but none stay to nest, Jersey being outside their normal breeding range which is central, south and east Europe. In book illustrations goldcrests and firecrests look fairly similar, but, in practice in the field, the white eye stripe of the firecrest is easily seen.

Spotted flycatchers, summer visitors, usually nest against the wall of a sheltered house or garden or the rock face of a quarry which has a creeper against it. The creeper can be a rose, honeysuckle, wistaria, or anything which will give support to the nest. A tree trunk with a suitable branch against it is also used. They are some of the latest migrants to arrive, often not being here until about mid-May and the eggs not usually being laid until the beginning of June. Many of those seen in Jersey are not nesting, merely being here on passage. Except in September some years, the spotted flycatcher is more likely to be seen than the pied flycatcher which does not nest and is a passage migrant only, mainly in the autumn. I exclude some Septembers because occasionally great numbers of pied flycatchers may be in Jersey over a very short period. In particular on the two days 9 and 10 September 1956, almost every wire fence, or lower branch of every tree or bush in the Island seemed to have a pied flycatcher on it. We had not noticed them the day before; the day after there were few, and shortly after that they had all gone. While there has not been exactly the same concentration of pied flycatchers again, the peak period for their migration is usually short and is in the first half of September. Four red-breasted flycatchers have been seen, all in autumn.

Stonechats are familiar nesting birds of the dunes, gorse commons and rough hillsides, usually, but not always, near the sea, and their numbers are increased in autumn by migrants. It is almost impossible to walk across a wild, open area on the coast without seeing one or hearing their insistent chacking call like two stones being knocked against one another. This is the note from which the bird derives its name. E. D. H. Johnson did a great deal of original work on them in Jersey in the 1950s and 1960s and his papers on them were published in 1961 and 1971 in *British Birds*, Vols. 54 and 64, and in the 1971 *Bulletin* of the Société Jersiaise. Whinchats are passage migrants only, none breeding here or staying the winter. They can be confused with the female stonechat which is also brown and lacks the black head and white collar of the male stonechat, but the whinchat has a prominent broad white eyestripe visible at all seasons, and as it flies away, a white patch shows on either side of its tail.

Dobson thought the wheatear might have its seasons of plenty followed by seasons of scarcity, because writers at different times in the past have assessed its status so differently. If so, then we are in a period of relative scarcity now. For some years after the Occupation the wheatear was a very common migrant, but it has been decreasing of late years. The migration period is long, being spread over several months in both spring and autumn, so that there are wheatears in the Island for some considerable time, but not usually in quantity. They are one of the earliest to arrive and, with the sand martins, herald the beginning of a new season of growth. Except for adult males in black and grey breeding plumage, wheatears are sandy-coloured birds exactly matching the dunes on which they are often seen. If disturbed they fly off, low over the turf, their snow-white rumps gleaming in the sun. Unfortunately, none has stayed to nest recently, but they may again. A few wheatears of the Greenland race come through each year, usually towards the end of the spring migration. They can be told by their slightly larger size and more upright stance.

Occasionally a brownish bird, not unlike a robin, will be seen in autumn, but with bright orange chestnut on its tail instead of its breast. This will be a redstart, or the closely-related black redstart. On spring migration the males of both species are magnificently coloured in black, white, clear grey and orange-red, but in autumn, when we see most redstarts, this striking breeding plumage has gone and the young of the year have not acquired it. The black redstart is the bird which colonised London's bombed buildings in the war, and Jersey had a few breeding pairs in 1964 and 1965. Their choice of nest site, the Fort then derelict on Mount Bingham, might have been expected, but the surprise and pleasure of hearing them singing in the centre of town never dulled. One used to sing in Bath Street, and F. R. Lawrence used to hear another above all the congestion and bustle, all the noise and roar of traffic, at Charing Cross, one of the busiest parts of the town of St Helier. After an interval of several years he heard one singing in the Sand Street/ Commercial buildings area in the spring and early summer of 1973. They continue to come through on migration and occasionally one or two spend the winter here near coastal cliffs or rocks as at Le Pulec, Grève de Lecq, Le Saie or La Rocque, where they feed on insects and grubs on the shoreline. In my experience, they are a late autumn migrant not usually coming until well into October and more are seen then, than on the return migration in spring. By contrast, the other species, the redstart, though in greater numbers and over a greater time, is only a passage migrant, never having bred or stayed the winter, and it is more a bird of the countryside, the fields, gardens and inland valleys, than of the coast.

Robins are here all the year round in quantity. They nest throughout the Island and are occasionally used by cuckoos inland as foster-parents for their young. There is some evidence of movement of robins through the Island, as birds bearing Jersey rings have been recovered in Manche, France, and along the south coast of England. It is difficult to pinpoint when migration is taking place as there is already a large resident population of robins, but at times in autumn there are more than usual and they behave differently, being more restive. None breed on Les Ecréhous, but large numbers, of which 19 were caught, were there on the morning of 30 October 1950. These were on their way south as was a party of about 20 black redstarts. A daily log of bird movements through both Les Ecréhous and Les Minquiers for a few years would be of great help in tracing the pattern of migration of some of these commoner birds. There would also be rarities. For instance, on 17 August 1958 there were three nightingales on Les Minquiers. Normally the migration route of nightingales lies more easterly in Europe than the Channel Islands, and they cross to England further up the Channel. There have been a few records on the mainland of Jersey, and we count ourselves lucky to have heard one here at St Ouen on 24 April 1959. We were having breakfast

by an open window when an incredible song began in a hedge
on the côtil below us. The bird sang from seven o'clock to
quarter past, and then again from eight o'clock to about
five past. The richness of the notes, whether flute-like or
rippling and bubbling, was beyond anything that we had
heard before in Jersey. The song alone was sufficient for
identification, but the bird was so engrossed in singing that
it allowed an approach to within a few yards while it continued singing undisturbed. Perhaps a few pass undetected
through the Island each year, particularly in autumn when
they are silent. Bluethroats have probably always done so,
but none was recorded until members of the ornithological
section of the Société Jersiaise began catching and ringing
birds at St Ouen's Pond. The first bluethroat was caught,
ringed and released in 1953, and on many autumns since
then a few have been caught. Hardly any have been sight
records: they are of birds which would have gone unnoticed
had they not flown into a net. More recently still, they
have been caught at Grouville Marsh.

Blackbirds and song thrushes nest commonly throughout
the Island, but in my experience mistle thrushes are much
less common than either of these, and may well be decreasing. These are the thrushes which nest early in the year and
sing loudly during stormy or windy weather. We used to have
several within earshot, but now I seldom hear one. The
numbers of blackbirds and song thrushes increase in autumn
as winter residents come from countries mainly to the north
east of Jersey, and with them come fieldfares and redwings.
The colder the European winter the greater the numbers.
Many pass straight over the Island, and on a still autumn
night they can be heard calling as they fly southwards.
Fieldfares ringed in Jersey one winter have been found in
Santander in Spain and Molinella in Italy in following
winters. One was recovered back north in summer at
Hedmark in Norway and another was killed by a cat at its
nest in Jamtland, Sweden. Redwings are equally far-travelled
some spending the winter here, but others going on further.
One ringed as a nestling near Kerppola in Finland was found
dead at St Martin, and one ringed in St Clement was later

found in south-east Spain. Fieldfares and redwings feed together sometimes in loose flocks in open fields, but redwings are perhaps more widely distributed and are often seen singly on lawns. Fieldfares tend to be more frequent on high ground in the interior of the Island, for instance, in the fields round La Hougue Bie.

Ring ouzels are passage migrants, usually, but not invariably, seen on the north coast cliffs or coastal areas in early spring. Only occasionally are they recorded in autumn. They stay a very short time before moving on, so I always feel chance has played a large part when I see one. There may well be more passing through the Island than the records indicate.

Since the increase of bearded reedlings in Britain and the Low Countries a few have been seen in Jersey. The first record here was in November 1965 when D. J. Clennett saw a small group in the reed-bed at St Ouen. Small parties arrived in November 1972 and October 1973 and stayed several weeks each winter with the numbers building up to 20 or 30 birds. It was hoped that the 1973 influx would stay permanently, but by mid-January they seemed to have gone. However, R. V. M. Burrow saw newly-fledged young with their parents on 26 May and they were still present in the reed-bed in October 1974.

Great tits and blue tits are common nesters using holes in trees, walls, buildings, rock faces and artificially-constructed nestboxes. Occasionally a pair will choose an unusual site, like the pair which nested in an upturned nine-inch flowerpot left out in a garden at La Rocque. The great tit entered through the drainage hole now in the roof and put a loosely-packed three-inch layer of brightly-coloured wools, moss and feathers across the whole of the bottom except for a neat round depression thickly lined with down and hair in the middle, where the eggs were laid. There is always an increase in flocks in winter, but some years, depending perhaps on their breeding success in Europe the previous spring, there are enormous numbers here on migration. Coal tits are comparatively rare winter visitors, but in the 1960s one or two pairs were suspected of breeding and in 1971 W. D. and S. F. Hooke had a pair which consistently carried food from their garden at Pont Marquet in a certain direction long enough to have reared a brood. A nest was found in St Brelade in 1974.

Long-tailed tits are most often seen in winter when parties of them search for food in the bare trees and hedgerows. Their distinctive notes as they call to one another usually attract attention first. They have been reported from all parts of the Island; exposed gardens in the west, trees near busy streets in St Helier and sheltered valleys in the east. One usually associates them with gorse at nesting time, but Dobson reports that while most nests he found were about seven feet up in gorse or honeysuckle, some were much higher and not in these traditional bushes. One was 35 feet up at the end of a branch of a fir tree, and another at least 40 feet up in ivy against an elm. The nests were sometimes in the open in the fork of a tree, the birds relying on the lichen which is always put on the outside to camouflage them.

Wherever there are sizable trees there may well be short-toed treecreepers which feed on insects in the crevices of the bark. A treecreeper will settle towards the base of the trunk and creep upwards, almost like a mouse, feeding all the time until it reaches fairly near the top, when it will fly down to the base of the next to begin the search for food again. They usually feed singly. Two species, the British treecreeper *Certhia familiaris* and the short-toed treecreeper *C. brachydactyla,* occur in Europe, the British treecreeper being in the British Isles and higher parts of the Continent, and the short-toed in the Channel Islands and lowland parts of the Continent. The differences in plumage are not enough to separate them in the field, but anyone coming here from a treecreeper area in Britain should try to hear a call note or song which will at once convince him that this is a different species. The nuthatch is strangely rare with only one record up to 1973, yet Jersey is well within its range.

For the last few years the reed bunting has been the only bunting in the Island in any quantity. A few pairs breed at St Ouen's Pond, and some may in Grouville Marsh, but the numbers are augmented in winter when several hundreds may be in the Island. They feed in open fields during the day, and from late afternoon until just before dusk they can be seen flying into the reeds at St Ouen and Grouville Marsh where they roost. In the late 1940s and 1950s yellow-hammers not only bred here in small numbers, but were a regular constituent of the winter flocks, feeding on arable fields left unploughed. During the 1960s and early 1970s they continued to breed, but were seen very seldom indeed in the presumably immigrant winter flocks. Dobson reported them as common some years and rare others. We seem to have gone, or be going, through a period of rarity. Small numbers of cirl buntings are still to be found breeding, and snow buntings are irregular winter visitors usually feeding on seeds of coastal plants. St Catherine and St Ouen are perhaps the most favoured bays. Three other buntings have been reported since the Occupation, the ortolan bunting once and the corn bunting and little bunting twice.

In winter the Island has large flocks of chaffinches, green-finches and goldfinches. Sometimes the flocks are mixed but more often one species predominates and the chaffinch flocks tend to be of one sex only. Tomato fields, when picking ends in autumn, are usually left for some time before being cleared, and seeds of rotting tomatoes and weeds provide food. Greenfinches also congregate in autumn on wild areas near the coast where some of their best food plants, like sea radish, occur. They can easily be attracted to bird tables by putting out peanuts which seem able to conjure greenfinches out of the air. Dobson thought that the numbers of goldfinches were irregular. They have increased recently and in my experience are commoner now than at any time during the last 25 years. They feed more on the smaller seeds and in particular will be present almost wher-ever there are thistles, teasel, chicory or groundsel. Small flocks are sometimes seen on the dunes where they may be feeding on the ray-flowered groundsel which flowers very early in the year and so produces its seeds at a time when other food is relatively scarce. In some winters no bramblings are here; in others there are thousands. The numbers probably depend on the weather elsewhere. They usually feed with chaffinches and it is always worth looking over a mixed flock of finches, as they fly off, to see if any birds have the conspicuous white rump of a brambling. If there are any in the Island, the fields of the south east are usually the best places to see them. Chaffinches, greenfinches and goldfinches nest regularly, but bramblings are northern birds and do not stay here in summer. And as they depart, linnets return in quantity to nest throughout the Island before leaving again in autumn. Occasional groups are seen in winter, but the vast majority has usually gone by the end of October.

Recoveries of ringed finches are perhaps beginning to show something of their general migration patterns, but it should be borne in mind that the number of recoveries is small compared with the vast numbers of birds involved. Some are ringed here and recovered abroad; others are ringed abroad and recovered here. Only one chaffinch has been recovered south of Jersey and that was one ringed at St Ouen in September and recovered in Portugal. All the other records are of chaffinches which journeyed to or from countries to the north east of Jersey, some as far away as Norway, Sweden and Finland. Unfortunately, almost all the ringing of chaffinches has been done in the autumn and winter, so the records are from birds here between October and March. Little attention has been paid to them in summer when nesting pairs are scattered thinly over the Island. It would be interesting to know if the nesting chaffinches remain here all year or not. There is a time in early autumn when it is difficult to find a chaffinch anywhere in Jersey. There is a possibility, therefore, that the majority of the summer population moves out, after breeding, leaving a gap which is filled a short time later by flocks which move in from the north east of Europe.

Linnets have been ringed not just in winter like chaffinches, but all year round, some on gorse commons, others at drinking places or in their feeding areas, so nesting birds have been included. There are few linnets in the depths of

9.—Map showing migration of linnets.

Linnets ringed in spring, summer and autumn in Jersey appear to go down the French channel coast to central Spain for the colder months. The two records from England were of birds which probably wintered in Jersey.

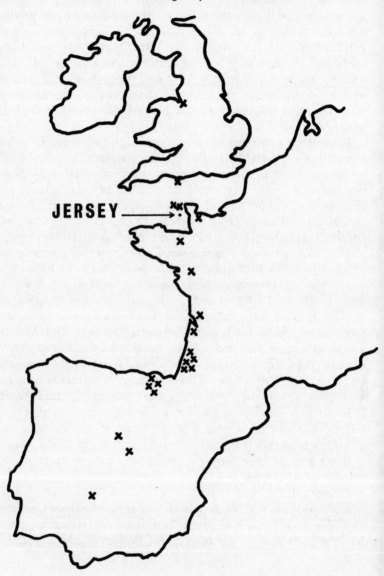

winter, but one ringed at Pontac in January 1967 was recovered in Shropshire in April, and another ringed at Portland Bill in October 1963 was found at St Clement in March 1964. Apart from two others which moved between Herm and Jersey, these are the only movements to or from the north. On the other hand, recoveries of linnets ringed between April and October show a remarkable autumn movement from Jersey down the west coast of France to the Biarritz/Bilbao region at the western end of the Pyrenees. A few go on further into Spain. One ringed at St Ouen on 8 September 1963 was over the Spanish border at Vizcaya the next day. A map is given showing the movements of individual linnets. A few goldfinches, ringed between July and October, have been recovered in the same Spanish/French border area as the linnets. It is not yet known if any of the goldfinches here in mid-winter stay all year or perhaps go north in spring to nest. Of the few greenfinches which have been recovered abroad, two have been in England, one in Belgium, and the others fairly close in France.

Bullfinches are widespread over the Island all year and nest in many copses and blackthorn thickets. Small parties are sometimes seen in winter, but there is no evidence of migration. Siskins have visited the Island in recent years and can occasionally be seen on alder trees in the inland valleys. Late in winter, probably when the alder seeds are finished, they feed in fields on weed seeds. Serins were recorded very rarely until 1971 since when they have been heard singing regularly in early summer along the Railway Walk to La Corbière. By 1974 there were three singing males and some were also present in 1975, so it is possible that the serin has bred here. This is in line with its northern spread elsewhere in Europe. Twite, redpoll, crossbill and hawfinch have been recorded at various times. House sparrows are very common, but tree sparrows exceptionally rare and they have not been known to breed here.

Starlings now nest commonly in Jersey in holes in trees or more often in holes in buildings, though a hundred years ago they were winter visitors only. Round the coast they

10.—Map showing migration of starlings.

All but two of the recorded movements of starlings to or from Jersey up to 1974 were within the angle shown. The more distant places are marked individually.

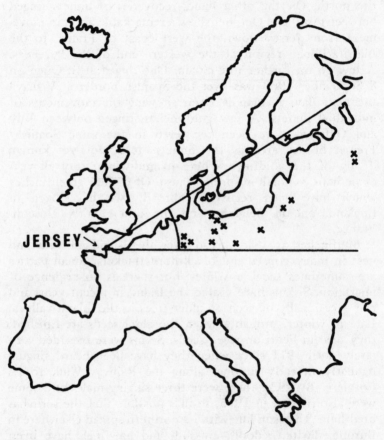

make great use of German fortifications built during the Occupation. One of the most spectacular ornithological sights is a flock of thousands of starlings twisting and weaving in the sky before a few peel off and begin an avalanche of birds pouring down into the reed-bed or wood in which they intend roosting. The site of the main roost may change after a year or two without any apparent reason. The reed-bed at St Ouen was used in 1935 according to G. F. B. de Gruchy, and since then the same reed-bed, the trees near Rocqueberg, Samarès, the woods of Noirmont Manor, and the trees of Westmount have been frequently chosen. But the picture is more complex than this for the resident population and the young of the year gather together in the evenings in July. These flocks gradually disperse again, and the huge flocks, which include migrants, begin building up in late autumn. They are biggest about the end of November and beginning of December when for some reason not understood, they begin moving about and dispersing. I have a suspicion that the number of starlings decreased in the 1970s and that the roosting flocks are not now as big as in the past. Some of the starlings which come to Jersey in winter from Europe travel very considerable distances, roughly from an east-north-east direction. A map of starlings ringed abroad and recovered here, or ringed here and recovered abroad, up to 1974 is given. The two furthest recoveries in Russia are from near Smolensk, and the ring in Finland was found in the nest of a tawny owl which presumably had caught and eaten the starling.

Records of golden orioles go back many years, but they are usually of single birds in spring. I have only seen two, the first a female in sober colours, but the second a male in brilliant yellow and jet black plumage in striking contrast to the soft sandy colours of Les Quennevais over which it was flying. On another occasion by Val de la Mare reservoir I heard its flute-like call-note, of great beauty, repeated many times, but saw no bird.

The jay was introduced into Jersey at La Haule about 1875, and, unfortunately, the introduction succeeded so most copses and woods now hold a pair. They eat some vegetable matter, but a large proportion of their food in the breeding season consists of eggs and young birds. The smaller species of birds have enough natural predators in the Island without man deliberately introducing another. The magpie, for instance, is one of Jersey's commoner birds and must destroy thousands of nests of other species yearly. In the breeding season they can be seen sitting on vantage points surveying the surrounding area for signs of nests. The years when we have magpies breeding near us, few, if any, young birds of any other species are reared on the côtil. Crows would seem to be the magpie's only predator, but they themselves can do a great deal of damage. Dobson mentions partial albinism in crows and it still persists some 30 years later. I once had one of these birds in the hand. The primaries and secondaries were white except for a black tip, and the tail feathers were each white towards the shaft. These partly white feathers were weak and dull unlike those of the head and mantle which were in fine condition with a good gloss. The amount of white varies from almost none to half the wing when, as in this case, the bird may be unable to support itself. Hooded crows have been seen on a few rare occasions, usually near the coast.

Dobson has two records of flocks of rooks visiting Jersey last century, but departing without nesting, and one incredible story of how the Rev. W. Lempriere attempted to introduce them at Rozel, sometime between 1865 and 1875, by importing rooks and building them artificial nests. This was not a successful venture. The first rookery in Jersey was at La Moye House in 1928, when eight pairs bred. The numbers increased, being nearly 50 in the early 1940s, but they are now very low. In 1942 the rookery in The Parade, St Helier, was established, also with eight nests. By 1946 there were 33, but since then it, too, has been declining, and it is doubtful if all the four nests in 1973 were successful as the rooks were constantly being harried by magpies. In 1975 there were two nests in The Parade, and five in La Moye House rookery. Small rookeries have existed elsewhere, but not for any length of time. Twenty years ago flocks of rooks were often overhead, but now they are seldom seen without a search. Jackdaws first stayed to breed in the Island in 1929, the year after rooks. In the British Isles a great many nest in buildings, often in chimneys. In Jersey they have been known to nest only in rock fissures in the cliffs. Their chacking is still heard overhead occasionally, perhaps from wintering birds, but the resident population, always small, seems to be decreasing. Choughs used to nest along the same south-west cliffs as the jackdaws do now. No nest has been known this century, and the last bird was seen in 1910.

Ravens nest on the cliffs of the coast in very small numbers, not more than· four pairs having been recorded in any one year. There was a gap during the late 1950s and early 1960s when no nest was known, but they are back again. Dobson comments on how the same site will be used over and over again and cites one that was used continuously from 1932 to at least 1944. When the ravens returned after the long gap in breeding, it was to one of the old sites. Once more it is possible to walk along the north coast cliffs in January and February and watch ravens rolling and tumbling in the sky in courtship flights, and hear them barking. Only the peregrines are missing.

5

INSECTS AND SOME RELATED CREATURES

Pâssecole, vole, vole; pâssecole, vole, vole,
Par sus la maîson à Jean Nicolle!

Traditional, *Jersey-French Nursery Rhyme*
Le Maistre, *Le Dictionnaire* 1966

ANY FARMER OR GARDENER, battling desperately
against mice, voles, moles and rabbits, must occasionally
be moved to think their numbers beyond count. When he
turns to another group of living creatures, the insects, spiders,
woodlice, and centipedes, he will literally find them so. In
almost any given area, and Jersey is no exception, these
creatures, the arthropods, which have external shells and
jointed limbs and bodies, exist in greater numbers than
all other living creatures put together. There is also a greater
number of different species than in any other group, and
nearly 3,000 were recorded in Jersey up to 1973. They range
in kind from butterflies and wild bees to bed-bugs and
millipedes; from the most beautiful or beneficial to the most
loathsome or destructive. In size they range from several
inches across to microscopic creatures in plankton. Obviously
any account, even only of the land and fresh-water forms,
as here, must be selective. The one which follows is directed
to the reader interested in natural history generally rather
than to the serious worker, but it may be that, because so
much is necessarily omitted, the account may serve to spur
readers to find out more. I have drawn heavily from the
Bulletins of the Société Jersiaise and particularly from the
work, published and unpublished, of H. G. L. Amy, D. J.
Clennett, R. Dobson, A. C. Halliwell, W. J. Le Quesne, and
R. and M. L. Long.

As with the flora, there is a substantial number of non-
British species, 20 per cent. of the grasshopper group, 17 per
cent. of the dragonflies and damselflies, and 10 per cent.
of the bees, wasps, and ants not occurring in Britain. These

are usually species which enjoy a warm mild climate and many of them occur either on Les Quennevais or on L'Ouaisné, areas which in summer are often reminiscent of the south of France. As one walks over these areas a flash of azure blue may suddenly appear low over the turf and then vanish as a blue-winged grasshopper, at rest almost invisible, opens its wings to become airborne. It moves, showing brilliant blue in its hind wings, but this is covered again when the insect comes to rest. Jersey has one grasshopper *Euchorthippus elegantulus* which occurs nowhere else in the world. It has developed here in isolation at some time since Jersey was an island. Its principal haunts seem to be the grassy dunes of the west where it prefers to cling vertically to grass stalks, so obtaining maximum camouflage from its slender body, unusually tapered head and striped markings.

Each species of grasshopper, cricket or bush cricket has its own specific, non-vocal call, and on a still evening their noise carries long distances. During the day I find them difficult to pick out against the background of birdsong, but to the enthusiast this presents no difficulty. The first record of the short-winged cone-head, one of the bush crickets, was obtained by D. J. Clennett who heard an unknown orthopterous noise in Samarès Marsh and tracked down and identified the creature which was making it.

The field cricket is sometimes kept as a family pet in France instead of a canary because of its musical call. It is becoming distinctly rare in Britain except in a few places, but it is still locally common in Jersey. We have a flourishing colony on our west-facing côtil at Val de la Mare. Their burrows, which are about eight inches long and three-quarters of an inch in diameter, are excavated in autumn and the insect hibernates inside until spring. In fine weather they then sit on a small earth platform at the entrance to their burrows and produce their pleasing, if somewhat monotonous, sound. The slightest disturbance will make them sharply click their wings together and dart back into their burrows. The burrow is dug almost horizontally in the earth, and beside it each insect has at least one tunnel through the grass. In theory their habitat is well-drained grassland and heaths, but as I write, there are at least three living in an arable field on the slope just below our côtil. Potatoes were lifted at the beginning of May, and shortly afterwards there were three inhabited burrows under the old potato haulms still scattered about the field. It is impossible for any burrows to have survived the digging, planting, hoeing, banking and lifting from February to May, so presumably the burrows are newly excavated.

The most spectacular 'grasshopper' is the great green bush-cricket, aptly named scientifically *Tettigonia viridissima,* the greenest of the green. A full-grown specimen can be up to two inches long in head and body with the legs and feelers spreading way out beyond. Its call, a seemingly continuous sound which is a vibration noise made by rubbing the upper fore-parts of its wings together, carries well over 100 yards, perhaps even two hundred. It is most often heard on warm still evenings when it continues well into the night.

A colony of migratory locusts was known for many years in the Landes district of France, but the individuals had always been in the solitary quiescent state. In the late 1940s they suddenly swarmed and a few locusts arrived in Jersey in 1946 and 1947. An immature male, which must have been bred here, was found at Les Platons in 1948. Locusts are always associated in people's minds with migrating swarms, but it is not so well known that many other insects also migrate. In some cases the numbers already in Jersey are merely augmented but in a few species, the Island's entire summer population is built up from immigrant stock and their progeny.

Any stretch of water, whether it be an open pool or a thin ribbon of a half-dried-up stream, will have its dragonflies in late summer, and they are at times seen well away from water. Some species, mainly those with vivid greens and blues in their colouring, fly steadily along a short beat, there and back for hours on end, hawking for their prey. Others, more often those with red in their colouring, will hang in the air in one place, then dart quickly to another. Most of the work on Jersey's dragonflies was done by

R. Dobson during the 1940s. Then the Island was rich in dragonflies, many different species occurring, and some of them in good quantity. The scarce and southern aeschnae are both common, and so is the brilliant green, blue and black emperor dragonfly. The Norfolk aeschna which, like some of our botanical species, is more at home in Mediterranean regions, has one of its northern outposts here in Jersey. It can be found regularly at St Ouen's Pond which would appear to be one of the best dragonfly areas in the Island. Unfortunately, there are signs that the dragonfly population of the Island is decreasing. While it is hoped that this may be only temporary, it may be due to the filling in of wet areas.

Like the crossbill and the waxwing among birds, the four-spotted dragonfly, one of the darters, has great irruption years when large numbers are on the move. The last known irruption to affect Jersey was in 1963 when many thousands arrived in the Island on 1 June. Offshore reefs and rocks were covered with them resting on the sea journey. They laid eggs in most of the Island's fresh water areas, whether natural or garden pools, but few adult insects were seen in the following years. The last irruption had been more than 20 years previously.

Damselflies, which look like delicate dragonflies and are closely related to them, occur frequently. W. J. Le Quesne has a story of how, in 1945, at the end of the Occupation, he saw German soldiers exploding hand grenades in a pool at Portelet, a pool in which a few years before he had found the common blue damselfly breeding. Later in the year he checked the pool and found the damselfly still there.

Adult ant-lions, large insects which could well be mistaken for dragonflies, were recorded in 1932 and 1960, and the remarkable larva which digs a pit for itself was found at L'Ouaisné in 1957. Green lacewings often come into houses, and there are many species both of these and the brown lacewings. Trout fishermen on local reservoirs speak of sudden hatches of mayflies, though from entomologists it would seem that few species are involved, and so with stoneflies and scorpion flies.

One section of the true bugs, that which includes creatures as attractive as some of the iridescent green and bronze shieldbugs, as fascinating as pond skaters, back-swimmers and water boatmen, or as loathsome as bed-bugs, has been well studied, mainly by Dr W. J. Le Quesne, and, up to 1973, 245 species had been found here. Most Jersey people have probably seen and looked with interest at the brightly-coloured, clown-faced bug *Pyrrhocoris apterus*, which has a striking red and black geometrical pattern on its back, and resembles an attractive beetle. It occurs here almost wherever there is a stand of its host plant tree mallow, and it is particularly common on Les Minquiers, Les Ecréhous and the Icho Rocks. In England it is very rare, being known regularly from only one area in Devon. The other section of the true bugs is almost too well-known to most Jersey gardeners since it contains frog-hoppers which are responsible for 'cuckoo spit', mealy bugs and all the various aphids which attack crops. Anyone parking a car under lime trees in St Helier may return to find its roof covered in honey dew, an appallingly sticky substance produced by aphids feeding on the leaves of the trees.

Adult caddis flies occur frequently, but they are unob-trusive creatures usually flying at dusk, so are seldom noticed. On the other hand few children playing by a stream or pond can have failed to notice caddis fly larvae. Some larvae are free-living or spin a net like *Philopotamus montanus* which may have a special Jersey form *caesareus,* but the majority exude a sticky silk thread which they wind round themselves and to which they stick various materials. Each individual caddis fly larva builds a home typical, in shape and materials, of its species, some species choosing sand, others small stones or twigs. As a result it is sometimes possible to identify a caddis fly by the case of its larva in the same way that it is possible to identify a bird by looking at its nest. Up to 1973, 34 different species had been recorded in Jersey, including *Agapetus fuscipes* which uses small stones to build a case flat on one side and domed on the other, *Heterocerus aterrimus* which builds a slender unattached case, and *Tidodes waeneri* which makes a very long case and attaches it to a stone or log.

In records of centuries ago there are occasionally mentions of most peculiar redevances or dues, apart from the usual wheat, hens, eggs, etc. For instance, a due to be paid on Midsummer Day to the Seigneur of La Hougue Boete consisted of a bunch of roses, and in Guernsey a lawsuit was brought in 1591 over a due of a dozen butterflies. One wonders what kind were provided. In Jersey, in the course of a year, a lepidopterist can reasonably hope to see 20 or more different species and, with inordinate luck and hard work, perhaps twice that number. Almost 50 have been recorded, but some records are doubtful and others are of vagrants like the purple emperor, one of which was found dead at Noirmont Manor in 1940, or the Camberwell beauty first recorded from Longueville in 1860 and not again until it was found at St Martin in 1947 and St Helier in 1950. Also, some years are better migration years than others. Each year the Island is almost entirely dependent on new stock coming from the Continent to replace the painted lady butterflies, the clouded yellows, and the red admirals. Neither the painted lady nor the clouded yellow hibernates at any stage, egg, caterpillar, chrysalis or butterfly, so each winter the very great majority, if not all, of the stock which stays in the Island is wiped out. The painted lady comes from Africa across Europe to reach here in quantity. The migration begins early in the year but Major Rybot reported seeing a migration at Elizabeth Castle from 3.30 to 4.30 in the afternoon of 4 August 1930. Eggs are laid, one brood hatches in autumn and these may journey back to Africa. Clouded yellows fluctuate in number considerably. Some years they are scarce and in others common, almost abundant. They lay eggs as soon as they arrive and are double brooded. With them very rarely, come pale clouded yellows. Each year large numbers of red admirals come as migrants from the south and are augmented later in the season by butterflies hatched from eggs of the first arrivals. There is evidence of a return migration late in autumn, but the majority stay and attempt to hibernate. Unfortunately, even our comparatively mild winter is too severe for them and most perish. Peacock and small tortoiseshell butterflies regularly hibernate successfully and emerge the following spring to lay eggs. After central heating is switched on in mid-winter in a little used room or store, they may come out of hibernation and be found fluttering round the room. Both are common in Jersey, the peacock being sedentary but the small tortoiseshell's numbers being increased by migration.

The large white and small white butterflies spend the winter in chrysalis form and the small white sometimes emerges as early as March in the warmth of greenhouses. Vast hoards of both also arrive on migration, some swarms being spectacular. On 8 June 1950 a yachtsman, sailing off Chausey, encountered a swarm of the large white, the cabbage white, which he described as like a snowstorm stretching for two miles. Butterflies were everywhere, in the air, on his boat and in the sea, but enormous numbers continued steadily in a north-easterly direction. The weather conditions at the time were unusual and ended in a freak thunderstorm the following day. Other insects, including beetles, bees and dragonflies were also reported as arriving in unusually large numbers the same weekend. Of the other white butterflies, the green-veined white is fairly common; the Bath white fluctuates enormously from none for years on end until a sudden immigration brings thousands, some of which stay to breed; the black-veined white has not been seen for more than a century and the wood white had not been seen for 99 years until one was captured in Bellozanne Valley in 1971.

A few orange tips and brimstones are seen each year, and an occasional comma, though this may be decreasing. In the past the swallowtail was recorded at long intervals, but it has been seen twice recently: in 1974 at La Coupe, and in 1971, when a female was seen laying an egg on fennel at La Moye. Rozel seems to produce most records of white admirals, but as in so many other branches of natural history one wonders if more lepidopterists might not produce more records. It seems strange, for instance, that of the extreme rarities large tortoiseshells appeared in the gardens of R. and M. L. Long at St John, and of R. Dobson at St Brelade in 1971; that Queen of Spain fritillaries frequented H. G. L. Amy's garden, and nearby, at Bel Royal for several years in the 1950s, and that only he and D. J. Clennett at St Ouen should have long-tailed blues in their gardens in 1967. These people are the Island's resident lepidopterists and, if every garden had one, many so-called rarities might cease to be considered rare.

The browns are perhaps the most numerous butterflies in Jersey. The grayling is more often seen on the dunes and cliffs than inland, but the other browns occur, sometimes abundantly, over most of the Island. The wall brown will usually be in full sunshine, the speckled wood in dappled shade, the gatekeeper along hedges particularly where there is bramble, the small heath will be on open grassy areas, and the meadow brown in a variety of places including meadows as its name implies. Only two ringlets have been seen, both near Rozel. Jersey is not large enough for there to be extensive woodland, so it is perhaps not surprising that some of the fritillaries, common in England, are either absent or rare. On the other hand, the Glanville fritillary, which in England is confined to the Isle of Wight, where it is scarce, is comparatively common here. It is the bright orange-brown and black butterfly, with yellowish patches on the underside, so often seen on the cliffs or near the coast in early summer. The rarely recorded fritillaries have the undersides marked with silver: the silver-washed, the dark green, the pearl-bordered and the Queen of Spain fritillary, which has large silver patches on the underside, and to me is the most beautiful of all. It is an immigrant which has bred here successfully and may yet do so again.

The blues, coppers and hairstreaks are well represented. The common blue and the holly blue are the most likely to be seen, but the brown argus, the small copper and the green hairstreak are all fairly common. The white-letter hairstreak reappeared at Rozel in 1941 after an absence of many years and, though still scarce, it has spread over most of the Island. The long-tailed blue, the short-tailed blue and the mazarine blue have also been reported a few times, the long-tailed blue laying eggs on lupin in a garden at St Ouen on its last appearance in 1967. Some years ago, after one of its previous visits, caterpillars were found in St Helier. The large copper was recorded last century, but without confirmation, and it has not been seen since. It may be that it bred here before the extensive marshes of the coastal plains were drained.

Two skippers, the Essex skipper and the large skipper, occur in good quantity, the large skipper sometimes being abundant. The small skipper does not occur here, and earlier records of it belong to the Essex skipper, which in those days was not separated from it. There is only one reliable record of a grizzled skipper and that is from last century when one was taken in Swiss Valley in 1871. The large chequered skipper, *le miroir,* a Continental butterfly, was found in the north east of the Island in 1946 and a breeding colony is or was known to exist in one area. Normally it is a sedentary, non-migratory butterfly, and though it occurs on the coast of France immediately opposite Jersey, lepidopterists consider it unlikely that it should suddenly cross the water in the numbers necessary to establish a breeding colony. They prefer the suggestion that sufficient eggs, caterpillars or chrysalis were unwittingly imported with hay from Normandy or Brittany by the Germans during the Occupation to form the nucleus of a breeding colony. *Le miroir* butterflies have been seen laying eggs on purple moor-grass which is fine and abundant in the area of the breeding colony, but the plant is not confined to this area, being equally plentiful elsewhere in the Island. More recently one specimen of *le miroir* was seen well away from the breeding area and it may be that, having obtained a foothold, the butterfly is now able to exploit other areas. On the other hand, this single butterfly might have been a stray, and it must be stated that in recent years, searches in the breeding area by the Island's lepidopterists have revealed only one specimen. They consider it unfortunate that selected species of butterflies have as yet no legal protection in the Island.

Many people wish to watch butterflies in their gardens, and lists of plants attractive to butterflies are often given. It is, however, seldom pointed out that butterflies are only sipping nectar at these flowers. If the butterflies are to be available, to be attracted, then they must have an adequate and correct food supply when they are caterpillars. In Jersey, as in all highly developed areas, it is this food supply which is likely to become in short supply and, in particular, nettle, which is the staple food of the caterpillars of three butterflies highly prized in gardens, the peacock, the red admiral and the small tortoiseshell, and thistles which are the favourite food of the caterpillar of the painted lady. The present fashion for tidying, gardening and 'improving' overgrown and unkempt areas is as destructive of wild life as the misuse of poisonous sprays.

That the cultivated brassicas are the host plants of caterpillars of some of the white butterflies is only too well known, but in most species of butterfly it is not usually a specially cultivated garden plant on which the caterpillar feeds. Many, like *le miroir's* caterpillar, feed on grasses; others, like the common blue's on clovers and vetches. The green hairstreak's can be found on gorse, broom and heather. The holly blue is interesting in that the species is double-brooded and the caterpillar of the spring brood feeds on holly, but that of the late summer brood feeds entirely on ivy. In England the first brood feeds on either holly or buckthorn, but there is no buckthorn *Rhamnus catharticus* in Jersey in the wild, and only one or two plants in gardens. The lack of this poses a problem for lepidopterists since it the only known food plant, elsewhere, of the caterpillar of the brimstone butterfly. Though normally scarce, some years this butterfly occurs here in sufficient quantity for successful breeding locally to be suspected. If so, on what did the caterpillar feed?

Anyone interested in birds can trace the progress of the seasons without a calendar. He can mark spring and early summer by the return of sand martins, wheatears, cuckoos and spotted flycatchers, more or less in that order, and autumn by seeing snipe, brent geese and fieldfare again.

Flowers will also tell the time of year—bluebells, burnet roses, autumnal squill reflecting the seasons. More specifically the sand crocus will be at its best about the first week in April, the Jersey buttercup about the first week in May, and the spotted rock-rose about the second week in June. What is not so well known is that many species of butterfly also appear at more or less set times. Those which hibernate as adults appear whenever the weather warms up in spring, but those which come through the winter as caterpillars or chrysalis each have their approximate emergence dates. The speckled wood appears in April and is one of the first to emerge. I associate spider-crabbing in the gullies at Le Pulec in May with bright emerald, newly-emerged green hairstreaks on Les Landes above Le Pulec, where they are in vivid contrast with the blue sheep's-bit on which they often settle. They are not so obvious on the yellow horseshoe vetch where they are closer to the background leaves and seem to vanish. Graylings and meadow browns will be emerging in June, gatekeepers in July, but if there are any commas they will probably not appear until September. Through the summer there may be several broods of some species. For instance, the small copper has three broods, one about April or May, a second about July, and a third about October. The green hairstreak is single-brooded in England, but double-brooded in France. Newly-emerged butterflies on the wing in August suggest that it is double-brooded in Jersey.

Butterflies are only a small section, in numbers an almost insignificant section, of the lepidoptera, the vast majority of which consists of moths. These range from being comparable to butterflies in size and beauty to being minute, dull in colour and a nuisance to man. Over 700 have been recorded in the Island and many more are undoubtedly here. In the 1930s, A. C. Halliwell, the Island's surgeon for many years, summarised the then knowledge. The larger moths were relatively well known as to species, but their frequencies were not, and Halliwell himself commented that much remained to be done on the smaller moths. In the 1960s and 1970s considerable work has been done to try to get a more balanced picture of the moth population. This work has been helped considerably by the use of mercury vapour lights which can be left on throughout the night in remote places. No heat is generated by these lamps, so moths attracted by their light are not harmed.

The most spectacular group is the Sphingidae, comprising the hawkmoths, which are remarkable for the size of both the moth and the caterpillar. The caterpillar of the privet

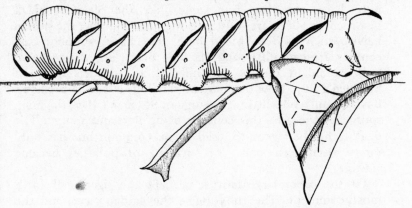

Privet hawkmoth caterpillar. (Natural size.)

hawkmoth is bright green, nearly three inches long and about half an inch thick, with lilac and white diagonal stripes across it at intervals. It is seldom noticed on privet or lilac, its chief hosts, but when it descends from the bush and moves away over the soil in search of a place to pupate, it becomes most obvious. The hummingbird hawkmoth is often seen hovering in front of flowers on calm days or at dusk in late summer. It stops in the air, hovering like a hummingbird, about an inch away from a flower, and exerts a long tongue with which it extracts nectar from the flower before flying to the next one. While the privet hawkmoth and the hummingbird hawkmoth are probably the commonest hawkmoths in Jersey, the poplar hawkmoth is widespread and regularly breeds and so does the small elephant hawkmoth, a particu-

larly beautiful moth of rose-red and gold. The convolvulus
hawkmoth varies in quantity, some years being very
common, but recently it has been scarce. It was thought to
be entirely a migrant, but breeding has now been proved.
Halliwell found the first pine hawkmoth in Jersey at Noirmont in 1929, and by 1939 he was sure they were breeding
successfully. It still does, and one flew into my kitchen at
Val de la Mare, St Ouen, in June 1974. Altogether 15 species
have been recorded, but some, like the oleander hawk
recorded in 1953, are only rare vagrants and one, the spurge
hawk which used to breed here, may have vanished. Last
century its caterpillar and its host plant, sea spurge, were
both abundant on the sandhills of St Brelade's Bay and
St Ouen's Bay. Now there are no sandhills left in St Brelade's
Bay and only very little sea spurge in St Ouen's Bay, the main
spurge of the area this century being Portland spurge. The
death's head hawkmoth used to be common but has only
rarely been seen since the spraying of potatoes became
routine.

Of the other large moths, perhaps the tigers call forth
most comment. The ruby tiger, the garden tiger, and the
Jersey tiger can be seen during the day and all come to light
commonly. The cream-spot tiger is only slightly less
common. The garden tiger and Jersey tiger, with their black-
spotted bright orange hindwings and dark brown and cream
forewings, are magnificent insects when newly emerged,
and so is the cream-spot which has yellower hindwings. Their
caterpillars can often be seen in spring or early summer when
they sit about, basking in the sunshine. All are large and
hairy, but the garden tiger's black caterpillar is one of the
most fascinating of all caterpillars, being clothed on its back
in inch-long silky black hairs which are white-tipped. The
hairs underneath are shorter and tawny and along the sides
there is a line of small blue spots like pinpricks. The Jersey
tiger is a south European moth, well known from Jersey
before it was found in the south west of England. It is
abundant in certain parts of the Mediterranean region and a
large number of the 'butterflies' in the Valley of Butterflies
in Rhodes are Jersey tiger moths. The ruby tiger moth is

Garden tiger
moth

Cream-spot tiger
moth

Jersey tiger moth

slightly smaller but no less brightly coloured, its hind wings and tail being ruby red. Orange-and-black-banded caterpillars of the cinnabar moth are common, often abundant, on ragwort in late summer. They pupate in autumn and remain in that state through winter and spring until about June, when they emerge as black and crimson moths. They can be confused with the equally common, unrelated six-spot burnets which are also black and crimson. The black of both has a beautiful metallic sheen when fresh, but the markings on the forewings are different, and the caterpillars of the two moths bear no resemblance to one another. The pale tussock, chiefly known for its brightly-coloured caterpillar which has tufts of yellow and pink hair, is common, but neither it nor the other closely-related moths of the same group are the agricultural pests here which they sometimes are elsewhere. The brown-tail, for instance, has long been known in Jersey. Halliwell described the caterpillar as abundant in 1930 when it fed on hawthorn, blackthorn and burnet rose on Les Quennevais and was in such quantity that the silken webs spun by the caterpillars caused huge patches of white which were visible from hundreds of yards away. Natural predators take a greater toll in times of plenty and so keep it well under control. The ravages of the brown-veined wainscot are also worse some years than others. Normally the reed-bed at St Ouen is pale straw-coloured all winter. New reeds begin to grow in April and by the end of May they are tall enough for the reed-bed to look green again. In August it develops a purple sheen from the flowerheads and, after they fruit, the reeds of that season die and become dry and straw-coloured. This succession is interrupted in years when the brown-veined wainscot reaches plague proportions. The caterpillar feeds inside a reed stem, on the pith, so kills the reed before it flowers. Some years, including 1974, large patches of the reed-bed are devastated.

The large emerald, green as its name implies, and the brimstone, sulphur yellow, are common and so is the large pale-cream swallow-tail moth which roosts in ivy. The peppered moth is often attracted to light but vanishes on a lichen-covered rock or wall during daytime. All these have looper caterpillars which advance in a series of looping movements instead of crawling and when at rest those of the large emerald and swallow-tail look exactly like twigs. Of the large-bodied, mainly brown moths, the oak eggar and fox moth are common all over the Island and the grass eggar and drinker local. The medium and smaller moths are legion and, as with all other groups, a fair proportion of them are species rare or unknown in Britain. For instance, the case moth *Luffia lapidella* which builds its case among, and from, grey lichen on a wall is extremely rare in the rest of the British Isles and further investigation may prove that those here are a local form. These micro moths are being actively studied, and the first paper by R. Long on the larger micros, the pyralid and plume moths, appeared in 1967.

Beetles have been studied by H. Last, who has visited Jersey on business over many years. He has now listed nearly 900 different species. Strangely the insect usually called a 'black beetle' is not a beetle, but an introduction from the East, the common cockroach, which is nearer to a grasshopper than a beetle. It still occurs in Jersey in spite of modern insecticides. There are two inoffensive native cockroaches, both of which live out-of-doors in vegetation. One, a pale-coloured insect, the tawny cockroach, sometimes called the 'Jersey fast runner', is plentiful; the other, the lesser cockroach, is local and mainly in St Ouen.

Of the beetles, many have a beautiful metallic sheen or iridescence. Some are harmless, even beneficial, and others are pests, but few people could name more than half a dozen, and two at least, ladybirds and glow-worms, are not usually recognised as beetles. Ladybirds are well known and well loved. Not only do most species eat aphids in the garden, but their colouring and shape appeal to young and old alike. It is one of the few beetles with a common name in most languages, and Jersey-French has three: *la pâssecole, la p'tite vaque du Bouôn Dgieu* and *une démouaîselle*. The seven-spot ladybird is the one usually illustrated, but about 20 different species have been recorded so far in Jersey. Some, like the seven-spot ladybird, have black spots on red; others have red spots on black, black spots on yellow, or

11.—Glow-worms have been seen at least once since 1968 in each of the marked squares.

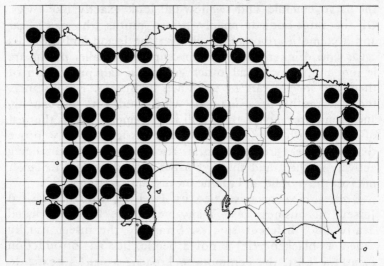

yellow spots on black, and the number of spots varies from two to twenty.

The glow-worm, another beetle useful in the garden because its larva eats small slugs and snails, has a different fascination. The wingless female glows on warm evenings to attract a flying male. Her light is cold and green and has such an ethereal quality about it that a new resident of Trinity, seeing one for the first time, rushed into his neighbour's house saying that some object had fallen from outer space and was still glowing in the hedge. There may not be as many as there used to be, but they still occur in quantity, sometimes even in great abundance. The best time to see them is a warm sultry evening in June between about ten o'clock and quarter to twelve. Such a night was 21 June 1974, and myriads of them were glowing brilliantly along the roadsides of the west of the Island. So many people in the late 1960s insisted, erroneously, that glow-worms had gone, that I began mapping their distribution. I have seen glow-worms, or had them reported on good authority, from all the areas marked on the accompanying map at some time since 1968. No particular search has been made, and I would

suggest that, if one were, they would be found all over the
Island except the south east. They are commonest in the
lime-rich south west and west, which is perhaps where snails,
their principal food, are most abundant.

Maybugs or cockchafers are highly alarming, almost
frighteningly large beetles which sometimes crash into a
room at night through an open window. It seems to me
that they have decreased in the last 20 years. The adult
insect is better known than the larva, even though the larva
does a considerable amount of damage. On the other hand,
the furniture beetle is better known by the ravages of its
larva, the woodworm, which is a pest in furniture and
rafters and flooring of houses. Unfortunately, one of the
worst pests of wood, the house longhorn beetle, was found
in a new house in 1957. The death watch beetle, another
notorious pest of timber, is common, and has even been
recorded in dog biscuits. There was a time during and shortly
after the Occupation when Colorado beetles were blown

Colorado beetle.

across from Normandy on to the beaches of the east coast
of Jersey in such quantity that there was a danger of the
Island's potato crop being ruined. And if any potatoes
escaped the ravages of the beetle they might not be allowed
into the United Kingdom in case they harboured the beetle
unknown to the importer. Extreme measures, commensurate
with the seriousness of the situation, were taken. These involved patrolling and spraying the east coast beaches, the reporting of every Colorado beetle seen inland, and eventually States
participation in the spraying of fields in France adjacent

to the nearby coast. It is now several years since one
was seen.

In 1682 Poingdestre, writing of earlier centuries, lamented
'. . . then the people generally applyed themselves to the
keeping of bees, which thrived there exceedingly, & made
a more excellent sort of hony, then is seene ordinarily;
which since by ye multiplying of apple trees hath by degrees
been neglected . . .' The honey was used to make a strong
drink, mead, which was displaced by perry, which in turn
gave way to cider. The neglect was still being lamented by
the Committee of the Jersey Agricultural and Horticultural
Society in 1836 for in their Report they state '. . . in an
Island like this, abounding in Bee food, the proper care of
these insects ought to be more generally studied', but, alas!
in 1837 still no cottager had a worthwhile apiary in spite
of prizes being offered. Today the Jersey Beekeepers'
Association flourishes. And the Island's wild bees must have
flourished for centuries. This presumption is not based on
records of bees from the past, but on the fact that Jersey
has been particularly rich in clovers, vetches and bird's-foot-
trefoils since botanical records began, and these species are
pollinated mainly by bees, some only by bumble bees.

Bumble bees or humble bees are a common sight and both
mining and leaf-cutting bees also occur, many with their
attendant parasitic or cuckoo bees. It may look as though
bumble bees are literally bumbling about, but it has recently
been discovered that the males of some species have regular
flight paths round certain areas, and that they stop at fixed
places along the track. In an hour and a half, one is known
to have flown 35 times round a path about 300 yards long.
Meanwhile the queen and workers are gathering nectar and
pollen. All bumble bees except the new queens die at the
approach of winter. The new queens survive and each founds
a colony the following year. Most species build nests underground, but not all, and I was shown one small colony in
the scanty remains of an old bird's nest in a thick overgrown
hedge at St Peter's Rectory. Mining bees live solitary lives
even though they may excavate their tunnels and nest
chambers close together. An excellent example of this can
be seen in the earth cliff under the wild medlar on the north

side of Snow Hill car park. Mining bees have used this area for at least 20 years. Yet another kind of solitary bee can be seen on rose bushes, where it cuts out pieces of leaves which it uses to construct a nest. One such bee took the pieces to a door of a house in St Ouen and built its nest in the keyhole.

Wasps are indelibly associated in people's minds with picnics and jam-making in autumn, but some wasps will have been on the wing since the first warmth of spring. Honey bees, both queens and workers, live through the winter in colonies, but only queen wasps ever survive; no workers do. In the course of summer, a stage is reached when there is no further point in the social wasps maintaining a nest or in the solitary wasps laying and provisioning any more eggs. Up to this date they have been engaged principally in collecting meat, spiders, caterpillars, insects, for their young, and have not been particularly interested in sweet food, but once the young are not being fed they begin gorging themselves on fruit, jam and other sugary substances.

The social wasps are best known. These build nests of paper in a hole in a bank or suspended from a branch in a thick hedge. One huge nest was suspended from a beam in an attic of a house in St Helier. In shape it was a squashed sphere about 14 inches across and 12 inches deep, and contained layer after layer of wasp-spun paper round the cells. It seems incredible that it was the labour of one season only and would not be used again. Of the solitary wasps there are a few species of mason wasps which build their nests from fine sand, and the digger wasps which excavate a hole are well represented. The main sandy areas of Jersey are in the south and west, which also happen to be the warmest places. It is not therefore surprising that many non-British species from south Europe occur, and at least one was new to science when first found on Les Quennevais. Hibernating queen wasps are often killed if found in winter. This is a mistake from a gardener's angle. Mason and sand wasps, after laying an egg in a nest put caterpillars in before sealing it up, and another group of digger wasps provides its young with nothing but paralysed spiders. The young of social wasps will eat more or less any flesh, and their diet contains innumerable garden pests.

About 20 species of ants have been recorded, and there may be more. There seems to be no habitat in which they are not present in quantity, and many houses are plagued by them. I once knew a house where a saucer containing a little syrup was always left just inside the back door. I was told the ants went straight to the syrup and left the rest of the house alone, whereas previously they had wandered all over. As with almost every group of insects non-British species occur. A huge nest of a south European species has existed for many years in Val de la Mare among gorse on a sloping côtil. Its exterior shell is formed of small pieces of dry grass and dead gorse in such a way that although the nest is five feet across and two feet high, it blends in with its surroundings and is difficult to see. In June 1974, cock's-foot, heath groundsel and common chickweed were growing on the lower parts of the nest, and the upper parts enclosed living branches of gorse. Rabbit droppings, collected by the ants, lie in quantity on the surface. The ants keep to a few well-worn narrow tracks on their way to food-gathering areas and the tracks can be traced, even when the ants are not using them, for considerable distances. One such track leads to a tree mallow, the leaves of which are being attacked by greenfly. The ants arriving at the tree mallow have small abdomens. They gorge on a sticky substance excreted on the mallow leaves by the aphids, and with greatly swollen abdomens crawl back to the nest to discharge the substance before returning for more.

Gall wasps, though not true wasps, are closely related to them. They are responsible for some of the commoner plant galls, one species producing the marble gall on pedunculate oak trees. This is the gall, usually, but erroneously, called an oak apple, so common on the oaks of the north coast cliffs. Each female of every alternate generation of this gall wasp lays her eggs singly in small twigs of pedunculate oak trees and the tissues of the oak react by forming marble galls round the eggs. The intervening generation lays eggs in the terminal buds of Turkey oak causing a different gall. Both Turkey oaks and pedunculate oaks are plentiful in

Jersey, so neither generation of this gall wasp *Andricus kollari* is presumably ever short of a host tree.

But galls can be caused by agencies other than gall wasps and some are the result of attacks by gall midges, as, for instance, the grey woolly heads produced by thyme shoots instead of flowers. A list of two-winged flies, which include the gall midges, was compiled by K. G. V. Smith in 1958, but there are obviously a great many more species still to be recorded, and D. G. Pope has recently listed the hoverflies of St Martin's separately. Each year about St Mark's Day, 25 April, there is usually a good hatch of St Mark's-fly, a large, harmless, dark fly which hangs in the air with its legs dangling underneath. There are occasional plagues of various flies, as when a cloud of crane-flies or daddy-long-legs was so dense that it darkened the sky round the airport buildings.

The state of knowledge up to 1973 of each group of insects was summarised by W. J. Le Quesne in the Centenary *Bulletin* of the Société Jersiaise. To give some idea of what might still need to be done, Dr Le Quesne compared the number of species recorded in Jersey in each group with the numbers on the mainland. Some would appear to be well worked, but others, perhaps the less attractive, are not. He also listed all the known papers on Jersey insects.

Spiders abound in Jersey, yet little is known about them by local people. In 1908, E. D. Marquand of Guernsey wrote of spiders in that island, '. . . people dislike or even dread them; by many they are regarded with feelings akin to horror; . . . but there are numbers to be found in every wayside bush and hedgebank which no-one could refuse to call beautiful, if elegance of form, brilliancy of colour, and delicacy of marking go to make anything beautiful'. This is equally true of Jersey, and the lack of sustained study is reflected in the comparatively small number so far recorded, which is less than 20 per cent. of those in the British Isles, and considerably less than those recorded in the other Channel Islands. Spiders and other allied orders in Jersey were listed by E. Browning of the British Museum of Natural History in 1956. As might be expected, many of them are rare or local in Britain, and occur only in the south of England, e.g., the two very large spiders *Segestria bavaria* and *S. florentina* and the smaller *Clubiona genevensis* which in Britain have variously been recorded only from the Isles of Scilly, Ramsey, Lundy and a few other areas usually coastal in the south west. Browning mentions finding *Ostearius melanopygius* at Bel Royal and in a German dug-out at Sorel Point. This spider may have been introduced into Britain from New Zealand, but two, *Heliophanus tribu-losus* and *Zodarium italicum*, from south Europe have not been recorded in Britain.

Not all spiders spin insect-catching webs, but, of those which do, each spins a web and forms a retreat typical of its species. On almost any loosely-built wall in Jersey, silken threads, woven together to look like fine pale grey woollen lace, may lead back into a closely woven circular tube going deep into a recess in the wall. This is the web and lair of a *Ciniflo* spider. Some webs are circular and in one plane but have two adjacent segments missing. These belong to *Zygiella* spiders and a single thread running through the middle of the gap connects the web centre to the spider's lair. A movement of this thread tells the spider when an insect may have been caught. Perhaps the most unusual in Jersey is that of the trapdoor spider *Atypus afinis* which spins a long silken tube, mostly in the ground, but part outside. Any insect which touches this projecting portion is seized through the tube and devoured.

Several kinds of harvestmen have been recorded, and two pseudoscorpions, but no scorpions proper. Among the many mites is a Mediterranean species, the plume-footed mite *Lucasiella plumipes* which has been found in St Ouen's Bay where it often climbs up the stems of Jersey thrift, a plant of south Europe. Another Mediterranean creature, *Scutigera coleoptera*, a long-legged creature related to the centipedes, is fairly common and frequently enters houses. Useful centipedes like *Lithobius forficatus* unfortunately are not as common, at least in our garden, as the destructive millepedes.

The word *Crustacea* is used so often in restaurants to mean only seafood, lobsters, crabs, prawns, etc., that it is easy to forget that there are also innumerable small land-living crustaceans here. They include woodlice and pill-bugs, both ubiquitous pests, and well shrimps, of which two kinds have been reported, one away back in Sinel's time, but another more recently down Dr F. Le Maistre's well at Vinchelez. Sandhoppers, *Talitrus*, bridge the gap between land and sea. In theory they scavenge along the tide line, but on very high spring tides they are pushed up on to the roads along the edge of the coast. The road from La Mare Slip to Millard's Corner used to be white with them every year on certain tides, but A. G. Harrison tells me that they have decreased considerably, and during the last year or two he has seen none on the road.

6

AMPHIBIANS AND REPTILES

... our greene and yellowe Lizards ... a
grace and ornament to this Island.

Poingdestre, *Caesarea* 1682

THE FIRST KNOWN MENTION of the Island's amphibians
and reptiles is in Poingdestre's *Caesarea* in 1682, when he
states: 'It is scarce credible what quantities wee haue of
Toades, Snakes, slowe worms, rats and mice with their
enemies the Stoates; . . .'.

There are still toads in quantity in the Island, but whereas
at one time they used to breed in the ponds and streams,
they are increasingly using artificial pools in gardens. It is
now possible to search many of the natural wet areas in
spring and early summer without finding toad spawn or
tadpoles, yet in Poingdestre's day they were in every pool
or spring and lived in all sources of drinking water. He
considered this was no bad thing, that they ensured the water
was wholesome, and he may well have been right. It is
possible that a number of the natural pools are so polluted
today that no toad will live in them.

In early spring a toad will leave its normal quarters for
its breeding area, probably the pool where it was a tadpole.
Great numbers will congregate at these pools, even some of
the smaller ones. In 1971 W. D. and S. F. Hooke reported
80 toads on the short drive of their Pont Marquet house,
all waiting to enter a small pool in the garden. As usual
with these breeding groups of toads, there was a great
preponderance of males. The breeding pools, at which the
males can sometimes be heard croaking, are distributed
throughout the Island and not restricted to one area. After
breeding the toads disperse to their quarters for the rest
of the year and live singly. In late summer we sometimes
have four or five in our garden, but by autumn only one.
This one, a magnificent creature, weighing eight ounces,
spends the summer and autumn days in a circular depression
which it has made in the soil at the foot of a clump of fennel.

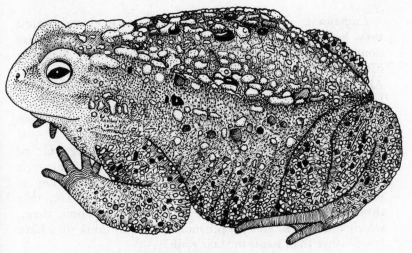

Common toad *Bufo bufo*.

It is difficult to see, as its colouring exactly matches the background mosaic of dead leaves, soil and greenery. In winter it retreats to a warmer place, either a cranny in a wall or the end of a short tunnel in the ground.

The toads of Jersey have been noted for their size for many years, but are not subspecifically different from those in Britain or on the Continent. Though large numbers still exist, there are decidedly less than in the past when stories of armies of toads, heard moving on the roads at night, were told to tourists. There may be a grain of truth in this, for on the two nights of 16 and 17 March 1974 C. G. Pile counted 150 dead toads, run over by cars, on a short stretch of the road in Vallée des Vaux below what used to be Nicolle Mill. This is exceptional. It is now possible to meet Jersey people who have not seen one for many years, and the number run over on the roads has decreased considerably. Even so, the lack of knowledge shown by Ward Rutherford in his book *The Untimely Silence*, 1973, is deplorable. He writes, 'There are neither frogs nor toads in Jersey, only a local amphibian called a *crapaud* which in any case does not croak. But then neither does a toad'. It would be difficult to find 28 printed words containing more errors.

Crapaud is the Jersey-French word for toad and, unless they have been successfully introduced recently, there are none in the other Channel Islands. Jerseymen were therefore often called *les crapauds* by the inhabitants of Guernsey, Alderney and Sark. Similarly men from Guernsey were *les ânes* because of the number of donkeys in St Peter Port; men from Alderney were *les lapîns* or *les vaques*, and men from Sark *les corbîns*.

There does not seem to be the unreasoning fear or prejudice in the Island against toads that there is in parts of France, though I must admit that I have found it impossible to accept records of frogs without first checking that they are not toads. Frogs seem to have an aura about them, which toads lack, and people much prefer to think they have frogs rather than toads in their garden.

Jersey seems only to have one species of frog, the agile or nimble frog, *Rana dalmatina*. At least all those recorded previously, and all those seen recently, have been this, though from time to time there are rumours, and I for one hope they are unfounded, that other species have been introduced. Sinel reported the common frog *Rana temporaria* in Jersey, in his Société Guernesiaise article in 1908, but in 1913 he showed some to Edward Britten, a mainland authority, who identified them as the agile frog *R. dalmatina*.

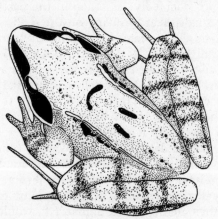

Agile frog *Rana dalmatina*.

Apart from the frog's ability to jump somewhat further than the common frog, the diagnostic features are its pointed snout, the hind legs so long that when they are folded, the heel is beyond the anus, and when stretched out forward the heel reaches or passes the snout, and there is a sub-articular tubercle on the inside of the inner toe at least two-thirds of the length of the toe.

Some old place names in St Martin may indicate frogs were there in the past, but, with one exception, all recent records of agile frogs have been in the western half of the Island. Similarly, all seven localities that I know for frog spawn, are in the western half, though in some of these localities it was a small amount of spawn one year only. L'Ouaisné is the best breeding area, but, unfortunately, is much disturbed by people hunting for spawn. I give the locality deliberately in the hope that parents and teachers may perhaps help to keep it as a safe breeding area for all time by discouraging children from collecting the spawn. It would also help the natural survival of the agile frog in Jersey if the frog could be removed from the list of subjects to be studied for external examinations. There is not enough frog spawn for each school to have some, yet toad spawn, which is common, is virtually ignored. Toad spawn would appear to offer just as much scope for study and the toad population at the moment could easily withstand the pressure.

Newts are reliably reported to be common in Jersey today. I seldom see one, but I can vouch for the fact that they are widespread, having seen them at Fauvic, La Fontaine ès Mittes, Mont Mado, Grosnez, and Noirmont. The only species is the palmate newt *Triticus helveticus*. Sinel recorded both the smooth newt and the palmate newt in 1908, but in his report of Britten's visit in 1913 he says, 'Our newt is not the Common Newt . . . but the Palmate Newt . . .'. The palmate newt has webs between its toes in the breeding season but not at other times of the year. Points of difference always present are that the palmate newt looks as though the extreme tip of its tail is permanently missing, and its throat is not spotted.

The only snake in Jersey is the grass snake, *Natrix natrix,* and it is entirely harmless. Every report of any other snake has turned out to be an error, the reptile in question being either a grass snake or a slow worm. They have obviously decreased since 300 years ago when Poingdestre could say their numbers were scarce credible, but Sinel's 1908 remark that they were diffused throughout the Island, with most in the north west and south west is still true. People of St Helier may not believe they have snakes in their midst, but after an article in the *Jersey Evening Post* asking for informa-tion about sightings, I was told of some on the slopes of Fort Regent behind Hill Street, and of one disturbed in a garden at Lower King's Cliff, where there was also a dis-carded skin. They were reported from most parishes, but, as in Sinel's day, most sightings have been in the western half of the Island. It is difficult to estimate their numbers. All that can be said is that while they are not common, there are more than most people would imagine.

Grass snakes are often confused with slow worms, but people who know grass snakes well in England, also find the Jersey ones strangely coloured. In England there are usually two white or yellow patches on the neck, one either side, with some black immediately behind, giving the appearance of a collar. It is from this that the grass snake gets its other name, the ringed snake. In Jersey, as Britten first pointed out in 1913, this collar is missing from the adults. Young ones have it, but it disappears as they age. The same variety of grass snake, var. *astreptophorus Seoane,* also occurs, according to Dr Frazer, in Cyprus and the Spanish peninsula. I do not know at what age the change takes place, but the grass snakes I have seen of about two feet long, have had a collar, while all those of about three feet and more have not.

There are no snakes in any of the other Channel Islands though some pets occasionally escape.

Three lizards occur in Jersey, the green lizard *Lacerta viridis,* the wall lizard *Lacerta muralis* and the slow-worm, a legless lizard, *Anguis fragilis.* When dealing with 'things detrimentall' Poingdestre says, 'As for our greene and yellowe

12.—Green lizards have been recorded at least once since 1965 in each of the marked squares.

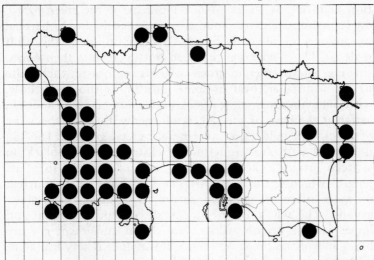

Lizards soe frequent in euery hedge, soe tame and harmelesse, though I place them here, because of theire kind, I doe not take them for any deformity, but on ye contrary a grace and ornament to this Island'. Since he wrote those words, numbers of islanders must have waited quietly and watched green lizards and been delighted by them. Alas! they are no longer in every hedge. Sinel, in an article on Channel Island lizards in the *Report and Transactions* of the Société Guernesiaise of 1907, bemoaned the fact that even in his day they were less common than formerly, blaming town extensions and dealers who had set a price on their heads, though he said they were as numerous as ever in the west and south west. We had at least nine in our garden in 1974. At present the older generation knows them well, but talk to any group of children and the chances are that few, other than those who know the west, will have seen one. The distribution map contains every record given to me relating to 1965 onwards, but does not purport to be complete. Nevertheless, the predominantly west and southwest pattern is interesting since people living all over the Island have been asked to contribute to it.

Sinel's 1907 article is full of detailed information, gathered it would appear entirely in Jersey, on the coloration at different stages of development of the green lizard, on its habitat and its mode of living, and it should be read by anyone interested in lizards. His description of the adult male is: 'Plates covering the head bottle-green at their edges, shading off to emerald green towards the centre, each plate having a circular, oval or sometimes linear spot of yellow, with occasionally a white speck in the very centre. The back, as far as the base of the tail, is adorned with a fine speckling of black and gold upon an emerald green ground. The tail is marked with short longitudinal close-set lines of black on a green ground, except for the terminal inch or so of its length, which is olive brown. The limbs are either spotted, or more often transversely barred, with black, on a green ground. The whole of the underside, except the throat and lower jaw, is bright yellow. The throat and lower jaw are blue, and in the breeding season this colour is very brilliant'. The female has little if any blue on the throat, and the young ones are brown and white, brown and green, green and yellow, at different stages of their development, always with white lines along their sides until they reach maturity at three years.

Lizards were being sent from Jersey to England as far back as 1761. In a letter dated 16 April that year, Jean Simon, a general merchant living in St John, wrote to his son in England, *'a l'egard des Laizards comme il n'a point encore fait de chaleur il s'en est veu tres peu mais comme il va en bref un navire d'icy a Londres j'aurai de vous en ramasser'.* By 1947 the pet trade in green lizards had reached such proportions that after representations by H. J. Baal, the States of Jersey passed the Wild Life Protection (Jersey) Law, 1947, which prohibits the buying, selling, killing or exporting of any of the four reptiles or three amphibians of Jersey. While there have been no prosecutions under the law, the Nature Conservation Advisory Body drew the attention of the police to the fact that green lizards were being offered for sale in St Helier recently, and action was taken.

Sinel recorded the wall lizard *Lacerta muralis* in 1907 from the cliffs, rocks and walls of a thin coastal belt from

13.—Wall lizards have been recorded at least once since 1970 in each of the marked squares.

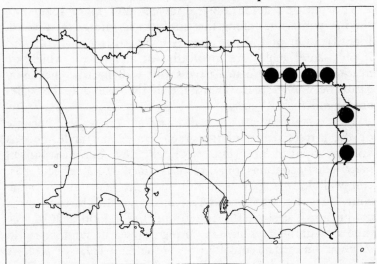

Bonne Nuit to Gorey. This is substantially its distribution today and it can still be found in quantity on the walls of Gorey Castle. He thought the rockless expanse of Gorey Common stopped its spread south, but he was at a loss to explain why it ranged no further west than Bonne Nuit where conditions appeared ideal. His fears in 1907 that it was dying out have proved unfounded.

He stated that the ranges of the wall lizard and green lizard did not overlap, i.e., that if one lizard was present in a certain area, the other was not, but W. A. Luff told a Société Guernesiaise meeting in October 1907 that he had seen both kinds on Gorey Castle. Later observations have also reported both, and on 24 April 1974, my family and I saw a green lizard and a wall lizard basking in the sun within six inches of one another on the slopes of the Castle. Sinel's description of the male wall lizard in its commonest Jersey colouring is:

'General ground colour a delicate silvery grey, upon which are close set spots of olive brown, each with a sage-green bordering. On the neck and limbs there is often a little marbling and speckling of white. Underside flesh colour, the sides pink, and the throat and lower jaw bright red.'

The female's colouring is browner and more sober and she has white lines along the sides like a young green lizard. Identification of the two species of lizard is straightforward if only adult males are involved, but any lizards which are not bright green are not necessarily wall lizards; they may easily be young green. The shape of the head and the scales are diagnostic at all ages.

To a certain extent the wall lizard suffers neglect because of the attractiveness of the green lizard, and little more is known about it now than in Sinel's day. The distribution map which contains only records since 1970 reflects this, and wall lizards may well still occur as far west as Bonne Nuit. Anyone who is interested in natural history, lives in the north east of the Island and has a good deal of free time on sunny days in late spring and early summer could make an important contribution to the knowledge of Jersey's wild life by studying wall lizards. The immediate points on which more information is needed are its relations with the green lizard, its exact distribution and its habitat require-ments, which seem, with our present knowledge, to restrict it to the coast.

The sand lizard *Lacerta agilis* does not exist in Jersey, earlier records of it being errors for the wall lizard, *L. muralis*.

Slow-worms are fairly common throughout the Island though they have decreased considerably since Poingdestre's time. Like all Jersey's other reptiles they are harmless to man, yet man's first reaction on finding a slow-worm is usually to kill it and ask questions afterwards. Their diet consists largely of slugs, with a few snails and insects, so they are a worthwhile asset in any garden. An adult slow-worm is about 12 to 14 inches long and they can be longer. The scales of their skin are so small and have such a high sheen that slow-worms look like pieces of brown-grey or steel-grey flexuous polished metal tubing, paler and, in the female, pinkish underneath. The head and tail look like continuations of the body, being nearly the same thickness. The young ones are yellow on top and black underneath, with a sharp demarcation line along the side. There is also a very thin black line running along the back. The effect is so different from adult slow-worms they are often not recognised as the same species. They feed at night when slugs come out, so are not often seen in daytime unless their resting place, a hole under stones, or a pile of leaves, is disturbed.

It is sometimes difficult to decide whether the report of a snake is correct or not without actually seeing it. In the same way that people seem to prefer having a frog to a toad, so they seem to prefer a snake to a slow-worm. A snake is exciting, with a sense of danger about it, whereas few people seem to want anything with a name as prosaic as a worm, however well they know that a slow-worm is not a worm but a lizard. Jersey-French names exist for all the amphibians and reptiles: the toad, *le crapaud*; the agile frog, *la rainotte*; the palmated newt, *la lezarde dg'ieau*; the green lizard, *la verte lezarde*; the wall lizard, *la grise lezarde*; the grass snake, *la tchilieuvre*; and the slow-worm, *l'orvet*. The same word *tchilieuvre* is used for goose grass (cleavers), whose green leafy stems snake up through a hedge.

There are fewer reptiles and amphibians in the other Channel Islands. The slow-worm is commonest, being in all the other main islands except Sark. Smooth newts and toads were introduced into Guernsey about 1930 and 1953 respectively, but they are thought to have died out. No toads have been seen for about 10 years. The green lizard was introduced earlier and still survives on the south coast. The frog situation is confusing. Jee and Brehaut state that both the common frog and the agile frog now exist on Guernsey. The common frog has been established on Sark for some time, but the occurrence of the agile frog is doubtful. (Its recorder perhaps jumped to conclusions.) Alderney's amphibian records are complicated by the release in the wild of species imported for garden pools.

7

FISH OF PONDS AND STREAMS

There is a little valley called Val des Vaux, situated at the
back of town; . . . a little stream of bright clear water comes
trickling down; . . .

O. Rooke, *The Channel Islands* 1857

AT THE ASSIZES of 1299 Drogo de Barentin of Rozel was
asked by what warrant he was keeping a fish pond on the
common land of the King, Edward II. Drogo's answer was
that he had not created a new pond, but that he had
renovated one which was attached to a mill on his own
land, not common land. Shortly afterwards, at the Assizes
of 1309, Philip de Carteret was asked by what warrant
he claimed 'to have his pond in the same parish free and
separate'. This is St Ouen's Pond, *La Mare au Seigneur,*
the largest natural sheet of fresh water in the Island. The
value of any pond would lie in the fish it contained, for
in those days, besides fresh meat being scarce, the Church
decreed that fish should be eaten on certain days. The
de Carterets were successful in their claim and in *Les
Chroniques* there is an account of how the Seigneur of
St Ouen, in the time of the French occupation from
1461-68, was fishing in his pond and was nearly taken
prisoner by the French, who approached stealthily along
the beach. Other landowners also claimed the right to keep
a pond, and later Poingdestre, who was Lieutenant Bailiff
of Jersey from 1668 to 1676, stated in his *Lois et coutumes
de l'Ile de Jersey* that anyone could construct a *vivier,*
a pond where fish are kept alive for the table, provided
it did not interfere with the water mills and streams of
the Island.

But what fish were kept in the ponds? In Camden's
Britannia 1607, it is stated of Jersey, 'on the west part
nere unto the sea, there is a lake . . . replenished with
fish, but carpes especially, which for bignesse and pleasant

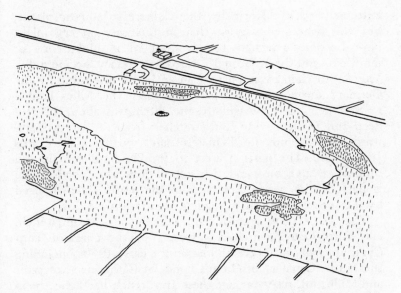

St Ouen's Pond, 1975.

tast are right commendable'. The carp is a fish of Asia and
south-east Europe, and was not introduced into ponds
in west Europe until the 12th or 13th centuries, and not
into Britain until as late as the 15th or 16th. When it was
introduced into the ponds of Jersey is not known, but there
are still carp in St Ouen's Pond and they are still claimed
to be of good size. Some of the reservoirs and a few private
pools also contain carp.

Camden implied that there were fish other than carp in
St Ouen's Pond, but, apart from eels, there are no records
of any others until recently. R. Dobson tells me that during
the Occupation he often put a trot line of a hundred hooks
out in the Pond to catch fish to supplement his family's
meagre diet, and the catch would invariably be carp and eels.
He caught no other species. Perch might perhaps have been
expected, but the only record of them, prior to their introduction by the Jersey Freshwater Angling Association in
the early 1960s, is of one caught by H. H. Willis in the South
Canal the year before the Association introduced them.
There has been much speculation over the origin of this
fish. Perch breed in fresh water areas in Normandy and
Brittany and their eggs which are laid in strings are

extremely sticky. Normally they adhere to aquatic plants, but the fishermen suggest that in this case an egg might have become attached to the foot of a duck, coot or moorhen and been brought across to Jersey accidentally. The South Canal was part of an anti-tank ditch dug by the Germans during the Occupation in case the Allies landed in St Ouen's Bay. Originally the ditch was about 12 feet deep and 60 feet wide, and stretched from the Pond northwards to Chemin de l'Ouzière and southwards towards Jubilee Hill. The parts nearest to the Pond still remain and support a large bird and fish population. The North Canal is part of the nature reserve and the South Canal is used by the Jersey Freshwater Angling Association.

The Association introduced roach, perch, bream, tench, and mirror carp, which is a variety of the common carp *Cypinus carpo*, into several areas in the early 1960s, including the South Canal at St Ouen's Pond, St Catherine's reservoir and Millbrook reservoir. Of these fish, tench had twice been mentioned previously. Lyte, in his sketch of the Island in 1808, reported that carp and tench were 'abundant in the ponds of gentlemen', and Sinel, in Ansted's *Channel Islands* (1893 edn.), recorded them as common, but gave no locality. Baal's article *The Fresh Water Fishes of Jersey* in the 1955 *Bulletin* of the Société Jersiaise contains much valuable information, but tench are not mentioned, and no fisherman alive today can remember them before they were introduced by the anglers' Association. Have they died out or were they recorded merely on hearsay? Mirror carp were in the pool at Avranche Manor before the Occupation, according to Baal, but he saw none afterwards. Willis tells me that a specimen mirror carp was found in a derelict pond at Maison de la Ruette, St Ouen, in 1962, when the pond was drained.

Three other species have been introduced at some time. Trinity Manor pool contains crucian carp *Carassius carassius,* a different species from the common carp. This pool was drained in October 1974 and crucian carp went downstream to the settling tanks of Grands Vaux reservoir from where the Waterworks Company is trying to remove them, the settling tanks being one of their trout-keeping areas. Crucian carp are in Millbrook reservoir, and the Rozel Manor pool on the east of La Grande Route de Rozel. Baal also recorded seeing them in the pool on the cliffs between Noirmont and Portelet. He gave no date, but C. G. Pile saw them there in the early 1950s. Unfortunately this pool was later temporarily emptied and crucian carp have not been seen there since. Rudd were first reported when the Jersey New Waterworks Company was clearing out La Hague reservoir in 1952. They colonised other waters in Jersey with remarkable speed and were soon common in most reservoirs and pools of the Island, and they still are today. It is possible that they were inadvertently spread by the Waterworks Company during pumping operations.

Baal, writing in 1955, stated that rainbow trout had been put into the reservoirs some years previously. Though the Waterworks Company rear them artificially in their hatcheries there is one stream in the Island where it has managed to breed and maintain itself naturally for more than 30 years. It is a North American fish which is frequently introduced into European waters, but seldom survives unaided. That it should do so in Jersey was most unexpected. Baal recorded two caught, just before the war, two miles out to sea in St Aubin's Bay. He assumed they had come down the stream at Millbrook and Pile tells me that in the 1950s he watched about 20 going to sea down another stream and negotiating various obstacles on the way.

Sea trout *Salmo trutta* are occasionally caught at sea just offshore. Elsewhere in these latitudes they migrate up streams to spawn, and Pile tells me he considers that they would have done so regularly in Jersey in the past. Now there are barriers, not negotiable by trout, at entrances to the suitable streams, but brown trout, of which sea trout are a migratory form, are present in many streams and reservoirs. Their status in the streams in Waterworks Valley is confused because trout were reared in a hatchery at Millbrook early this century. But brown trout cannot spread naturally to unconnected waterways, and they were in other stream systems in Jersey before they are known to have been introduced there. They have been in the Grands Vaux streams throughout living memory and the

ability of these streams to produce large numbers was
amply demonstrated by Grands Vaux reservoir becoming
stocked with trout naturally shortly after it was completed.
Indications are that other stream systems are equally productive. When reporting a brown trout, caught in 1938 in the
brook which runs across Grouville Common, Baal queried
whether trout still existed in the Island as a native species.
This implies that he considered they had been native at one
time and though by 1955 he seemed to have changed his
mind, the Island's anglers are of the opinion that brown
trout are still of indigenous stock in the streams of
St Peter's Valley, Vallée des Vaux, Grands Vaux, and in
the stream running down to the reservoir at St Catherine.

The Waterworks Company now runs a trout hatchery
at Handois. Both brown and rainbow trout are reared, and
the fish are used as indicators of pollution in the reservoirs
and feeder systems. Their value has been shown on numerous
occasions. In one case, many years ago, A. Rabet who was in
charge of the hatchery was watching trout fry in a stream
when they suddenly turned over and died in a matter of
seconds. After diverting the water, he raced up the feeding
stream and found a man washing out an arsenical-spray
container in the stream. Almost equally frightening incidents
still occur in spite of closer liaison between the Waterworks
Company and the Department of Agriculture, but is it not
time that the pollution of any stream or fresh water area,
whether used by the Waterworks Company or not, was
made a criminal offence?

In 1808 Lyte could write, 'Eels are common in all the
waters here', but this is not true today. Any wet areas
which have easy access from a stream below, e.g., Millbrook
and La Hague reservoirs and St Ouen's Pond, still contain
large numbers, but some of the other reservoirs have massive
dams which are built out from steep dry rocky slopes. Rabet
tells me he has never seen an eel at Handois, and R. M.
Clarke, the Engineer Manager and Director of the
Waterworks Company, has only seen one, an enormous
creature whose head was projecting from stones below
the island. Lower down Waterworks Valley there are
plenty of eels, but there is no simple water connection

between Handois and a treatment plant above Dannemarche. At Grands Vaux, Pile has seen elvers attempting to negotiate a spill-stream of the dam, though there are no reports of eels in the reservoir. This may be because of the difficulty of seeing them, but each time the mudpond has been cleared in recent years, no eels have been found. Val de la Mare reservoir has another huge dam and, once again, none has been seen recently, though they are in good quantity in the stream below. There is less water-spillage here than at Grands Vaux and their entrance may be totally blocked. When this dam was finished in 1959, the Seigneur of St Ouen asked the Waterworks Company to clean out his pools at the Manor and remove the eels which were damaging the bottom. These pools are at the head of the stream which feeds the north arm of the reservoir. Rabet says that many of these eels were enormous. Five years later, when the pools were cleared again, fewer eels were found. There were none in the mud-pond just above the north arm of the reservoir when it was cleaned in 1973 and none again in 1974, though two were seen between the clearings.

Eels can cross damp grass and some of the Island's anglers are unable to accept that any reservoir can be free of eels. A negative record is difficult to prove, but it would appear safe to say that the eels in Val de la Mare, Handois or Grands Vaux must be few in number, whereas in the other reservoirs they are common.

Elvers in great quantity still find the entrances from the beach. One of them is where the Waterworks Valley stream, i.e., the Mill Brook, discharges at Millbrook. When the Sewerage Department was working on the outlet on the beach, J. Vaines, from whom a good deal of the following information comes, tells me that pools left overnight would be full of elvers in the morning. The Gorey brook discharges at the *Welcome* inn. In the old days sewage went out at the same place, so there has been some interference with the brook's course, and, in particular, there is a step where the brook joins the now disused sewer. This step is only negotiable on a neap tide or higher. At low tide, elvers can be seen clinging to the brick-lined walls waiting for the water to be high enough to enable them to go up into the brook.

Some elvers are not as fortunate as this. Those entering at the town outfall, which discharges water from Grands Vaux and Vallée des Vaux, meet more severe physical barriers in the underground channels, in particular, a cascade under Town Mills where there are vertical drops of several feet.

From other entrances, elvers travel far into the heart of Jersey. When the pool at Beau Desert, St Saviour, was cleaned in 1973 large quantities of eels were found. Did the elvers come up the Dicq entrance and then travel through the Longueville Manor stream and up Swiss Valley? Most streams and wet ditches still contain eels and the last news item about them was on 7 August 1974 when 1.44 inches of rain fell in 10 to 12 minutes at Dr F. Le Maistre's weather station at his home, La Brecquette, L'Etacq, and eels over a foot long were found swimming in his normally dry yard.

Sticklebacks were common in 1893 according to Sinel, and in 1955 Baal stated that the three-spined stickleback was common in all the Longueville and Greve d'Azette streams. He also recorded it from the stream past Tesson Mill in St Peter's Valley. I saw some in a brook at the north end of St Ouen's Pond in the early 1950s, but I have not seen any recently. Rabet tells me that some years they are plentiful at Grands Vaux, and after the very dry summer of 1959 when the Waterworks Company pumped water from Grands Vaux to Handois, sticklebacks suddenly appeared in great abundance at Handois where previously he had seen none. They became a nuisance in the filters, but trout, which feed on them, have been re-introduced, and they are now less common.

Sinel also listed loach as one of the common fishes in 1893. In the 1944 *Bulletin* of the Société Jersiaise Baal wrote, 'For many years it has been known that a species of loach was to be found in Grands Vaux and Les Vaux streams, but it was thought to be the common loach *Nemacheilus barbatula*; it was for us to find out that it was the rare species *Corbitis taenia* or Spined loach . . .'. In 1950, when the Waterworks Company was working on the stream in Grands Vaux, large numbers of common loach were found and were identified as such by R. F. Le Sueur, the marine biologist. R. G. Smith, the fishing correspondent of the *Jersey Evening Post*, told me his son caught a common loach in the stream below Grands Vaux in the late 1960s. In October 1974 H. H. Willis showed me a common loach which he had found just below the Grands Vaux dam when the Waterworks Company were looking for the crucian carp which had come downstream from Trinity Manor. These three records confirm the presence of the common loach. But what of the spined loach? In 1955 Baal listed both.

If little is known about loach in Jersey even less is known about the brook lamprey. This was recorded from several brooks, including the Grands Vaux stream near Mal Assis Mill by Baal in his 1955 article. A systematic study of the fish population of the brooks, open or culverted, would be well worthwhile.

Flounders can live in either fresh or salt water, though they must return to the sea to breed. They prefer the muddier parts of the coast and, where a slow-moving brook runs down to the sea, they may swim well inland. Grasett Park housing estate now stands on the site of Bashford's Nurseries. In the old days, water for the nurseries came from a pond in the corner opposite the Recreation Grounds at Grève d'Azette. Fifty years ago, W. J. Guise can remember spiking flounders in that pool. He also remembers them about 400 yards inland up the brook through Grouville, and he was told they had been found in the stream which flows down St Peter's Valley through the marsh. In 1943 or 1944 he was working part-time for Baal, who then lived in a house at the foot of Beach Road. The stream past the Recreation Grounds eventually runs through a deep culvert in the garden of this house and then enters a pipe to go under the road, sea-wall, etc., at the Dicq. In those days it did not emerge again until it was several hundred yards down the beach. This was during the Occupation and wood was scarce. Occasionally pieces came floating down stream and were trapped at a grating in the culvert. One evening Baal descended a ladder into the culvert to retrieve a piece of wood for the fire and received a tremendous shock when something white leapt from under his feet in the stream. Next day he mentioned it to Guise who immediately suggested flounders, and that evening he descended into the brick-lined culvert. He caught two flounders, one of a pound and the other a pound and three quarters. He thinks there were more, and he would have liked to have walked further up the channel to under St Luke's Crescent, but it was dark and, as this was the Occupation, he had no torch.

It is of interest that flounders were then in good quantity round the entrance to that stream. Vaines tells me that the Germans erected a wire mesh a few yards in front of the outlet down on the beach. He and his father spiked many flounders in the sand in front of the wire until the Germans discovered what they were doing. After that the Germans had the fish. Now, according to Guise, who is an authority on flat fish, there are far fewer on the beaches, and Vaines says that trot lines on that particular beach produce few, if any, flat fish. This may account for the fact that there are no further sightings of flat fish inland.

8

MOLLUSCS OF INLAND AREAS

Colînmachon, mouontre-mé tes cônes:
J'té dithai où'est tan péthe et ta méthe:
I' sont dans la bâsse-fôsse à tchilyi des roses!

Child's Ditty
F. Le Maistre, *Le Dictionnaire* 1966

MOST STREAMS AND PONDS of the Island contain fresh water mussels, limpets and snails, but snails are not confined to water, and a few even prefer a dry habitat provided there is an occasional shower of rain. Molluscs were first listed for the Channel Islands by Dr F. C. Lukis, a keen Guernsey conchologist, in 1862. While the Guernsey records were considered more or less complete, those of Jersey were not and Eugene Duprey gave a comprehensive list in an article, *'Coquilles de Jersey, marine (zone littorale), fluviatiles et terrestres'*, which appeared in the *Bulletin* of the Société Jersiaise for 1877. As might be expected, most species were marine, though there was a surprising number of fresh water and land species. In later years he added a few more records but, except for an examination of shells in peat deposits, no further work was done until recently. Dr J. Chatfield and the Rev. G. Long are currently working on the present-day snail population, and when the results are published later this year it will be of great interest to see how many species have survived since Duprey's time, and, indeed, how many of those in the peat deposits are still here. Names of snails are in the process of changing, so both English and Latin names are given to minimise confusion.

With the decrease in wet ditches and marshes, and with the great use today of pesticides, many directed specially against slugs and snails, one almost invariably imagines that their numbers will have decreased. This is not necessarily so, and indeed the Island has gained at least one species, Jenkin's spire snail *Potamopyrgus jenkinsi.* Until the middle

of last century its ancestors lived in New Zealand in fresh
water, but in 1859 it was found in brackish water at Graves-
end, and by 1893 it was in fresh water in Britain. Now it
exists in enormous quantities in most rivers and streams
in Europe, including Jersey's. In England 5,000 per square
metre has been mentioned as a fairly normal number. The
narrow spiral shells are only a few millimetres long, and
most of the other molluscs found in the Island's streams are
equally small. Pea mussels *Pisidium spp* have been found in
every waterway examined. These and the lake orb mussel
Sphaerium lacustre which has been recorded from Samares,
are bivalves and look like minute shiny cockles. The river
limpet *Ancylastrum fluviatilis* is so small, Duprey recorded
frequently finding it on the water beetle *Acilius sulcatus*
which itself is only about 17mm. long. The shell is
limpet-shaped, with the point bent over like that of a
slit limpet.

The great majority of Jersey's fresh water and land mollusc
species have spiral shells, the spiral varying from being flat
to being very tall, in which case the shell is a narrow cornet.
Occasionally the walls of a tall shell are the same diameter
for a good part of its height, producing a cylindrical shell.
Sometimes the first curving whorl near the opening is huge
and constitutes most of the shell with all the remaining
whorls packed into small tight twists at the top. Colours are
mainly those of the background with olive-green, brown and
straw-colour predominating. Few are brightly coloured. The
texture varies from rough to highly polished and shining,
and some of these are transparent. At least one species
has a hairy shell. All the snails and slugs mentioned in the
following account have been found in Jersey since 1970,
but it is not the complete list to date. Also there are probably
others so far unrecorded. The frequencies of many species,
that is, whether they are rare, occasional or common, is as
yet unknown and so is their distribution in Jersey. In the
hope of encouraging readers to search their own areas, rather
than to concentrate search on a few known, probably unim-
portant places, the exact locality where each species has so
far been found is not given.

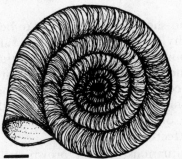

White-lipped ramshorn
Planorbis leucostoma.

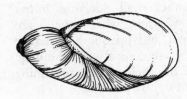

Pfeiffer's amber snail
Succinea pfeifferi.

Chrysalis snail
Lauria cylindracea.

The great ramshorn snail *Planorbarius corneus*, whose
shell is a large flat spiral, is often introduced into gold-
fish pools to keep algae in check, but there are two,
not so well known, less eye-catching ramshorns, the white-
lipped ramshorn *Planorbis leucostoma* and the white ramshorn *P. albus* which occur naturally in pools. Their shells
are much smaller but their shape is similar. In the same pools
there may be wandering snails *Lymnaea peregra*, dwarf
pond snails *L. truncatula*, and large numbers of marsh snails
L. palustris. Most of these are amphibious and can live out
of water if necessary for some considerable time. This enables
the dwarf pond snail to live in damp fields where it climbs
up the vegetation. Unfortunately this snail is the intermediate
host of the liver fluke and it may leave the infective stage
of the parasite on grass which is later eaten by grazing

animals. There no sheep in Jersey today to be infected by it, but C. L. Gruchy, the States veterinary surgeon, tells me that the dwarf pond snail is so widespread that cattle put to graze on wet land anywhere in the Island are likely to get liver fluke. He considers that roughly 40 per cent. of all Jersey cattle slaughtered here have it in their liver, but unless there are other complications the general health of cattle seems unaffected.

In very wet situations, opaque brown shells of the shiny glass snail may be found. 'Glass' snails are so-called because their shells have the high gloss and smooth texture of polished glass. Among other snails with thin transparent shells, which have been found in the marshy areas and wet meadows of Jersey, are the amber snail *Succinea putris* and Pfeiffer's amber snail *S. pfeifferi,* whose shells are translucent like amber when small, but opaque and darker brown when older. In shape they are conical with the huge bottom whorl taking up most of the shell and the remaining spirals being remarkably small and tightly packed.

The dampness in leaf litter of a wood or hedge-bottom provides sufficient moisture for some snails, and a sift through it will produce a good number. Most are only a few millimetres across and are easily overlooked. Those found in Jersey include the prickly snail *Acanthinula aculeata* which has a rough keel running round the middle of the squat spirals, the chrysalis snail *Laura cylindracea* which, as its specific name implies, has a somewhat cylindrical shell, and the slippery snail *Cochlicopa lubrica* whose very shiny, almost transparent shell is formed of graduated well-differentiated spirals. Even smaller, will be the dwarf snail *Punctum pygmaeum*, and the herald snail *Carychium minimum.* The dwarf snail's shell is a squat cone, and that of the herald snail a thin cornet, but the largest dimension of each is only about two millimetres. When examined under a lens, the rounded snail, *Discus rotundatus,* which is very common here, looks like a piece of well-coiled rope.

The very great majority of shells spiral dextrally, i.e., if a shell is placed with the point upwards, a track from the point following round the spirals down to the opening in

Hairy snail
Hygromia hispida.

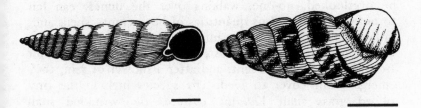

Two-toothed door
snail *Clausilia bidentata.*

Pointed snail
Cochlicella acuta.

the bottom whorl would always be turning in a clockwise direction like a right-handed screwdriver. The tree snail *Balia perversa,* which tucks itself away in holes in the bark of trees, has been found once in Jersey and is one of the few species with a sinistral, or left-handed, spiral. So is the two-toothed door-snail *Clausilia bidentata* which is not uncommon in hedge-bottoms and on walls. The name door-snail refers to the snail's internal structure.

Any large stone which just breaks the surface of an otherwise grassy area is likely to be used as an anvil by thrushes to break open snail shells. The commonest broken shells are those of the larger banded snails which must therefore occur fairly frequently. Only the dark-lipped *Helix nemoralis* has been found. I have never seen the Roman or edible snail *H. pomatia* in Jersey, though empty shells, presumably from kitchen rubbish, can be picked up occasionally. On the other hand I have seen French workers assiduously and systematically searching a wall and collecting garden snails *H. aspersa*, which I understand taste more or less the same, but are tougher. It seems a pity that the garlic glass snail *Oxychilus alliarius* which occurs in gardens is too small, even if edible, to be of any practical value. Several snails smell of garlic, but this one does most pungently when handled. Even more surprising is that some snails have hairy shells. The hairy snail, *Hygromia hispida,* whose small shell is covered with short curving hairs, is common all over the Island.

While many snails have to be searched for and can easily be overlooked, no-one, walking over the dunes, can fail to notice the enormous quantities of both empty shells and, in late summer, of the living animals. These snails are adapted to life in a dry habitat. Most, though not all, take shelter from the heat and drought, and after a shower of rain, they emerge from cover to feed. The species include the tiny ribbed grass snail *Vallonia costata,* the wrinkled snail *Helicella caperata,* the pointed snail *Cochlicella acuta,* and the banded snail *H. virgata.* The banded snail probably causes more comment than any other. In St Ouen's Bay large numbers can be seen from July onwards, even in the hottest, driest weather, clinging to tall stems of the dune vegetation. Sometimes the shells are so closely packed along a branch of sea radish that there is no room for more and the branch is bending over because of their weight. The Pisan snail *Theba pisana,* another dune snail, was listed only for Jersey by Dr F. C. Lukis in Ansted and Latham's *Channel Islands* (1862 edn.), and he is reported to have introduced it from Jersey into Guernsey in 1860. It still occurs on shell sand in the south east of Jersey and it now flourishes in Guernsey.

Slugs and snails are descended from common ancestors, but whereas snails have external shells, usually housing the animal, slugs have very small shells which, except in a few species, are buried unseen beneath the skin. One of the commonest in Jersey is probably the netted slug *Agricolimax reticulatus* which is the fairly small whitish creature often found humped up inside lettuce. The dark grey garden slug *Arion hortensis* is also well known. The larger black slug *A. ater,* which can be up to 150mm long, occurs, and the huge giant, the great grey slug *Limax maximus,* which can be up to 200mm. long, has recently been re-found.

We tend to class all slugs together as obnoxious garden pests, utterly revolting in themselves, but they do differ most interestingly, both in shape and habits, in the same way that other groups of animals differ, and some may be beneficial. A few are carnivorous, like the shelled slug *Testacella maugei,* which was once reported from St Saviour's Road. It may still be here, and that it has not been recorded again may be a reflection of this dislike that most people have for slugs, and indeed for almost any invertebrate. Not so, one enterprising Scotsman. The following extract is from the book *A Summer Stroll,* by an unknown author G.L., and from internal evidence it was written about 1808: 'St. Ouen's Pool, is a fresh water lake of some extent, celebrated for its excellent carp, as well as for a superior species of Leeches, which are in high request among the London Apothecaries, so much so, that an industrious scotchman, last year, is said in three pedestrian trips, to have carried three thousand of this singular livestock to the metropolis, where he sold them at a shilling each'.

9

THE FUTURE

Haro! Haro! Haro! A l'aide mon Prince! On me fait tort.

Jersey *Clameur*

THE NATURAL HISTORY of Jersey is changing. It always has and always will, since no living population, even without man, remains static. The trouble is that the rate of that change has increased tremendously this century, largely as a result of man's activities. Bulldozers and other heavy machinery enable him to change large tracts of habitat almost overnight; with pesticides and herbicides he can alter the plants, animals, insects and birds of a whole field or hedgerow in a few hours; his buildings and his roads obliterate the wild life which was previously on their sites. In many cases the result of these changes is to reduce those parts of the fauna and flora which give Jersey its character. It may be part of a plant and animal association, common in Jersey, which is destroyed, or it may be a single species known only to a few specialists which is lost. Each, individually, may be thought to matter little, but the cumulative effect, if the trend continues, will be serious.

There are many hopeful signs for the future, among them being an awareness that the countryside of Jersey is threatened. At one time any land of little or no agricultural value and useless for building development was derogatively termed waste land. It is now becoming more widely understood that some of this land, the sand dunes, the remaining marshy areas, the inland wooded côtils, the cliffs and the heathlands, are of immense importance from a natural history point of view.

One of the first positive steps to preserve the countryside was the purchase by Mr Carlyle Le Gallais of some of the beautiful wooded côtils of Vallée des Vaux which were about to be cleared and sold as building land. He was one of the founder members of the National Trust for Jersey in 1936, and he gave the côtils to the Trust in 1937 as its first property. In 1975, the Trust, which is a Jersey organisation and has no connection with the National Trust of England, owns 51 properties, which include dunes, coastal headlands, wooded côtils and farms.

In European Conservation Year, 1970, the Island Development Committee, after consultation with the Public Works and the Agricultural Committees, set up a Nature Conservation Advisory Body to supply information and advice on Jersey's natural history. Included on the Advisory Body are members from each of the departments concerned, so that close co-operation exists in matters as varied as the management of Les Quennevais and trying to stop the spread of Dutch elm disease. The Island Development Committee has discussed the possibility of establishing a natural history centre in St Ouen's Bay, where the States own a good deal of land. If this were to come about, it would have far-reaching effects.

Members of the Société Jersiaise, from its foundation in 1873, have actively studied many aspects of the Island's natural history. Records are published in the reports of the various sections in the Société's *Bulletin*. Over the years, a representative natural history collection has been built up in the Société's museum at 9, Pier Road, St Helier. This is used by both visiting and Island naturalists so avoiding the waste of wild life involved in private collecting. Members continue to provide detailed information on natural history in Jersey to British and continental scientists engaged on special studies. In 1949 the late Guy Malet de Carteret, Seigneur of St Ouen, declared St Ouen's Pond, *La Mare au Seigneur*, to be a nature reserve, and the Ornithological Section of the Société have managed it since then, operating a bird-ringing station at the north-east corner.

There is no logic in the way legal protection is given to some species of wild life, yet not to others. Every reptile and amphibian is protected in Jersey, and all birds except six species: crow, jay, magpie, starling, woodpigeon, and house sparrow, which are considered injurious. This is excellent and so is the *Importation of Miscellaneous Goods Act* which forbids the importation of grey squirrels and coypu. But why was mink not added as soon as it was known that they were equally serious pests if they escaped? And why is no flower, mammal or butterfly, to name but a few other groups, given the slightest protection? These groups are now receiving attention from the British parliament with a view to giving selected species legal protection, and the States of Jersey should also consider them.

Nevertheless, the best way to conserve a particular species is to see that the plant and animal association, of which it is part, continues to flourish. Most wild life communities in an intensively-farmed and well-populated area like Jersey are the result of a balance having been struck between the various constituents themselves and man. To remove man's traditional activities completely may produce undesirable changes—so we return to man. Is it possible for him so to use the land of Jersey that, in this century and the next, he does not obliterate a wild life community which has developed infinitely slowly? The future of Jersey's natural history lies largely in his hands.

BIBLIOGRAPHY

Actes des Etats de Jersey 1524-1800 (1897-1917), Société Jersiaise.

Anon., *Les Chroniques de Jersey 1585* (ed. E. Mourant, Jersey, 1858).

D. T. Ansted and R. G. Latham, *The Channel Islands* (London, 1862); also 1893 edition (ed. by E. T. Nicolle).

C. C. Babington, *Primitiae Florae Sarnicae* (London, 1839).

G. R. Balleine, *A History of Jersey* (London, 1950).

G. E. H. Barrett-Hamilton, 'The bank vole in Jersey', *Zoologist* (1896), Vol. 20, p. 98.

R. J. Berry, 'History in the evolution of *Apodemus sylvaticus* (*Mammalia*) at one edge of its range', *J. Zool.*, (1969), Vol. 159, pp. 311-28.

I. R. Bishop and M. J. Delaney, 'The Ecological Distribution of Small Mammals in the Channel Islands', *Mammalia* (1963), Vol. 27, pp. 99-110.

I. R. Bishop and M. J. Delaney, 'Life history of small mammals in the Channel Islands in 1960-1'. *Proc. zool. Soc. Lond.* (1963), Vol. 141, pp. 515-26.

J. Braithwaite and F. Macleu, *Two Knapsacks in the Channel Islands.* (Jersey, 1896.)

W. Camden, *Britannia* (1607 ed.).

J. Chevalier, *Journal de Jean Chevalier 1643-1651* (Société Jersiaise, 1906).

A. R. Clapham, T. G. Tutin, and E. F. Warburg, *Flora of the British Isles* (Cambridge, 1962).

S. P. Clark, 'Field experience of feral mink in Yorkshire and Lancashire', *Mammal Review*, Vol. 1, No. 2 (1970).

Code of Laws for the Island of Jersey 1771.

G. B. Corbet, '*Plecotus austriacus* in England and the Channel Islands', *Proc. zool. Soc. Lond.*, Vol. 143, pp. 511-15.

G. B. Corbet, *The identification of British Mammals* (London, 1964).

The Earl of Cranbrook, 'Long-tailed Field Mice from the Channel Islands', *Proc. zool. Soc. Lond.* (1957), Vol. 128, pp. 597–600.

The Earl of Cranbrook and P. Crowcroft, 'The white-toothed shrews of the Channel Island', *Ann. Mag. nat. Hist.* (13) (1958), Vol. I, pp. 359–64.

P. Crowcroft and G. K. Godfrey, 'On the taxonomy of the Jersey vole (*Clethrionomys glareolus caesarius* Miller)', *Ann. Mag. nat. Hist.* (13) (1959), Vol. 2, pp. 737-43.

G. F. B. De Gruchy, *Medieval Land Tenures in Jersey* (privately published, Jersey, 1957).

M. J. Delaney and M. J. R. Healey, 'Variation in the long-tailed field mouse (*Apodemus sylvaticus* [L.]) in the Channel Islands', *Proc. Roy. Soc.* (1967), Vol. 166, pp. 408-21.

R. Dobson, *Birds of the Channel Islands* (London, 1952).

Documents Historiques relatifs aux Iles de la Manche 1199–1244, Société Jersiaise.

J. G. Dony, C. M. Rob, and F. H. Perring (1974) *English Names of Wild Flowers, Bot. Soc. Brit. Isles* (London 1974).

E. H. Du Feu, *A Bryophyte Flora of Jersey* (Société Jersiaise, 1966).

E. H. Du Feu and J. Paton, *Supplement to a Bryophyte Flora of Jersey* (Société Jersiaise, 1972).

U. K. Duncan, *Guide to the Study of Lichens* (Arbroath, 1959).

G. H. Dury, *Land Utilisation Survey of Britain: The Channel Islands* (London, 1950).

J. R. Ellerman and T. C. S. Morrison, *Checklist of Palearctic and Indian Mammals* (London, 1951).

Extentes de l'Ile de Jersey 1274, 1331, 1528, 1607, 1668, 1749 (1877–1883) Société Jersiaise.

P. Falle, *An account of the Island of Jersey* (1694); also *An account of the Island of Jersey with additional notes by the editor* (1837, ed. by E. Durell).

J. F. D. Frazer, 'The Reptiles and Amphibia of the Channel Islands and their distribution'. *Brit. J. Herp.* (1949).

Gazette de l'Ile de Jersey 1789.

J. Hawkes, *The Archaeology of the Channel Islands, Vol. II: The Bailiwick of Jersey* (Société Jersiaise, 1937).

P. Heylin, *A full relation of two journeys: the one into the mainland of France. The other into some of the adjacent islands* (1656).

N. Jee, *Guernsey's Natural History* (Guernsey, 1967).

Jersey Agricultural and Horticultural Society *Reports 1834–1839*. (Later the *R.J.A.H.S.*).

E. D. H. Johnson, 'Stonechats in Jersey', *British Birds* (1971), Vol. 64, pp. 201-13, 267-79.

'G.L.', *A Summer Stroll* (c. 1808).

P. A. Larkin, 'Ecology of Mole (*Talpa europaea*) Populations' (D. Phil. Unpub. thesis, Univ. of Oxford, 1948).

Le Lievre, *Guide to Jersey* (1861).

R. Long, 'Rhopalocera (LEP.) of the Channel Islands', *Entomologist's Gaz.* (1970), Vol. 21, pp. 241-51.

F. Le Maistre, *Le Dictionnaire Jersiais-Français* (Don Balleine Trust, 1966).

J. H. Le Patourel, *The Mediaeval Administration of the Channel Islands 1199–1399* (Oxford, 1937).

L. V. Lester-Garland, *A Flora of the Island of Jersey* (London, 1903).

Lettres Closes 1205–1327 (Société Jersiaise, 1893).

T. Lyte, *A Sketch of the History and Present State of the Island of Jersey* (1808).

R. R. Marett, *A Jerseyman at Oxford* (Oxford, 1941).

C. B. M. McBurney and P. Callow, 'The Cambridge Excavations at La Cotte de St Brelade, Jersey—a preliminary report', *Proc. Prehist. Soc.* (1971), Vol. 37, pp. 167–207.

D. Messervy, *Journal de Daniel Messervy 1769–1772* (Société Jersiaise, 1896).

Michelin *Les Guides Verts: Normandie* (Paris).

A. D. Middleton, *The Grey Squirrel* (London, 1931).

G. S. Miller, *Catalogue of the Mammals of Western Europe* (London, 1927).

E. T. Nicolle, *Mont Orgueil Castle: its History and Description* (Jersey, 1921).

C. Noury, *Géologie de Jersey* (1886).

J. B. Payne, *Armorial of Jersey* (Jersey, 1861).

W. Plees, *An account of the Island of Jersey* (1817).

J. Poingdestre, *Les Lois et Coutumes de l'Ile de Jersey.*

J. Poingdestre, *Caesarea or a Discourse on the Island of Jersey* (Société Jersiaise, 1889).

'Rolls of the Assizes held in the Islands in 1299', unpub. English trans., Société Jersiaise.

'Rolls of the Assizes held in the Islands in 1309' (Société Jersiaise, 1903).

Seigneurial Court of St Lawrence, *Records for 1707.*

M. Shorten, *Squirrels* (London, 1934).

J. Sinel, *The Geology of Jersey* (Jersey, 1912).

L. Sinel, *The German Occupation of Jersey, 1940–1945, a Complete Diary* (Jersey, 1945).

K. G. V. Smith, 'The Diptera of Jersey, Channel Islands', *Ent. Gaz.* (1958), Vol. 9, No. 4, pp. 203–11.

Société Guernesiaise, *Report and Transactions 1882–1975.*

Société Jersiaise, *Annual Bulletins 1873–1975.*

H. N. Southern (ed.), *Handbook of British Mammals* (Oxford, 1964).

J. Stevens, *Victorian Voices* (Jersey, 1969).

INDEX

Adder's-tongue spearwort: 15
Albinism: 72, 152
Alder: 5, 31, 149
Alderney: 4, 62-5, 67, 69, 72, 74, 75, 80, 86, 89, 90, 92, 105, 110, 125, 187
Amphibians: 205
Amy, H.G.L.: 154, 161
Andesite: 7
Angelica: 36
Ant-lion: 157
Ants: 154, 174
Aphids: 158, 169
Apple of Peru: 44
Apple trees: 11, 30, 54, 172
Archirondel: 40, 135
Argentum: 34
Arthropods: 154
Arums: 35
Ash: 31
Attenborough, T.W.: 48
Aubin, P.A.: 95
Auk, Little: 126
Avocet: 122
Avranche: 190

Baal, H.J.: 66, 78, 79, 85, 97, 99, 101, 104, 117, 184, 191, 192, 194, 195
Babington, C.C.: 1
Back-swimmers: 158
Balleine, Rev. G.R.: 11, 100
Barker, W.B.: 109
Barrett—Hamilton, G.E.H.: 101
Bats:
    Greater horseshoe, 67, 78, 79; Grey long-eared, 67, 78, 79; Leisler's, 79; Natterer's, 79; Noctule, 79; Pipistrelle, 67, 78, 79; Serotine, 79
Baudrette Brook: 47
Beau Desert: 194

Beaumont: 31
Beauport: 54
La Becquetterie: 119
Bed-bugs: 154, 158
Beech: 31
Bees: 154, 160, 172
Beetles: 160, 169-172
Belcroute: 1
Belette: 83, 84
Belladonna lily: 32
Belle Hougue: 79, 109
Bellozanne: 82, 160
Bel Royal: 29, 161
Bernacles: 113
Bilberry: 18
Bindweed: 43, 51, 52
Bird's-foot trefoil: 172
Bishop, I.R.: 66, 75, 76, 99, 102
Bittern: 112
Bittern, Little: 112
Bittersweet: 45
Blackbird: 143
Blackcap: 134, 137
Black Death: 100
Blackthorn: 32, 33, 149, 168
Blanches Banques: 25, 133
Bluebell: 23, 50, 53, 164
Blue butterfly:
    Common, 161, 163; Holly, 161, 163; Long-tailed, 161; Mazarine, 162; Short-tailed, 161
Bluethroat: 143
Bogbean: 15
Bonne Nuit: 99, 185, 186
Bouley Bay: 44, 81
Bracken: 22, 24
Bramble: 14, 22, 24
Brambling: 146, 147
Branchage: 35
Bream: 190
Brehaut, R.: 86
Brimstone: 160, 163

Britten, E.: 180, 181, 182
Brook lamprey: 195
Brooklime: 36
Brooks, Mrs J.: 47
Broom: 19, 163
Brown argus: 161
Browning, E.: 175
Buckler-fern: 44
Buckthorn: 163
Buddleja: 39
Bulbous meadow-grass: 27
Bullfinch: 149
Bunting:
    Cirl, 146; Corn, 146; Little, 146;
    Ortolan, 146; Reed, 145; Snow,
    146
Bunting, R.H.: 105
Burdock: 54
Burhou: 92, 110
Burnet rose: 15, 25, 26, 164, 168
Burrow, R.: 85, 123, 144
Bustards: 116
Butterflies: 159-164
Butterfly bush: 39
Buxton, C.E.: 117
Buzzards: 116

Caddis flies: 158, 159
Callow, P.: 2
Camden, W.: 8, 188, 189
Camberwell beauty: 159
Campions: 19, 35, 50
Cape-gooseberry: 45
Carp: 188, 189, 203
Carteret, Sir George: 29, 92
Cat's-ears: 21, 24
Centipedes: 176
Chaffinch: 13, 108, 146, 147
Chamomile: 26
Charles II: 82, 83, 87, 88
Chatfield, Dr J.: 197
Chemin de l'Ouzière: 190
Cherry: 31
Chestnut: 13, 29, 30, 32
Chevalier, J.: 88, 100

Chicory: 38, 146
Chickweed: 174
Chiffchaff: 134, 137
Chough: 153
Clennett, D.J.: 76, 144, 154, 155,
    161
Climate: 8, 9
Clouded yellow: 159
Clovers: 37, 44, 163, 172
Clown-faced bug: 158
Clarke, R.M.: 192
Cockchafer: 171
Cockcroaches: 169
Cock's-foot: 14, 38, 54, 174
Code of Laws 1771: 93
Comfrey: 38
Comma: 160, 164
Cone-head: 155
Conglomerate: 7
Coot: 117, 118
Copper butterfly:
    Large, 162; Small, 161, 164
Corbet, Dr G.B.: 78
La Corbière: 18, 19, 21, 128,
    135, 137, 149
Cormorant: 110
Corncrake: 117
Corncockle: 41
Cornflower: 41
Cornish moneywort: 35
Corn marigold: 41
Cornsalad: 43
Corn spurrey: 20
La Cotte: 2, 61, 89, 98, 103
Couch grass: 43
La Coupe: 160
Cowslip: 24
Coypu: 206
Crabbé: 62, 73
Crab grass: 43
La Crabière: 99
Crake, Spotted: 117
Crallan, G.E.J.: 79
Cranbrook, Earl of: 66, 74, 98
Crane-flies: 175

Crane: 116
Crapaud: 180
Crossbill: 149, 157
Crowcroft, Dr P.: 66, 74, 101, 102
Crows: 152, 205
Crucian carp: 190, 191, 195
Crustacea: 177
Cuckoo: 127, 130, 142, 163
Cuckoo flower: 50, 53
Cuckoo spit: 158
Curlew: 119, 122
Curlew, Stone: 122
Cypresses: 35

Daffodils: 22, 37
Damselflies: 154, 157
Dannemarshe: 32, 193
de Carteret, G. Malet: 205
Deer: 3, 60
de Gruchy, G.F.B.: 60, 79, 89,
    96, 115, 138, 151
Delaney, M.J.: 66, 75, 76, 98, 102
Devil's-bit scabious: 24, 51
Devil's Hole: 85
Le Dicq: 194, 195
Divers: 108
Dobson, R.: 115, 116, 127, 128,
    130, 136, 138, 141, 145, 146,
    152-4, 157, 161, 189
Dog's mercury: 23
Le Don Ferey: 44
Le Don Gaudin: 31
Le Don Le Gallais: 32
Le Don Powys: 31
Dotterel: 122
Douet de la Mer: 125
Doves:
    Collared, 127, 139; Rock, 126;
    Stock, 127; Turtle, 127
Dragonflies: 154, 156, 157, 160
Druce, Dr G.C.: 27
Ducks:
    Long-tailed, 115; Mandarin,
    116; Tufted, 113, 114
du Feu, Miss E. H.: 55
Duke of Argyll's tea-plant: 45

Dumaresq, P.: 81
Duncan, U.: 54
Dunes: 15
Dunlin: 118, 122
Dunnock: 129, 130, 134
Duprey, E.: 197, 198
Durell, E.: 14, 80, 88
Dury, G.H.: 16
Dutch elm disease: 29, 57, 205
Dwarf rush: 21

Les Ecréhous: 87, 110, 125, 142,
    158
Edward I: 90
Edward II: 91, 188
Edward III: 91, 100
Eel: 189, 192-194
Eel grass: 113
Eider: 115
Elder: 35
Elizabeth Castle: 83, 100, 114,
    159
Elms: 29, 30, 33, 57, 58, 145
L'Etacq: 18, 19, 85, 118, 119, 135,
    136, 194
Euonymus: 34
Evening-primrose: 26, 40

Falcon, Greenland: 116
Falle, Rev. P.: 12, 70, 80, 88, 93,
    95, 106, 113
Family crests: 97
Fauvic: 87, 181
Fenugreek: 44
Ferret: 86, 91, 95
Fief des Arbres: 29, 30
Field cricket: 155
Fieldfare: 143, 163
Firecrest: 139
Five Oaks: 99
Fliquet: 71
Flounders: 195, 196
Fly agaric: 57
Flycatchers: 140, 163
Fontaine-es-Mittes: 181
Forget-me-not: 26, 36, 52

Fort Regent: 129, 141, 182
Foxglove: 54
Fox, Red: 60, 61, 64, 67, 80-82
Fritillary:
    Dark green, 161; Glanville, 161;
    Pearl-bordered, 161; Queen of
    Spain, 161; Silver-washed, 161
Frogs: 180, 181, 187
Froghoppers: 158
Frazer, Dr J.F.D.: 182
Fuel: 11-13
Fulmar: 109
Fungi: 55-58

Gadwall: 114
Galingale: 36
Galls: 29, 174, 175
Gall midges: 175
Gall wasps: 174
Gannet: 109, 110
Garganey: 115
Garlics: 39
Gatekeeper: 161, 164
Geology: 6-8
German ivy: 40
Getlif, Mrs B.: 85
Glaciations: 1, 2
Gladiolus: 39
Glow-worm: 169, 170
Godfray, Dr A.C.: 79
Godfray, G.C.: 68
Godfrey, Miss G.: 66, 101, 102
Godwits: 119, 121
Goldcrest: 139
Goldeneye: 115
Goldfinch: 146, 147, 149
Golden-saxifrage: 23
Good-King-Henry: 38
Goosander: 115
Goose:
    Barnacle, 114; Bean, 114;
    Brent, 111-113, 163; Greylag,
    114; Pink-footed, 114
Gorey: 99, 117, 124, 185, 193
Gorey Castle: 29, 32, 40, 90, 129,
    185

Gorse: 13, 14, 22, 24, 145, 163,
    174
Goshawk: 116
Grainville: 92
Le Grand Becquet: 109
Grands Vaux: 114, 121, 190,
    191, 193-195
Granite: 7
Grasett Park: 195
Grasses, Agricultural: 38
Grasshoppers: 6, 154, 155
Grayling: 161, 164
Greater celandine: 53
Greater stitchwort: 35
Great fen-sedge: 76
Great green bush-cricket: 156
Grebes: 108, 109
Green alkanet: 35
Greenfinch: 146, 147, 149
Green Island: 14, 39
Greenshank: 121
Grève d'Azette: 194, 195
Grève de Lecq: 62, 81, 82, 135,
    142
Grosnez: 18, 24, 35, 109, 110,
    125, 135, 136, 138, 181
La Grosse Tête: 31
Groundsel: 146, 174
Grouville: 112, 113, 120, 127,
    192, 194
Grouville Marsh: 15, 48, 117,
    119, 129, 133, 143, 146
Gruchy, C.L.: 97, 200
Guernsey: 4, 62-5, 67, 69, 73-5,
    80, 86, 88, 89, 92, 101, 103-
    105, 159, 175, 187, 202
Guillemot: 126
Guillemot, Black: 126
Guise, W.J.: 195
Gull:
    Black-headed, 123; Common,
    124; Glaucous, 125; Greater
    black-backed, 123; Herring,
    23, 123; Lesser black-backed,
    123; Little, 125; Iceland, 125

La Hague: 26, 96, 191, 192
Hair-grass: 27, 50
Hairy finger-grass: 43, 54
Hairstreak:
    Green, 161, 164; White-letter, 161
Halliwell, A.C.: 154, 164, 166, 168
Hamon, Adv. F.C.: 109, 124
Handois: 192, 193, 194
Hares: 60, 61, 64, 87-89, 94
Hare's-ear: 26
Hare's-tail: 27, 41
Harriers: 116
Harrison, A.G.: 177
Harvestmen: 176
Harvie-Brown, J.: 135
La Haule: 36, 92, 99, 122, 151
Havre des Pas: 73
Hawfinch: 149
Hawkes, Mrs J.: 3, 5
Hawkmoths: 165, 166
Hawthorn: 32, 33, 168
Hazel: 5, 31, 32
Healy, M.J.R.: 66, 98
Heathers: 14, 22, 24, 163
Hedgehog: 59, 60, 61, 63, 67-69
Hedge mustard: 54
Hedges: 32-35
Hedge woundwort: 52
Hemlock: 54
Hemlock water-dropwort: 23, 26, 54
Hemp: 38
Hemp-agrimony: 23
Henry III: 89
Herm: 4, 62-5, 67, 69, 73-5, 80, 86, 94, 101, 149
Herons: 112
Heylin, P.: 17
Hinton, M.A.C.: 3, 98, 103
Hobby: 116
Le Hocq: 99
Holly: 31, 163
Honey bells: 39
Honey fungus: 57

Honeysuckle: 23, 145
Hooke, W.D. and Mrs S.F.: 145, 178
Hoopoe: 129
Horehounds: 52
Hornbeam: 32
Horsetail: 43, 54
La Hougue Bie: 120, 121, 144
La Hougue Boëte: 159
Hover-flies: 175
Hutchinsia: 26

Icho Tower: 87, 112, 158
Ile Agois: 35, 98
Ile au Guerdain: 31, 44
Iris: 36
Isles of Scilly: 75, 90
Ivy: 23, 43, 145, 163
Ivy-leaved toadflax: 43

Jack: 39, 52
Jackdaw: 152
Jay: 151, 205
Jee, N.: 86, 105
Jersey buttercup: 21, 164
Jersey cudweed: 15
Jersey fern: 36
Jersey grasshopper: 6, 155
Jersey lily: 22
Jersey orchid: 46, 48, 53
Jersey thrift: 26, 50, 51, 176
Jersey-French names:
    amphibians, 180; birds, 130; flowers, 49-54; insects, 169; islanders, 180; mammals, 68, 72, 75, 105; reptiles, 187
Jethou: 94
Johnson, E.D.H.: 116, 140
Johnson, Mrs G.F.: 116
Jones, P.: 109
Jubilee Hill: 86, 190

Kangaroo apple: 45
Kempt Tower: 6, 86
Kestrel: 115
Kingfisher: 129

Kite, Red: 116
Kittiwake: 109, 124
Knapweed: 54
Knot: 121

Lacewings: 157
Ladybirds: 169
Lady-fern: 44
Lady's bedstraw: 26
Lady's tresses: 48, 52
Les Landes: 24, 56, 136, 164
Lapwing: 120-122
Larkin, P.A.: 72
Last, H.: 169
Lattice stinkhorn: 56
Laurent, A.P.: 34
Lawrence, F.R.: 124, 141
Le Brocq, N.: 113
Le Cocq, K. and Mrs F.: 109
Le Couteur, Col. Sir John: 38, 72
Leeches: 203
Le Gallais, C.: 204
Leland's map: 92
Le Maistre, Dr F.: 37, 50, 72, 105,
    130, 154, 177, 194, 197
Le Marquand, W.: 94, 95
Lemprière, Rev. W.: 152
Le Quesne, Dr W.J.: 154, 157,
    158, 175
Lester-Garland, L.V.: 15, 16, 18,
    44
Le Sueur, R.F.: 124, 194
Lichens: 43, 44, 54, 55, 145, 168,
    169
Linnet: 147-149
Liver fluke: 199
Liverworts: 55
Lizard:
    Green, 16, 178, 182-185, 187;
    Legless *see* slow-worm; Wall,
    182, 184-187
Loach: 194, 195
Locust: 156
Lords and ladies: 35, 53
Long, Rev. G.: 197
Long, Mrs M.L.: 135, 154, 161

Long, R.: 127, 154, 161
Longueville: 126, 159, 194
Luff, W.A.: 185
Lukis, Dr F.C.: 197, 202
Lyte, T.: 13, 14, 190, 192

Magpie: 151, 152, 205
Maidenhair fern: 44
Mal Assis Mill: 195
Male-ferns: 44
Mallard: 113, 114
Mammoth: 2, 3
La Mare Slip: 177
Marett, Julia: 35
Marett, Dr R.R.: 116
Marquand, E.D.: 175
Marram: 25
Marshes: 15
Marsh helleborine: 49
Marsh mallow: 15
Marsh marigold: 41
Marten: 84, 86
Martin:
    House, 106, 131; Sand, 131,
    138, 141, 163
Marvel of Peru: 10
Maufant: 8
Mayflies: 157
Maybug: 171
Mayweed: 16, 41
McBurney, Dr C.B.M.: 2, 8
Meadow brown: 161, 164
Medlar: 32
Melesches: 92
Merganser, Red-breasted: 114
Merlin: 116
Messervy, D.: 8
Mexican fleabane: 39, 43, 53
Microtus: 3, 65, 67, 103
Middleton, A.D.: 95
Mielles: 15
Milkwort: 21
Millard's Corner: 177
Millbrook: 190, 191, 192, 193
Millipedes: 176
Mink: 59, 60, 61, 67, 87, 206

Les Minquiers: 87, 109, 110, 125, 142, 158
Le Miroir: 162, 163
Mole: 59-63, 67, 69-73
Mont-a-la-Brune: 86
Montbretia: 52, 53
Mont de la Ville: 93
Mont Mado: 181
Mont Matthieu: 57
Mont Orgeuil *see* Gorey Castle
Moorhen: 117, 118
Mosses: 55
Moths: 166-169
Mourant, Dr A.E.: 7, 8
Le Mourier: 85, 91, 97
Mouse-ear Hawkweed: 36
Mouse-ears: 20, 54
Mouse:
 House, 59, 61, 62, 65-67, 98-100, 104, 128; Wood, 3, 6, 59, 61, 62, 64, 66, 67, 98, 103-105, 178; Yellow-necked, 98
La Moye: 14, 90, 96, 129, 135, 138, 152, 160
Mushrooms: 56
Mussels: 198
Myxomatosis: 14, 94

Navelwort: 36, 43
Neanderthal man: 2, 3
Neolithic sites: 5
Nettle: 163
New Beaumont Hill: 30
Newts: 181, 187
Nicolle Mill: 179
Nightingale: 142
Nightjar: 128
Nightshades: 45, 51
Noirmont: 14, 41, 79, 80, 89, 91-93, 96, 129, 135, 138, 151, 159, 166, 181, 191
North Canal: 190
Noury, Père C.: 7
Nuthatch: 145

Oaks: 5, 23, 28, 29, 31, 174

Oat-grasses: 27, 38
Occupation: 13, 30, 35, 42, 150, 157, 162, 171, 189, 190, 195, 196
Orange tip: 160
Orchid:
 Bee, 49; Common spotted-, 48, 53; Early purple, 46; Early spider, 49; Green-winged, 26, 46, 48; Heath spotted-, 48, 53; Jersey or loose-flowered, 46-48, 53; Lady, 49; Lesser butterfly, 49; Lizard, 49; Man, 49; Marsh, 47, 48; Pyramidal, 49
Oriole, Golden: 151
Osier: 34, 50, 54
Osprey: 116
L'Ouaisné: 5, 15, 27, 34, 115, 120, 133, 135, 155, 157, 181
Ouzel, Ring: 144
Owls: 99, 128
Oxalis: 23, 41, 42
Ox-eye daisy: 21, 24
Oystercatcher: 119, 122

Painted lady: 159, 163
Pale clouded yellow: 159
Pampas grass: 39
Pansy: 26, 50
Partridges: 60, 87, 88, 116
Peacock: 160, 163
Pear: 32
Pennywort: 26
Perch: 189, 190
Peregrine: 116
Petit Port: 23, 119, 121
Petrels: 109, 110
Phalaropes: 121, 122
Pheasant: 116
Phillimore, Sir W.: 96
Phillips, Dr H.: 55
Pigeons: 126
Pile, C.G.: 128, 179, 191, 193
Pillbugs: 177
Pillwort: 15
Le Pinnacle: 5

Pintail: 115
Pipits: 128, 133
Piquet, J.: 27, 41
Plantain: 54
Les Platons: 156
Plees, W.: 13, 72, 84, 88, 94
Plémont: 125
Plover:
    Golden, 121; Grey, 119;
    Kentish, 122; Little ringed,
    122; Ringed, 118, 122
Plume-footed mite: 176
Pochard: 113, 114
Poingdestre, J.: 59, 66, 68, 70,
    73, 76, 84, 88, 92, 93, 95, 98,
    103, 105, 126, 172, 178, 182,
    188
Polecat x ferret: 59-61, 67, 86, 95
Pond skaters: 158
Pont Marquet: 145, 178
Pope, D.G.: 175
Poppy: 5, 41
Portelet: 79, 120, 157, 191
Potatoes: 38, 45
La Pouquelaye: 96
Pourpier: 43
Primrose: 24, 35, 50, 53
Privet: 34, 35
Pseudoscorpions: 176
Puffball: 56
Puffin: 125
Le Pulec: 76, 123, 142, 164
La Pulente: 122, 135
Purple emperor: 159
Purple loosestrife: 36

Quail: 116
Quaking grass: 52
Queen's Valley: 117
Les Quennevais: 15, 25, 27, 32, 46,
    54, 72, 151, 155, 168, 173,
    205

Rabbit: 13, 14, 54, 59-61, 64, 67,
    88-95, 174
Rabet, A.: 192, 194

Rabies: 81, 82
Ragged-Robin: 36, 50
Ragwort: 168
Rail, Water: 117
Raised beaches: 1
Ramshorns: 199
Rat:
    Black, 59-61, 65, 67, 83, 100-
    101, 104, 178; Brown, 59-61,
    65, 67, 100-101
Raven: 153
Razorbill: 125
Read, T.: 80
Red admiral: 159, 163
Redpoll: 149
Redshank: 119, 122
Redshank, Spotted: 121
Redstarts: 141, 142
Redwing: 143
Red valerian: 43
Reedling, Bearded: 144
Reeds: 168
Reptiles: 178, 182-187, 205
Rhinoceros, Woolly: 2, 3
Rhyolite: 7
Richens, Dr R.H.: 29, 30
Ringlet: 161
River limpet: 198
Roach: 190
Robin: 128, 142
Rockrose: 18, 21, 164
La Rocque: 119, 122, 142
Rolland, A.: 85
Roller: 129
Romeril, J.: 117
Rook: 152
Rooke, O.: 14, 188
Rostron, J.: 75, 76, 99
Le Rouge Nez: 44
Rough dog's-tail: 27
La Rousse: 112
Rowan: 32
Royal fern: 44
Royal Jersey Agricultural and
    Horticultural Society: 37, 172
Royal Square: 97, 126, 127

Rozel: 18, 40, 41, 85, 90, 97, 130,
  135, 152, 160, 161, 188, 190,
  191
Rudd: 191
Ruff: 121
Rustyback: 43
Rutherford, W.: 179
Rybot, Maj. N.V.L.: 159
Rye-grass: 38

St Andrew's Park: 36
St Aubin: 1, 15, 36
St Aubin's Bay: 13, 36, 112, 113,
  118, 122, 191
St Brelade: 26, 44, 76, 79, 81, 99,
  115, 121, 135, 145, 166
St Catherine: 16, 39, 41, 139,
  146, 190, 192
St Clement: 47, 48, 91, 116, 119,
  134, 143, 149
St Helier: 15, 38, 39, 69, 90-93,
  97, 99, 101, 113, 117, 124,
  126, 129, 133, 142, 145, 152,
  158, 159, 162, 173, 182
St John: 23, 91, 96, 120, 122,
  161, 184
St John's-wort: 21, 51
St Lawrence: 15, 29, 72, 91, 131,
  135
St Luke's Church: 95
St Mark's fly: 175
St Martin: 37, 72, 76, 131, 143,
  159, 175, 181
St Mary: 23, 44, 62, 73, 97, 120
St Ouen: 5, 15, 16, 26, 27, 30, 31,
  34, 37, 39, 41, 45, 47, 48, 62,
  68, 75, 76, 78, 85, 86, 91, 94,
  96, 97, 99, 109, 110, 112-4,
  116-24, 128, 129, 131, 133,
  135, 138, 142, 143, 146, 147,
  149, 151, 157, 161, 162, 166,
  168, 169, 173, 176, 188-90,
  192, 194, 202, 203, 205
St Peter: 15, 26, 45, 76, 87, 120,
  128, 172

St Peter's Valley: 34, 36, 68, 192,
  194, 195
St Saviour: 46, 95, 96, 122, 194,
  203
Le Saie: 32, 142
Saltmarsh: 15, 16, 19
Samares: 15, 81, 90, 93, 122, 151,
  155, 198
Samphire: 19
Sand crocus: 20, 21, 164
Sanderling: 118, 119
Sand-grass: 20, 27
Sandhoppers: 177
Sandpipers: 119, 121
Sand sedge: 26
Sark: 4, 62-65, 67, 69, 73-75, 80,
  86, 90, 92, 101, 125, 187
Saw-wort: 24
Scaup: 115
Scarlet pimpernel: 49
Scorpion flies: 157
Scutigera: 176
Scoters: 109, 114, 115
Scurvy-grass: 19
Sea beet: 19
Seablite: 16
Sea holly: 26
Seahorses: 124
Sea lavenders: 16, 19
Seal, Grey: 87
Sea-purslane: 16
Sea radish: 146, 202
Serin: 149
Seymour Tower: 112
Shag: 110
Shaggy ink caps: 56
Shale: 7
Shearwaters: 109
Sheep: 13, 14
Sheep's-bit: 36, 50, 51, 164
Shelduck: 114
Shieldbugs: 158
Shield-fern: 44
Shrew:
  Common, 16, 59-63, 66, 67,

Shrew: Common (continued),
  73-78, 128, Lesser white-
  toothed, 16, 59, 60, 62, 63,
  66, 67, 73-78, 128; Water, 105;
  White-toothed, 63, 67, 74, 75
Shore-lark: 131
Shorten, M.: 95
Shoveler: 113, 114
Shrikes: 134
Shrubby orache: 34
Sinel, J.: 3, 66-68, 72, 74, 79, 84,
  86, 88, 89, 94-99, 101, 104,
  180, 182-185, 190, 194
Sinel, L.: 13
Siskin: 149
Skipper:
  Essex, 162; Grizzled, 162;
  Large, 162; Large chequered,
  162; Small, 162
Skuas: 109
Skylark: 12, 131
Slow-worm: 178, 182, 186, 187
Slugs: 202, 203
Small heath: 161
Smew: 115
Smith, K.G.V.: 175
Smith, R.G.: 195
Snails: 171, 197-202
Snake, Grass: 178, 182
Snipe: 119, 120, 122, 163
Snow Hill: 1, 97, 173
Snowy mespilus: 32
Solomon's seal: 52
Sorel: 81
South Canal: 190
South Hill: 1
Sparrowhawk: 115
Sparrows: 107, 149, 205
Speckled wood: 161, 164
Speedwells: 20, 40
Spiders: 175, 176
Spindle: 34
Spleenworts: 19, 36, 43
Spoonbill: 112
Spotted rockrose: 18, 21, 164
Spurge-laurel: 23

Spurges: 53, 166
Squills: 22, 164
Squirrel:
  Grey, 97, 98, 206; Red, 59-61,
  64, 67, 95-98
Starling: 149, 150, 205
Sternbergia: 39
Stevens, Mrs J.: 34
Steventon, D.: 122
Stickleback: 194
Stint, Little: 121
Stoat: 59-62, 64, 67, 72, 82-86,
  95, 178
Stock: 51
Stonechat: 136, 140
Stonecrop: 51
Stoneflies: 157
Storksbill: 52
Submerged forest: 5
Surville: 81
Swallow: 131, 132
Swallowtail: 160
Swan: 113
Sweet flag: 41
Swift: 129
Swiss Valley: 31, 162, 194
Sycamore: 29, 31, 40

Tamarisk: 34
Teal: 113, 114
Teasel: 146
Tench: 190
Terns: 109, 125
Tesson Mill: 194
Thistles: 146, 163
Thorn apple: 45, 51
Thrift: 19, 26, 50, 51, 176
Thrushes: 143
Thyme: 26, 36, 175
Timothy: 38
Tit:
  Blue, 144; Coal, 144, 145;
  Great, 144; Long-tailed, 145
Toad: 16, 69, 178-181, 187
Tomatoes: 38, 45
Tortoiseshell butterfly: Large, 161

Tortoiseshell butterfly (continued), Small, 160, 163
Town Mills: 8, 113, 194
Treecreepers: 145
Tree lupin: 40
Tree mallow: 158, 174
Trinity: 23, 79, 91, 120, 134, 170, 190, 195
Les Trois Roches: 120
Trout: 191, 192
Turnstone: 118, 119, 122, 123
Tussock-sedge: 23
Twite: 149
Two-winged flies: 175

Upstone, M.E.: 55

Vaines, J.: 193, 196
Val de la Mare: 76, 94, 99, 114, 117, 127, 151, 155, 166, 174, 193
Vallée des Vaux: 97, 112, 117, 134, 179, 188, 192, 194, 204
Vetches: 26, 163, 164, 172
Victoria Village: 99
Vinchelez: 177
Vinson, W.K.: 57
Violet: 35, 50, 51
Viviers: 188
Vole:
    Bank, 3, 6, 59-61, 65-67, 101-104, 128; Field, 3, 62, 65, 67; Water, 15, 59-61, 65, 67, 104, 105

Wagtails: 130, 133, 134
Wall brown: 161
Wallflower: 51
Wall-rue: 43
Warbler:
    Aquatic, 138; Cetti's, 134, 138, 139; Dartford, 134, 135; Garden, 134, 137; Great reed,

Warbler (continued)
    138; Reed, 128, 138; Sedge, 138; Willow, 137; Wood, 137
Wasps: 154, 173, 174
Water beetle: 198
Water boatman: 158
Waterworks Valley: 32, 34, 191-193
Waxwing: 134, 157
Weasel: 84
Well shrimp: 177
West Mount: 151
West Park: 124
Wheatear: 133, 138, 141, 163
Whimbrel: 121
Whinchat: 140
White butterfly:
    Black-veined, 160; Bath, 160; Green-veined, 160; Large, 160, 163; Small, 160, 163; Wood, 160
White admiral: 160
Whitethroat: 137
Whitethroat, Lesser: 137
Wigeon: 113, 114
Willis, H.H.: 189, 190, 195
Willowherb: 36
Willows: 12, 23, 32-34
Winter daffodil: 39
Woodcock: 120
Wood-lark: 131
Woodlice: 177
Woodpecker, Greater-spotted: 130
Woodpigeon: 127, 205
Wood-sorrel: 23, 41, 50
Wren: 129, 134
Wryneck: 129, 130

Yarrow: 53
Yellow archangel: 23
Yellowhammer: 146

Zostera: 113